Thomas Bond Lindsay

The Satires of Juvenal

Thomas Bond Lindsay

The Satires of Juvenal

ISBN/EAN: 9783337372002

Printed in Europe, USA, Canada, Australia, Japan

Cover: Foto ©Thomas Meinert / pixelio.de

More available books at **www.hansebooks.com**

Appletons' Classical Series.

THE

SATIRES OF JUVENAL

EDITED BY

THOMAS B. LINDSAY, Ph. D.

BOSTON UNIVERSITY

NEW YORK ·:· CINCINNATI ·:· CHICAGO

AMERICAN BOOK COMPANY

FROM THE PRESS OF

D. APPLETON & COMPANY

PREFACE.

THE text of this edition agrees in the main with that of Bücheler's edition of Jahn. A list of passages where I have thought best to make use of other readings or other orthography will be found at the end of the volume; differences in punctuation are marked only where the meaning is materially affected. I have compared most of the important editions, and used *Hosius' Apparatus Criticus ad Iuvenalem* (1888), and *Beer's Spicilegium Iuvenalianum* (1885), as well as such special articles as were at my command.

Several of the satires are omitted, and in those which are retained I have omitted all lines that seemed to me likely to offend a rational delicacy. My wish was to make the best work of Juvenal readable without awkwardness even in mixed classes.

The notes are the result of several years' experience, careful study, and a comparison of the views of the best editors, especially Ruperti, Heinrich, Jahn, Mac-Leane, Mayor, Weidner, and Bücheler. I have also had the benefit of my own MS. copy of Ribbeck's lectures on Juvenal.

No index, except the index of proper names, is given, because an incomplete one seems of little value, and the complete index in Jahn's edition of 1851 is easily accessible to scholars.

I wish to express my thanks to several friends and former pupils for valuable aid in connection with both the MS. and the proof-sheets.

T. B. LINDSAY.

BOSTON UNIVERSITY, *May, 1890.*

CONTENTS.

LIST OF ILLUSTRATIONS.

(*Cf. alphabetical list on page* 223.)

INTRODUCTION.

We know very little of the life of Juvenal. He rarely speaks of himself, and is seldom mentioned by other Latin writers. The sources of our information are—

1. Thirteen versions of a Life of Juvenal which have come down to us from an unknown source, in connection with various MSS. of his works. No one of these is accurate or trustworthy. Seven are given at the end of Jahn's edition.

2. Scattered references in his own writings serving to fix dates and places. Many of these references, however, occur in passages the authenticity of which is disputed.

3. The following inscription, discovered at Aquinum :

C[ere]ri sacrum [D. Iu]nius Iuvenalis
trib. coh[ortis I] Dalmatarum, II vir quin-
q[uennalis] flamen divi Vespasiani
vovit dedicav[it q]ue sua pec[unia]

4. Passages in Martial (VII, 24; 91; XII, 18), in Sidonius Apollinaris (Carm. IX, 270), in Johannes Malala

(Chron. X, p. 341, Chilm.), and in Rutilius Namatianus (I, 603).

From these sources we gather the following probable account:

DECIMUS IUNIUS IUVENALIS, the son or foster-son of a rich freedman, was born at Aquinum, about 54 A. D. He attended school, probably at Rome, studied rhetoric and practiced declamation, without, however, any view to either teaching or law, as a profession. He wrote some satirical verses on the actor Paris, the favorite of Domitian, possibly the lines (87–96) which were afterward inserted in the seventh satire. From Martial's statements, as well as from his own works, we conclude that he lived for some time in Rome. He served in the army as *tribunus cohortis*, and was at one time banished, probably to Egypt. He lived to the age of eighty.

Satire was a distinctively Roman literary production. The name was given by *Ennius* (239 B. C.) to a collection of poems in various metres, dealing with various subjects. *Lucilius* (ca 148 B. C.) gave to satire the character that it afterward retained; a rambling account of matters and things, half philosophy, half ridicule. *Horace* (65 B. C.) polished and refined this form of composition, and gave it more of the genial spirit of the later essay. Following Horace came *Persius* (34 A. D.), whose style is rough and at times obscure, and whose treatment is more directly philosophical than that of his predecessors.

Sixteen satires have come down to us as the writings of Juvenal; the genuineness of several, and of parts of others, has been questioned, particularly by Otto Ribbeck in his *Der echte und der unechte Iuvenal*, Berlin, 1865. Most editors, while admitting Ribbeck's clear insight and critical ability, and conceding that each of the two sections into which he divides the works attributed to Juvenal has marked characteristics, hesitate to adopt the theory as a whole, and the text stands in the main as given in the MSS. The division into five books seems to have been an arbitrary arrangement made by the early commentators.

The MSS. of Juvenal are divided into two classes. To the first class belongs the Montepessulanus 125, or *Pithoeanus* (*P.*), a MS. of the ninth century, which contains corrections made by a later hand (*p.*). Here belonged too the now lost MS. used by G. Valla in his edition of 1486, and another lost MS. formerly in the monastery of St. Gall, the scholia of which are still accessible. The second class contains a large number of later and less trustworthy MSS., among which must be reckoned the corrections in *P*.

The classification of the scholia follows that of the MSS.

Horace lived when the Roman state, emerging from the horrors of civil war, seemed about to enter upon a new life under the wise leadership of Augustus; his satire, sympathizing with the time, strikes only at those lesser follies that might be reached by a laugh. In fact, the satires of Horace have very little of the bitter irony and the scathing criticism which we connect with the word satire, but contain a pleasant, rather loquacious, discussion of matters of general interest, with side blows at an unhappy miser, a foolish scribbler, a conceited dandy, or a rich glutton; a general contempt for the folly of men that refuse to enjoy their present happiness in their impatient struggles for something more. In fact, Horace treats vice as folly, not so much a thing to be harshly censured as one to be sharply ridiculed.

Juvenal lived about a century later, when the seeds of moral degradation, sown long ago, had produced their fruit, when the glory of the empire had faded into a despotic, self-glorifying rule, when the practically unlimited power which, in the hands of Augustus, had been bounded by his own self-respect and the self-respect of the nation, had crossed or leveled all such bounds, and was used for the gratification of the worst passions of its possessors. Rome was full of adventurers from all lands, anxious to acquire wealth and power by any arts; the spirit of earnest devotion to the state and to personal duty, which had marked the earlier Romans, had given place to self-seeking; pride had become vanity, frugality had become avarice; the curse that attends unearned wealth had fallen upon the great city. It was to reprove the sins of such an age that Juvenal wrote. Here was no time for pretty philosophic generalities; here was no time to compose poems on the beauty of content, lying beside some gently murmuring stream, or, crowned with roses, sipping Falernian wine amid a company of pleasant friends; here was no time to laugh at vice, to say what foolish fellows bad men were. No; here was a time for fierce invective, for denunciation like that of the Hebrew prophets; here was a time to cry out that sin was the death of all that was good and fair in family and state. Here was room for contempt indeed, but a contempt too deep and bitter for a laugh. And Juvenal has this contempt, a contempt tinged with despair, for he loved Rome, the ideal Rome, the Rome of the republic, when patriotism ruled in the Forum and family affection in the home; and it was a sense of this terrible change, the sure sign of approaching dissolution, that gave to the lash of Juvenal its severest sting. "*Facit indignatio versum.*"

DATES OF THE ROMAN EMPERORS.

Augustus	. 27 B. C.–14 A. D.
Tiberius	14–37 A. D.
Caligula	37–41 A. D.
Claudius	41–54 A. D.
Nero	54–68 A. D.
Galba	68–69 A. D.
Otho	69 A. D.
Vitellius	69 A. D.
Vespasian	69–79 A. D.
Titus.	79–81 A. D.
Domitian	81–96 A. D.
Nerva	96–98 A. D.
Trajan	98–117 A. D.
Hadrian	117–138 A. D.
Antoninus Pius . . .	138–161 A. D.
Marcus Aurelius . . .	161–180 A. D.

DATES OF ROMAN WRITERS.

Plautus	254–184 B. C.
Ennius	239–169 B. C.
Terence	185–159 B. C.
Lucilius	148–103 B. C.
Cicero	106–43 B. C.
Lucretius	98–55 B. C.
Vergil	70–19 B. C.
Horace	65–8 B. C.
Livy	59 B. C.–17 A. D.
Ovid	43 B. C.–17 A. D.
Persius	34–62 A. D.
Quintilian	35–95 A. D.
Martial	43–103 A. D.
Tacitus	54–118 A. D.
Juvenal	54 (?)–134 (?) A. D.
Statius	61–98 A. D.
Pliny the Younger	62–113 A. D.
Suetonius	75–160 A. D.

2

P, codex Montepessulanus 125 olim Pithoeanus.

p, codicis Pithoeani manus emendatrix.

S, scholiorum lectio aut ex scholiis ducta.

ω, codices reliqui omnes aut multi.

ς, codicum reliquorum pars.

The Appian Way.

SATURA I.

SEMPER ego auditor tantum? numquamne reponam,
Vexatus totiens rauci Theseide Cordi?
Inpune ergo mihi recitaverit ille togatas,
Hic elegos? inpune diem consumpserit ingens
Telephus aut summi plena iam margine libri   5
Scriptus et in tergo necdum finitus Orestes?
Nota magis nulli domus est sua, quam mihi lucus
Martis et Aeoliis vicinum rupibus antrum
Vulcani.   Quid agant venti, quas torqueat umbras
Aeacus, unde alius furtivae devehat aurum   10
Pelliculae, quantas iaculetur Monychus ornos,
Frontonis platani convulsaque marmora clamant

---

2. Cordi *PS*, Codri *pω*.

Semper et adsiduo ruptae lectore columnae.
Expectes eadem a summo minimoque poeta.
Et nos ergo manum ferulae subduximus, et nos　　　15
Consilium dedimus Sullae, privatus ut altum
Dormiret.　Stulta est clementia, cum tot ubique
Vatibus occurras, periturae parcere chartae.
Cur tamen hoc potius libeat decurrere campo,
Per quem magnus equos Auruncae flexit alumnus,　　20
Si vacat ac placidi rationem admittitis, edam.　　　21
Patricios omnis opibus cum provocet unus,　　　　24
Quo tondente gravis iuveni mihi barba sonabat;　　25
Cum pars Niliacae plebis, cum verna Canopi
Crispinus, Tyrias umero revocante lacernas,
Ventilet aestivum digitis sudantibus aurum,
Nec sufferre queat maioris pondera gemmae:
Difficile est saturam non scribere.　Nam quis iniquae　30
Tam patiens urbis, tam ferreus, ut teneat se,
Causidici nova cum veniat lectica Mathonis
Plena ipso, post hunc magni delator amici
Et cito rapturus de nobilitate comesa
Quod superest, quem Massa timet, quem munere palpat 35
Carus et a trepido Thymele summissa Latino?　　36
Quid referam, quanta siccum iecur ardeat ira,　　45
Cum populum gregibus comitum premit hic spoliator
Pupilli prostantis, et hic damnatus inani
Iudicio—quid enim salvis infamia nummis?
Exul ab octava Marius bibit et fruitur dis
Iratis; at tu victrix provincia ploras!　　　　50
Haec ego non credam Venusina digna lucerna?
Haec ego non agitem? sed quid magis? Heracleas,
Aut Diomedeas, aut mugitum labyrinthi

---

46. premat *s.*　47. at *pω.*

Et mare percussum puero fabrumque volantem, 54
Cum fas esse putet curam sperare cohortis, 58
Qui bona donavit praesepibus et caret omni
Maiorum censu, dum pervolat axe citato 60
Flaminiam puer Automedon? nam lora tenebat
Ipse, lacernatae cum se iactaret amicae.
Nonne libet medio ceras implere capaces
Quadruvio, cum iam sexta cervice feratur,
Hinc atque inde patens ac nuda paene cathedra 65
Et multum referens de Maecenate supino,
Signator falso, qui se lautum atque beatum
Exiguis tabulis et gemma fecerit uda?
Occurrit matrona potens, quae molle Calenum
Porrectura viro miscet sitiente rubetam, 70
Instituitque rudes melior Lucusta propinquas
Per famam et populum nigros efferre maritos.
Aude aliquid brevibus Gyaris et carcere dignum,
Si vis esse aliquid. .Probitas laudatur et alget,
Criminibus debent hortos, praetoria, mensas, 75
Argentum vetus et stantem extra pocula caprum. 76
Si natura negat, facit indignatio versum, 79
Qualemcumque potest, quales ego vel Cluvienus. 80
    Ex quo Deucalion nimbis tollentibus aequor
Navigio montem ascendit sortesque poposcit,
Paulatimque anima caluerunt mollia saxa, 83
Quidquid agunt homines, votum, timor, ira, voluptas, 85
Gaudia, discursus, nostri farrago libelli est.
Et quando uberior vitiorum copia? quando
Maior avaritiae patuit sinus? alea quando
Hos animos? neque enim loculis comitantibus itur

---

67. signato falso *Madvig.* 68. fecerit *Sω*, fecerat *P.* 69. occurrat
Heinrich. 70. rubeta *P.* 74. aliquis *s.* 85. timor *add. p.*

Ad casum tabulae, posita sed luditur arca.   90
Proelia quanta illic dispensatore videbis
Armigero! simplexne furor sestertia centum
Perdere et horrenti tunicam non reddere servo?
Quis totidem erexit villas, quis fercula septem
Secreto cenavit avus? nunc sportula primo   95
Limine parva sedet, turbae rapienda togatae.
Ille tamen faciem prius inspicit et trepidat, ne
Suppositus venias ac falso nomine poscas.
Agnitus accipies; iubet a praecone vocari
Ipsos Troiugenas—nam vexant limen et ipsi   100
Nobiscum—" Da praetori, da deinde tribuno!"
Sed libertinus prior est: " Prior," inquit, " ego adsum;
Cur timeam dubitemve locum defendere, quamvis
Natus ad Euphraten, molles quod in aure fenestrae
Arguerint, licet ipse negem? sed quinque tabernae   105
Quadringenta parant; quid confert purpura maior
Optandum, si Laurenti custodit in agro
Conductas Corvinus oves, ego possideo plus
Pallante et Licinis?"—Expectent ergo tribuni,
Vincant divitiae, sacro ne cedat honori,   110
Nuper in hanc urbem pedibus qui venerat albis,
Quandoquidem inter nos sanctissima divitiarum
Maiestas, etsi funesta Pecunia templo
Nondum habitat, nullas nummorum ereximus aras,
Ut colitur Pax atque Fides, Victoria, Virtus,   115
Quaeque salutato crepitat Concordia nido.
    Sed cum summus honor finito computet anno
Sportula quid referat, quantum rationibus addat,
Quid facient comites, quibus hinc toga, calceus hinc est
Et panis fumusque domi? Densissima centum   120

---

106. purpura *Spω*, purpurae *P*.   114. habitas *p*.

Quadrantes lectica petit, sequiturque maritum
Languida vel praegnans et circumducitur uxor.
Hic petit absenti, nota iam callidus arte,
Ostendens vacuam et clausam pro coniuge sellam.
" Galla mea est," inquit, " citius dimitte; moraris?   125
Profer, Galla, caput! noli vexare, quiescet."
Ipse dies pulchro distinguitur ordine rerum :
Sportula, deinde forum iurisque peritus Apollo
Atque triumphales, inter quas ausus habere
Nescio quis titulos Aegyptius atque Arabarches.   130
Vestibulis abeunt veteres lassique clientes   132
Votaque deponunt, quamquam longissima cenae
Spes homini; caulis miseris atque ignis emendus.
Optima silvarum interea pelagique vorabit   135
Rex horum, vacuisque toris tantum ipse iacebit.
Nam de tot pulchris et latis orbibus et tam
Antiquis una comedunt patrimonia mensa.
Nullus iam parasitus erit.   Sed quis ferat istas
Luxuriae sordes? quanta est gula, quae sibi totos   140
Ponit apros, animal propter convivia natum!
Poena tamen praesens, cum tu deponis amictus
Turgidus et crudum pavonem in balnea portas.
Hinc subitae mortes atque intestata senectus;
Et nova, nec tristis, per cunctas fabula cenas;   145
Ducitur iratis plaudendum funus amicis.
   Nil erit ulterius quod nostris moribus addat
Posteritas; eadem facient cupientque minores.
Omne in praecipiti vitium stetit; utere velis,
Totos pande sinus!   Dices hic forsitan : " Unde   150
Ingenium par materiae? unde illa priorum

---

126. quiescet *F*, quiescit *pω*. 143. crudum *p*, crudus *P*. 144. in-
festata *Madvig*. 150. dices *P*, dicas *pω*.

Scribendi quodcumque animo flagrante liberet
Simplicitas, ' cuius non audeo dicere nomen?
Quid refert, dictis ignoscat Mucius an non?'
Pone Tigellinum : taeda lucebis in illa,   155
Qua stantes ardent, qui fixo pectore fumant,
Et latum media sulcum deducis harena."
Qui dedit ergo tribus patruis aconita, vehatur
Pensilibus plumis atque illinc despiciet nos?
" Cum veniet contra, digito compesce labellum :   160
Accusator erit qui verbum dixerit : ' hic est.'
Securus licet Aenean Rutulumque ferocem
Committas, nulli gravis est percussus Achilles
Aut multum quaesitus Hylas urnamque secutus;
Ense velut stricto quotiens Lucilius ardens   165
Infremuit, rubet auditor, cui frigida mens est
Criminibus, tacita sudant praecordia culpa.
Inde irae et lacrimae. Tecum prius ergo voluta
Haec animo ante tubas ; galeatum sero duelli
Paenitet." Experiar quid concedatur in illos,   170
Quorum Flaminia tegitur cinis atque Latina.

---

156. pectore *P*, gutture *pω*. 157. deducis *pω*, deducit *P*. 159. despiciaet *P*, despiciat *s*. 161. versum *P*, verum *pω* 169. animo ante tubas *codd. Prisc.*, animante tuba *p*, anime ante tubas *Valla*. 171. legitur *P*.

The Campagna.

SATURA III.

Quamvis digressu veteris confusus amici,
Laudo tamen, vacuis quod sedem figere Cumis
Destinet atque unum civem donare Sibyllae.
Ianua Baiarum est et gratum litus amoeni
Secessus. Ego vel Prochytam praepono Suburae;   5
Nam quid tam miserum, tam solum vidimus, ut non
Deterius credas horrere incendia, lapsus
Tectorum adsiduos ac mille pericula saevae
Urbis et Augusto recitantes mense poetas?
Sed dum tota domus raeda componitur una,   10
Substitit ad veteres arcus madidamque Capenam.
Hic, ubi nocturnae Numa constituebat amicae,
Nunc sacri fontis nemus et delubra locantur
Iudaeis, quorum cophinus faenumque supellex;
Omnis enim populo mercedem pendere iussa est   15
Arbor, et eiectis mendicat silva Camenis;
In vallem Egeriae descendimus et speluncas
Dissimiles veris: quanto praesentius esset

Numen aquis, viridi si margine cluderet undas
Herba nec ingenuum violarent marmora tofum!   20
Hic tunc Umbricius : " Quando artibus," inquit, " honestis
Nullus in urbe locus, nulla emolumenta laborum,
Res hodie minor est, here quam fuit, atque eadem cras
Deteret exiguis aliquid ; proponimus illuc
Ire, fatigatas ubi Daedalus exuit alas.   25
Dum nova canities, dum prima et recta senectus,
Dum superest Lachesi quod torqueat, et pedibus me
Porto meis, nullo dextram subeunte bacillo ;
Cedamus patria : vivant Artorius istic
Et Catulus ; maneant, qui nigrum in candida vertunt, 30
Quis facile est aedem conducere, flumina, portus,
Siccandam eluviem, portandum ad busta cadaver,
Et praebere caput domina venale sub hasta.
Quondam hi cornicines et municipalis harenae
Perpetui comites notaeque per oppida buccae   35
Munera nunc edunt, et verso pollice vulgus
Quem iubet occidunt populariter ; inde reversi
Conducunt foricas ; et cur non omnia? cum sint,
Quales ex humili magna ad fastigia rerum
Extollit, quotiens voluit Fortuna iocari.   40
Quid Romae faciam ? mentiri nescio ; librum,
Si malus est, nequeo laudare et poscere ; motus
Astrorum ignoro ; funus promittere patris
Nec volo nec possum ; ranarum viscera numquam
Inspexi ;   45
                      me nemo ministro
Fur erit, atque ideo nulli comes exeo, tamquam
Mancus et exstinctae, corpus non utile, dextrae.

---

    19. aque *pω*. 37. quem *pω*, qum *P*, cum *s*. 48. exstinctae—dextrae
Pω, exstincta—dextra *Eremita*.

Quis nunc diligitur, nisi conscius, et cui fervens
Aestuat occultis animus semperque tacendis? 50
Nil tibi se debere putat, nil conferet umquam,
Participem qui te secreti fecit honesti;
Carus erit Verri, qui Verrem tempore quo vult
Accusare potest. Tanti tibi non sit opaci
Omnis harena Tagi quodque in mare volvitur aurum, 55
Ut somno careas ponendaque praemia sumas
Tristis et a magno semper timearis amico.
  Quae nunc divitibus gens acceptissima nostris,
Et quos praecipue fugiam, properabo fateri,
Nec pudor opstabit. Non possum ferre, Quirites, 60
Graecam urbem; quamvis quota portio faecis Achaei!
Iam pridem Syrus in Tiberim defluxit Orontes,
Et linguam et mores et cum tibicine chordas
Obliquas nec non gentilia tympana secum
Vexit. 65
Rusticus ille tuus sumit trechedipna, Quirine, 67
Et ceromatico fert niceteria collo!
Hic alta Sicyone, ast hic Amydone relicta,
Hic Andro, ille Samo, hic Trallibus aut Alabandis, 70
Esquilias dictumque petunt a vimine collem,
Viscera magnarum domuum dominique futuri.
Ingenium velox, audacia perdita, sermo
Promptus et Isaeo torrentior. Ede quid illum
Esse putes. Quemvis hominem secum attulit ad nos: 75
Grammaticus, rhetor, geometres, pictor, aliptes,
Augur, schoenobates, medicus, magus: omnia novit
Graeculus esuriens; in caelum miseris, ibit.
In summa, non Maurus erat neque Sarmata nec Thrax,
Qui sumpsit pinnas, mediis sed natus Athenis. 80

---

78. miseris *Aroviensis*, iusscris *pω*, — seris *P.*

Horum ego non fugiam conchylia? me prior ille
Signabit fultusque toro meliore recumbet,
Advectus Romam quo pruna et cottona vento?
Usque adeo nihil est, quod nostra infantia caelum
Hausit Aventini, baca nutrita Sabina?   85
Quid quod adulandi gens prudentissima laudat
Sermonem indocti, faciem deformis amici,
Et longum invalidi collum cervicibus aequat
Herculis Antaeum procul a tellure tenentis?   89
Haec eadem licet et nobis laudare; sed illis   92
Creditur.
Nec tamen Antiochus nec erit mirabilis illic   98
Aut Stratocles aut cum molli Demetrius Haemo:
Natio comoeda est.   Rides, maiore cachinno   100
Concutitur; flet, si lacrimas conspexit amici,
Nec dolet; igniculum brumae si tempore poscas,
Accipit endromidem; si dixeris, " Aestuo," sudat.
Non sumus ergo pares: melior, qui semper et omni
Nocte dieque potest aliena sumere vultum   105
A facie, iactare manus, laudare paratus.   106
Scire volunt secreta domus atque inde timeri.   113
Et quoniam coepit Graecorum mentio, transi
Gymnasia atque audi facinus maioris abollae: 115
Stoicus occidit Baream delator, amicum
Discipulumque senex ripa nutritus in illa,
Ad quam Gorgonei delapsa est pinna caballi.
Non est Romano cuiquam locus hic, ubi regnat
Protogenes aliquis vel Diphilus aut Hermarchus,   120
Qui gentis vitio numquam partitur amicum,
Solus habet; nam cum facilem stillavit in aurem
Exiguum de naturae patriaeque veneno,

---

104. *damnarat Iahn,* omni *Pω,* omnis *Weidner.*   113. *delebat Pinzger.*

Limine summoveor, perierunt tempora longi
Servitii; nusquam minor est iactura clientis.   125
   Quod porro officium, ne nobis blandiar, aut quod
Pauperis hic meritum, si curet nocte togatus
Currere, cum praetor lictorem impellat et ire
Praecipitem iubeat, dudum vigilantibus orbis,
Ne prior Albinam et Modiam collega salutet?   130
Da testem Romae tam sanctum, quam fuit hospes   137
Numinis Idaei, procedat vel Numa vel qui
Servavit trepidam flagranti ex aede Minervam :
Protinus ad censum; de moribus ultima fiet   140
Quaestio : 'Quot pascit servos? quot possidet agri
Iugera? quam multa magnaque paropside cenat?'
Quantum quisque sua nummorum servat in arca,
Tantum habet et fidei; iures licet et Samothracum
Et nostrorum aras, contemnere fulmina pauper   145
Creditur atque deos, dis ignoscentibus ipsis.
Quid quod materiam praebet causasque iocorum
Omnibus hic idem, si foeda et scissa lacerna,
Si toga sordidula est et rupta calceus alter
Pelle patet, vel si consuto vulnere crassum   150
Atque recens linum ostendit non una cicatrix?
Nil habet infelix paupertas durius in se,
Quam quod ridiculos homines facit. 'Exeat,' inquit,
'Si pudor est, et de pulvino surgat equestri,
Cuius res legi non sufficit;   155
Hic plaudat nitidi praeconis filius inter   157
Pinnirapi cultos iuvenes iuvenesque lanistae.'
Sic libitum vano, qui nos distinxit, Othoni.
Quis gener hic placuit censu minor atque puellae   160

---

130. ne *pω*, nec *P*.   141. agri *pω*, agros *P*.   142. iugera *om. P.*
add. pω.

Sarcinulis inpar? quis pauper scribitur heres?
Quando in consilio est aedilibus? agmine facto
Debuerant olim tenues migrasse Quirites.
Haud facile emergunt, quorum virtutibus obstat
Res angusta domi; sed Romae durior illis   165
Conatus : magno hospitium miserabile, magno
Servorum ventres, et frugi cenula magno.
Fictilibus cenare pudet, quod turpe negabis
Translatus subito ad Marsos mensamque Sabellam
Contentusque illic Veneto duroque cucullo.   170
Pars magna Italiae est, si verum admittimus, in qua
Nemo togam sumit, nisi mortuus.   Ipsa dierum
Festorum herboso colitur si quando theatro
Maiestas, tandemque redit ad pulpita notum
Exodium, cum personae pallentis hiatum   175
In gremio matris formidat rusticus infans :
Aequales habitus illic similesque videbis
Orchestram et populum; clari velamen honoris
Sufficiunt tunicae summis aedilibus albae.
Hic ultra vires habitus nitor; hic aliquid plus   180
Quam satis est interdum aliena sumitur arca.
Commune id vitium est; hic vivimus ambitiosa
Paupertate omnes; quid te moror? omnia Romae
Cum pretio.   Quid das, ut Cossum aliquando salutes?
Ut te respiciat clauso Veiento labello?   185
Ille metit barbam, crinem hic deponit amati :
Plena domus libis venalibus; accipe et istud
Fermentum tibi habe : praestare tributa clientes
Cogimur et cultis augere peculia servis.
   Quis timet aut timuit gelida Praeneste ruinam, 190

---

164. emergunt *pω*, mergunt *P*.   168. negabis *Valesius*, necabis *P*,
negavit *ω*.   186. deponit, amati *Francke*.   187. libis *s*, libris *P*.

Aut positis nemorosa inter iuga Volsiniis, aut
Simplicibus Gabiis, aut proni Tiburis arce?
Nos urbem colimus tenui tibicine fultam
Magna parte sui; nam sic labentibus obstat
Vilicus et, veteris rimae cum texit hiatum,   195
Securos pendente iubet dormire ruina.
Vivendum est illic, ubi nulla incendia, nulli
Nocte metus.   Iam poscit aquam, iam frivola transfert
Ucalegon, tabulata tibi iam tertia fumant:
Tu nescis; nam si gradibus trepidatur ab imis,   200
Ultimus ardebit, quem tegula sola tuetur
A pluvia, molles ubi reddunt ova columbae.
Lectus erat Codro Procula minor, urceoli sex,
Ornamentum abaci, nec non et parvulus infra
Cantharus et recubans sub eodem marmore Chiro,   205
Iamque vetus Graecos servabat cista libellos,
Et divina opici rodebant carmina mures.
Nil habuit Codrus; quis enim negat? et tamen illud
Perdidit infelix totum nihil: ultimus autem
Aerumnae est cumulus, quod nudum et frusta rogantem 210
Nemo cibo, nemo hospitio tectoque iuvabit.
Si magna Asturici cecidit domus, horrida mater,
Pullati proceres, differt vadimonia praetor;
Tunc gemimus casus urbis, tunc odimus ignem.
Ardet adhuc, et iam accurrit qui marmora donet,   215
Conferat impensas: hic nuda et candida signa,
Hic aliquid praeclarum Euphranoris et Polycliti,
Phaecasiatorum vetera ornamenta deorum,
Hic libros dabit et forulos mediamque Minervam,
Hic modium argenti; meliora ac plura reponit   220

---

203. Codro—sex *om. P. add. p.* 210. frusta s, frustra *PS.* 218.
Phaecasiatorum *Roth,* haec Asianorum *PS,* fecasianorum *pω.*

Persicus orborum lautissimus et merito iam
Suspectus, tamquam ipse suas incenderit aedes.
Si potes avelli circensibus, optima Sorae
Aut Fabrateriae domus aut Frusinone paratur,
Quanti nunc tenebras unum conducis in annum.   225
Hortulus hic puteusque brevis nec reste movendus
In tenuis plantas facili diffunditur haustu.
Vive bidentis amans et culti vilicus horti,
Unde epulum possis centum dare Pythagoreis.
Est aliquid, quocumque loco, quocumque recessu,   230
Unius sese dominum fecisse lacertae.
     Plurimus hic aeger moritur vigilando; sed ipsum
Languorem peperit cibus inperfectus et haerens
Ardenti stomacho; nam quae meritoria somnum
Admittunt? magnis opibus dormitur in urbe.   235
Inde caput morbi. Raedarum transitus arto
Vicorum inflexu et stantis convicia mandrae
Eripient somnum Druso vitulisque marinis.
Si vocat officium, turba cedente vehetur
Dives et ingenti curret super ora Liburno,   240
Atque obiter leget aut scribet vel dormiet intus;
Namque facit somnum clausa lectica fenestra.
Ante tamen veniet: nobis properantibus obstat
Unda prior, magno populus premit agmine lumbos,
Qui sequitur; ferit hic cubito, ferit assere duro   245
Alter, at hic tignum capiti incutit, ille metretam.
Pinguia crura luto, planta mox undique magna
Calcor, et in digito clavus mihi militis haeret.
Nonne vides, quanto celebretur sportula fumo?
Centum convivae, sequitur sua quemque culina.   250
Corbulo vix ferret tot vasa ingentia, tot res

---

227. diffunditur ω, defunditur *P*.   240. liburno *Pω*, liburna *S*.

Inpositas capiti, quas recto vertice portat
Servulus infelix et cursu ventilat ignem.
Scinduntur tunicae sartae modo; longa coruscat
Serraco veniente abies, atque altera pinum   255
Plaustra vehunt; nutant alte populoque minantur.
Nam si procubuit, qui saxa Ligustica portat
Axis, et eversum fudit super agmina montem,
Quid superest e corporibus? quis membra, quis ossa
Invenit? obtritum vulgi perit omne cadaver   260
More animae.   Domus interea secura patellas
Iam lavat et bucca foculum excitat et sonat unctis
Striglibus et pleno componit lintea guto!
Haec inter pueros varie properantur, at ille
Iam sedet in ripa taetrumque novicius horret   265
Porthmea, nec sperat caenosi gurgitis alnum
Infelix, nec habet quem porrigat ore trientem.
    Respice nunc alia ac diversa pericula noctis:
Quod spatium tectis sublimibus, unde cerebrum
Testa ferit, quotiens rimosa et curta fenestris   270
Vasa cadant, quanto percussum pondere signent
Et laedant silicem.   Possis ignavus haberi
Et subiti casus inprovidus, ad cenam si
Intestatus eas; adeo tot fata, quot illa
Nocte patent vigiles te praetereunte fenestrae.   275
Ergo optes votumque feras miserabile tecum,
Ut sint contentae patulas defundere pelves.
Ebrius ac petulans, qui nullum forte cecidit,
Dat poenas, noctem patitur lugentis amicum
Pelidae, cubat in faciem, mox deinde supinus.   280
Ergo non aliter poterit dormire?   Quibusdam
Somnum rixa facit: sed quamvis inprobus annis

---

259. e *P*, de *pω*.   281. *delebat Heinecke.*

3

Atque mero fervens cavet hunc, quem coccina laena
Vitari iubet et cómitum longissimus ordo,
Multum praeterea flammarum et ahenea lampas;   285
Me, quem luna solet deducere vel breve lumen
Candelae, cuius dispenso et tempero filum,
Contemnit.   Miserae cognosce prooemia rixae,
Si rixa est, ubi tu pulsas, ego vapulo tantum.
Stat contra starique iubet: parere necesse est;   290
Nam quid agas, cum te furiosus cogat et idem
Fortior?   'Unde venis?' exclamat; 'cuius aceto,
Cuius conche tumes? quis tecum sectile porrum
Sutor et elixi vervecis labra comedit?
Nil mihi respondes? aut dic aut accipe calcem!   295
Ede ubi consistas; in qua te quaero proseucha?'
Dicere si temptes aliquid tacitusve recedas,
Tantundem est: feriunt pariter, vadimonia deinde
Irati faciunt; libertas pauperis haec est:
Pulsatus rogat et pugnis concisus adorat,   300
Ut liceat paucis cum dentibus inde reverti.
Nec tamen haec tantum metuas; nam qui spoliet te
Non derit, clausis domibus postquam omnis ubique
Fixa catenatae siluit compago tabernae.
Interdum et ferro subitus grassator agit rem: 305
Armato quotiens tutae custode tenentur
Et Pomptina palus et Gallinaria pinus,
Sic·inde huc omnes tamquam ad vivaria currunt.
Qua fornace graves, qua non incude catenae?
Maximus in vinclis ferri modus, ut timeas ne   310
Vomer deficiat, ne marrae et sarcula desint.
Felices proavorum atavos, felicia dicas
Saecula, quae quondam sub regibus atque tribunis

---

296 *ante 295 posuit Pinzger.*   304. catenaestluit *tum* ta *super* a *P.*

Viderunt uno contentam carcere Romam.

His alias poteram et pluris subnectere causas :   315
Sed iumenta vocant, et sol inclinat; eundum est.
Nam mihi commota iandudum mulio virga
Adnuit: ergo vale nostri memor, et quotiens te
Roma tuo refici properantem reddet Aquino,
Me quoque ad Helvinam Cererem vestramque Dianam 320
Converte a Cumis: saturarum ego, ni pudet illas,
Auditor gelidos veniam caligatus in agros."

---

322. auditor *P*, adiutor *pω*.

Domitian.

Coin of Domitian.

SATURA IV.

Cum iam semianimum laceraret Flavius orbem   37
Ultimus, et calvo serviret Roma Neroni,
Incidit Adriaci spatium admirabile rhombi
Ante domum Veneris, quam Dorica sustinet Ancon,   40
Implevitque sinus; nec enim minor haeserat illis,
Quos operit glacies Maeotica ruptaque tandem
Solibus effundit torrentis ad ostia Ponti,
Desidia tardos et longo frigore pingues.
Destinat hoc monstrum cumbae linique magister   45
Pontifici summo.   Quis enim proponere talem
Aut emere auderet, cum plena et litora multo
Delatore forent? dispersi protinus algae
Inquisitores agerent cum remige nudo,
Non dubitaturi fugitivum dicere piscem   50
Depastumque diu vivaria Caesaris, inde
Elapsum veterem ad dominum debere reverti.
Si quid Palfurio, si credimus Armillato,
Quidquid conspicuum pulchrumque est aequore toto,
Res fisci est, ubicūmque natat: donabitur ergo   55

---

41. implevitque *Spω*, implevit *P*.   43. torrentis *S*, torpentis *Ps*.

Ne pereat. Iam letifero cedente pruinis
Autumno, iam quartanam sperantibus aegris,
Stridebat deformis hiems praedamque recentem
Servabat: tamen hic properat, velut urgueat Auster.
Utque lacus suberant, ubi quamquam diruta servat   60
Ignem Troianum et Vestam colit Alba minorem,
Obstitit intranti miratrix turba parumper;
Ut cessit, facili patuerunt cardine valvae;
Exclusi spectant admissa obsonia patres.
Itur ad Atriden; tum Picens: " Accipe," dixit,   65
" Privatis maiora focis; genialis agatur
Iste dies; propera stomachum laxare saginae,
Et tua servatum consume in saecula rhombum;
Ipse capi voluit."—Quid apertius? et tamen illi
Surgebant cristae; nihil est quod credere de se   70
Non possit, cum laudatur, dis aequa potestas.
Sed derat pisci patinae mensura. Vocantur
Ergo in consilium proceres, quos oderat ille;
In quorum facie miserae magnaeque sedebat
Pallor amicitiae. Primus, clamante Liburno   75
" Currite, iam sedit! " rapta properabat abolla
Pegasus, attonitae positus modo vilicus urbi—
Anne aliud tunc praefecti?—quorum optimus atque
Interpres legum sanctissimus omnia, quamquam
Temporibus diris, tractanda putabat inermi   80
Iustitia. Venit et Crispi iucunda senectus,
Cuius erant mores qualis facundia; mite
Ingenium; maria ac terras populosque regenti
Quis comes utilior, si clade et peste sub illa
Saevitiam damnare et honestum adferre liceret   85

---

67. saginae *Iahn*, saginam *P*, saginis *Spω*, sagittis *S*, sagina *Buecheler*.
78. *delebat Heinrich.*   83. terras *pω*, terra *P*, terram *Iahn.*

Consilium? sed quid violentius aure tyranni,
Cum quo de pluviis aut aestibus aut nimboso
Vere locuturi fatum pendebat amici?
Ille igitur numquam direxit bracchia contra
Torrentem, nec civis erat qui libera posset 90
Verba animi proferre et vitam inpendere vero.
Sic multas hiemes atque octogensima vidit
Solstitia, his armis illa quoque tutus in aula.
Proximus eiusdem properabat Acilius aevi
Cum iuvene indigno quem mors tam saeva maneret 95
Et domini gladiis tam festinata; sed olim
Prodigio par est in nobilitate senectus:
Unde fit, ut malim fraterculus esse Gigantis!
Profuit ergo nihil misero, quod comminus ursos
Figebat Numidas Albana nudus harena 100
Venator; quis enim iam non intellegat artes
Patricias? quis priscum illud miratur acumen,
Brute, tuum? Facile est barbato inponere regi.
Nec melior vultu, quamvis ignobilis, ibat
Rubrius, offensae veteris reus atque tacendae. 105
Montani quoque venter adest abdomine tardus, 107
Et matutino sudans Crispinus amomo,
Quantum vix redolent duo funera; saevior illo
Pompeius tenui iugulos aperire susurro, 110
Et qui vulturibus servabat viscera Dacis
Fuscus, marmorea meditatus proelia villa,
Et cum mortifero prudens Veiento Catullo, 113
Grande et conspicuum nostro quoque tempore monstrum;
Caecus adulator dirusque a ponte satelles, [115
Dignus Aricinos qui mendicaret ad axes
Blandaque devexae iactaret basia raedae.

---

97. in *pω*, cum *Pithoeus*. 116. dignus qui *Haupt*.

Nemo magis rhombum stupuit : nam plurima dixit
In laevum conversus; at illi dextra iacebat   120
Belua.   Sic pugnas Cilicis laudabat et ictus
Et pegma et pueros inde ad velaria raptos.
Non cedit Veiento, sed ut fanaticus oestro
Percussus, Bellona, tuo divinat et, " Ingens
Omen habes," inquit, " magni clarique triumphi :   125
Regem aliquem capies, aut de temone Britanno
Excidet Arviragus : peregrina est belua; cernis
Erectas in terga sudes? "—Hoc defuit unum
Fabricio, patriam ut rhombi memoraret et annos.—
" Quidnam igitur censes? conciditur? "—" Absit ab illo 130
Dedecus hoc," Montanus ait; " testa alta paretur,
Quae tenui muro spatiosum colligat orbem.
Debetur magnus patinae subitusque Prometheus;
Argillam atque rotam citius properate! sed ex hoc
Tempore iam, Caesar, figuli tua castra sequantur."—   135
Vicit digna viro sententia : noverat ille
Luxuriam imperii veterem noctesque Neronis
Iam medias aliamque famem, cum pulmo Falerno
Arderet.   Nulli major fuit usus edendi
Tempestate mea : Circeis nata forent an   140
Lucrinum ad saxum Rutupinove edita fundo
Ostrea, callebat primo deprendere morsu ;
Et semel aspecti litus dicebat echini.
Surgitur, et misso proceres exire iubentur
Consilio, quos Albanam dux magnus in arcem   145
Traxerat attonitos et festinare coactos,
Tamquam de Chattis aliquid torvisque Sycambris
Dicturus, tamquam ex diversis partibus orbis
Anxia praecipiti venisset epistula pinna.

---

148. ex *Weidner*, cc *Ribbeck*, et *P*, a *s*, *om*. *ω*.

Atque utinam his potius nugis tota illa dedisset   150
Tempora saevitiae, claras quibus abstulit urbi
Inlustresque animas inpune et vindice nullo!
Sed periit, postquam cerdonibus esse timendus
Coeperat: hoc nocuit Lamiarum caede madenti.

The Triclinium.

SATURA V.

Sɪ te propositi nondum pudet atque eadem est mens,
Ut bona summa putes aliena vivere quadra;
Si potes illa pati, quae nec Sarmentus iniquas
Caesaris ad mensas, nec vilis Gabba tulisset:
Quamvis iurato metuam tibi credere testi.   5
Ventre nihil novi frugalius; hoc tamen ipsum
Defecisse puta, quod inani sufficit alvo:
Nulla crepido vacat? nusquam pons et tegetis pars
Dimidia brevior? tantine iniuria cenae?
Tam ieiuna fames cum possit honestius illic   10
Et tremere et sordes farris mordere canini?
    Primo fige loco, quod tu discumbere iussus
Mercedem solidam veterum capis officiorum.
Fructus amicitiae magnae cibus; inputat hunc rex
Et quamvis rarum tamen inputat. Ergo duos post   15
Si libuit menses neglectum adhibere clientem,
Tertia ne vacuo cessaret culcita lecto:
"Una simus," ait. Votorum summa! quid ultra

---

10. possit *Ps*, possis *ω*.   17. nc *pω*, nec *P*.

Quaeris? Habet Trebius, propter quod rumpere somnum
Debeat et ligulas dimittere, sollicitus ne   20
Tota salutatrix iam turba peregerit orbem
Sideribus dubiis aut illo tempore, quo se
Frigida circumagunt pigri serraca Bootae.
Qualis cena tamen? Vinum, quod sucida nolit
Lana pati; de conviva Corybanta videbis.   25
Iurgia proludunt; sed mox et pocula torques
Saucius et rubra deterges vulnera mappa,
Inter vos quotiens libertorumque cohortem
Pugna Saguntina fervet commissa lagona.
Ipse capillato diffusum consule potat   30
Calcatamque tenet bellis socialibus uvam,
Cardiaco numquam cyathum missurus amico;
Cras bibet Albanis aliquid de montibus aut de
Setinis, cuius patriam titulumque senectus
Delevit multa veteris fuligine testae,   35
Quale coronati Thrasea Helvidiusque bibebant
Brutorum et Cassi natalibus. Ipse capaces
Heliadum crustas et inaequales berullo
Virro tenet phialas: tibi non committitur aurum;
Vel, si quando datur, custos adfixus ibidem   40
Qui numeret gemmas, ungues observet acutos.
"Da veniam: praeclara illic laudatur iaspis."
Nam Virro, ut multi, gemmas ad pocula transfert
A digitis, quas in vaginae fronte solebat
Ponere zelotypo iuvenis praelatus Iarbae: 45
Tu Beneventani sutoris nomen habentem
Siccabis calicem nasorum quattuor ac iam
Quassatum et rupto poscentem sulpura vitro.

---

38. berullo *PS*, berillos *pω*.   39. phialas *pω*, phiala *P*.   42. illic *ω*,
illi *P*.   43. ut *pω*, et *P*.

Si stomachus domini fervet vinoque ciboque,
Frigidior Geticis petitur decocta pruinis: 50
Non eadem vobis poni modo vina querebar?
Vos aliam potatis aquam.   Tibi pocula cursor
Gaetulus dabit aut nigri manus ossea Mauri,
Et cui per mediam nolis occurrere noctem,
Clivosae veheris dum per monumenta Latinae: 55
Flos Asiae ante ipsum, pretio maiore paratus,
Quam fuit et Tulli census pugnacis et Anci
Et, ne te teneam, Romanorum omnia regum
Frivola.   Quod cum ita sit, tu Gaetulum Ganymedem
Respice, cum sities.   Nescit tot milibus emptus   60
Pauperibus miscere puer: sed forma, sed aetas
Digna supercilio.   Quando ad te pervenit ille?
Quando rogatus adest calidae gelidaeque minister?
Quippe indignatur veteri parere clienti,
Quodque aliquid poscas, et quod se stante recumbas.   65
Maxima quaeque domus servis est plena superbis.
Ecce alius quanto porrexit murmure panem
Vix fractum, solidae iam mucida frusta farinae,
Quae genuinum agitent, non admittentia morsum:
Sed tener et niveus mollique siligine fictus   70
Servatur domino.   Dextram cohibere memento;
Salva sit artoptae reverentia! finge tamen te
Inprobulum, superest illic qui ponere cogat:
" Vis tu consuetis, audax conviva, canistris
Impleri panisque tui novisse colorem?"—   75
" Scilicet hoc fuerat, propter quod saepe relicta
Coniuge per montem adversum gelidasque cucurri
Esquilias, fremeret saeva cum grandine vernus
Iuppiter et multo stillaret paenula nimbo!"—

---

51. *delebat Pinzger.*   66. *delebat Heinrich.*   70. fictus *P*, factus *ω*.

Aspice, quam longo distinguat pectore lancem,   80
Quae fertur domino squilla, et quibus undique saepta
Asparagis, qua despiciat convivia cauda,
Dum venit excelsi manibus sublata ministri :
Sed tibi dimidio constrictus cammarus ovo
Ponitur, exigua feralis cena patella.   85
Ipse Venafrano piscem perfundit: at hic, qui
Pallidus adfertur misero tibi caulis, olebit
Lanternam ; illud enim vestris datur alveolis, quod
Canna Micipsarum prora subvexit acuta ;
Propter quod Romae cum Boccare nemo lavatur,   90
Quod tutos etiam facit a serpentibus atris.
Mullus erit domini, quem misit Corsica, vel quem
Tauromenitanae rupes, quando omne peractum est
Et iam defecit nostrum mare, dum gula saevit,
Retibus adsiduis penitus scrutante macello   95
Proxima, nec patimur Tyrrhenum crescere piscem.
Instruit ergo focum provincia : sumitur illinc
Quod captator emat Laenas, Aurelia vendat.
Virroni muraena datur, quae maxima venit
Gurgite de Siculo ; nam dum se continet Auster,   100
Dum sedet et siccat madidas in carcere pinnas,
Contemnunt mediam temeraria lina Charybdim :
Vos anguilla manet longae cognata colubrae,
Aut glacie aspersus maculis Tiberinus, et ipse
Vernula riparum, pinguis torrente cloaca   105
Et solitus mediae cryptam penetrare Suburae.
   Ipsi pauca velim, facilem si praebeat aurem :
" Nemo petit, modicis quae mittebantur amicis
A Seneca, quae Piso bonus, quae Cotta solebat

---

80. distinguat *P*, distendat ω.   91. *om. Ps, damnarat Iahn.*   105.
torpente *Rutgers.*

Largiri; namque et titulis et fascibus olim   110
Maior habebatur donandi gloria: solum
Poscimus, ut cenes civiliter; hoc fac et esto,
Esto, ut nunc multi, dives tibi, pauper amicis!"
   Anseris ante ipsum magni iecur, anseribus par
Altilis et flavi dignus ferro Meleagri   115
Fumat aper; post hunc tradentur tubera, si ver
Tunc erit et facient optata tonitrua cenas
Maiores. "Tibi habe frumentum," Alledius inquit,
"O Libye; disiunge boves, dum tubera mittas!"
Structorem interea, ne qua indignatio desit,   120
Saltantem spectes et chironomunta volanti
Cultello, donec peragat dictata magistri
Omnia; nec minimo sane discrimine refert,
Quo gestu lepores et quo gallina secetur.
Duceris planta, velut ictus ab Hercule Cacus,   125
Et ponere foris, si quid temptaveris umquam
Hiscere, tamquam habeas tria nomina. Quando propinat
Virro tibi sumitve tuis contacta labellis
Pocula? quis vestrum temerarius usque adeo, quis
Perditus, ut dicat regi: "bibe"? Plurima sunt, quae 130
Non audent homines pertusa dicere laena;
Quadringenta tibi si quis deus aut similis dis
Et melior fatis donaret homuncio, quantus
Ex nihilo, quantus fieres Virronis amicus!
"Da Trebio! pone ad Trebium! vis, frater, ab ipsis   135
Ilibus?"—O nummi, vobis hunc praestat honorem,
Vos estis fratres! Dominus tamen et domini rex
Si vis tu fieri, nullus tibi parvolus aula
Luserit Aeneas nec filia dulcior illo:

---

   112. faciet *P*.   116. fumat *pω*, spumat *P*.   138. tu *ω*, tunc
P.

Iucundum et carum sterilis facit uxor amicum. 140
Sed tua nunc Mycale pariat licet et pueros tres
In gremium patris fundat semel : ipse loquaci
Gaudebit nido, viridem thoraca iubebit
Adferri minimasque nuces assemque rogatum,
Ad mensam quotiens parasitus venerit infans.— 145
Vilibus ancipites fungi ponentur amicis,
Boletus domino ; sed quales Claudius edit
Ante illum uxoris, post quem nil amplius edit.
Virro sibi et reliquis Virronibus illa iubebit
Poma dari, quorum solo pascaris odore ; 150
Qualia perpetuus Phaeacum autumnus habebat,
Credere quae possis subrepta sororibus Afris :
Tu scabie frueris mali, quod in aggere rodit,
Qui tegitur parma et galea metuensque flagelli
Discit ab hirsuta iaculum torquere capella. 155
Forsitan inpensae Virronem parcere credas?
Hoc agit ut doleas ; nam quae comoedia, mimus
Quis melior plorante gula? ergo omnia fiunt,
Si nescis, ut per lacrimas effundere bilem
Cogaris pressoque diu stridere molari. 160
Tu tibi liber homo et regis conviva videris :
Captum te nidore suae putat ille culinae
Nec male coniectat ; quis enim tam nudus, ut illum
Bis ferat, Etruscum puero si contigit aurum
Vel nodus tantum et signum de paupere loro? 165
Spes bene cenandi vos decipit. " Ecce dabit iam
Semesum leporem atque aliquid de clunibus apri,
Ad nos iam veniet minor altilis." Inde parato

---

140. *delebat Iahn.* 141. Mygale *P*, Migale *S.* 142. semel *P*, simul
pω. 146. ponentur *pω*, potentur *PS.* 148. post quem *pω*, post-
quam *P*.

Intactoque omnes et stricto pane iacetis.
Ille sapit, qui te sic utitur.   Omnia ferre   170
Si potes, et debes.   Pulsandum vertice raso
Praebebis quandoque caput nec dura timebis
Flagra pati, his epulis et tali dignus amico !

---

169. iacetis *P*.

A Roman Reading.

SATURA VII.

Et spes et ratio studiorum in Caesare tantum:
Solus enim tristes hac tempestate Camenas
Respexit, eum iam celebres notique poetae
Balneolum Gabiis, Romae conducere furnos
Temptarent, nec foedum alii nec turpe putarent   5
Praecones fieri; cum desertis Aganippes
Vallibus esuriens migraret in atria Clio.
Nam si Pieria quadrans tibi nullus in umbra
Ostendatur, ames nomen victumque Machaerae
Et vendas potius, commissa quod auctio vendit   10
Stantibus, oenophorum, tripodes, armaria, cistas,
Alcithoen Pacci, Thebas et Terea Fausti.
Hoc satius, quam si dicas sub iudice, " Vidi,"

---

9. utcumque *P.*

4

Quod non vidisti; faciant equites Asiani
Quamquam, et Cappadoces faciant equitesque Bithyni, 15
Altera quos nudo traducit Gallia talo.
Nemo tamen studiis indignum ferre laborem
Cogetur posthac, nectit quicumque canoris
Eloquium vocale modis laurumque momordit.
Hoc agite, O iuvenes! circumspicit et stimulat vos   20
Materiamque sibi ducis indulgentia quaerit.
Si qua aliunde putas rerum spectanda tuarum
Praesidia atque ideo croceae membrana tabellae
Implentur, lignorum aliquid posce ocius et quae
Componis, dona Veneris, Telesine, marito ;   25
Aut clude et positos tinea pertunde libellos.
Frange miser calamum vigilataque proelia dele,
Qui facis in parva sublimia carmina cella,
Ut dignus venias hederis et imagine macra.
Spes nulla ulterior; didicit iam dives avarus   30
Tantum admirari, tantum laudare disertos,
Ut pueri Iunonis avem. Sed defluit aetas
Et pelagi patiens et cassidis atque ligonis.
Taedia tunc subeunt animos, tunc seque suamque
Terpsichoren odit facunda et nuda senectus.   35
    Accipe nunc artes. Ne quid tibi conferat iste,
Quem colis, et Musarum et Apollinis aede relicta,
Ipse facit versus atque uni cedit Homero
Propter mille annos, et si dulcedine famae
Succensus recites, maculosas commodat aedes.   40

---

15. *delebat Pinzger*, Bitini *cum* Asiani (14) *locum permutare voluit*
Hermann. 16. Gallia *pω*, gallica *PS.* 18. cogetur *pω*, cogitur *P.* 20.
o *primo omissum* add. *P*, vos *P*, nos *ω*, vel nos *superscr p.* 22. exspec-
tanda *ω.* 23. crocea *P corr. p.* 24. implentur *PS*, impletur *pω.* 27.
calamum *P*, calamos *pω.* 39. et *Ps*, sed *vel* at *vel* aut *s*, tu *Hermann.*
40. maculosas *S, Heinrich*, maculonis *Γ*, maculonus *s.*

Haec longe ferrata domus servire iubetur,
In qua sollicitas imitatur ïanua portas.
Scit dare libertos extrema in parte sedentis
Ordinis et magnas comitum disponere voces.
Nemo dabit regum, quanti subsellia constant,   45
Et quae conducto pendent anabathra tigillo,
Quaeque reportandis posita est orchestra cathedris.
Nos tamen hoc agimus tenuique in pulvere sulcos
Ducimus et litus sterili versamus aratro.
Nam si discedas, laqueo tenet ambitiosi   50
Consuetudo mali; tenet insanabile multos
Scribendi cacoethes et aegro in corde senescit.
Sed vatem egregium, cui non sit publica vena,
Qui nil expositum soleat deducere, nec qui
Communi feriat carmen triviale moneta,   55
Hunc, qualem nequeo monstrare et sentio tantum,
Anxietate carens animus facit, omnis acerbi
Inpatiens, cupidus silvarum aptusque bibendis
Fontibus Aonidum.   Neque enim cantare sub antro
Pierio thyrsumque potest contingere maesta   60
Paupertas atque aeris inops, quo nocte dieque
Corpus eget: satur est, cum dicit Horatius " Euhoe!"
Qui locus ingenio, nisi cum se carmine solo
Vexant et dominis Cirrhae Nysaeque feruntur
Pectora vestra, duas non admittentia curas?   65
Magnae mentis opus nec de lodice paranda
Attonitae, currus et equos faciesque deorum
Aspicere et qualis Rutulum confundat Erinys.
Nam si Vergilio puer et tolerabile desset

---

50. ambitiosum *Iahn versu 51 damnato.* 58. bibendis *pω,* vivendis *P.*
61. quo *Pω,* cum *Ribbeck.* 63. qui *Ps,* quis *pω.* 66. ne de Iode *P*,
codice *S corr. pω.*

Hospitium, caderent omnes a crinibus hydri,   70
Surda nihil gemeret grave bucina.   Poscimus ut sit
Non minor antiquo Rubrenus Lappa cothurno,
Cuius et alveolos et laenam pignerat Atreus.
Non habet infelix Numitor quod mittat amico :
Quintillae quod donet habet; nec defuit illi   75
Unde emeret multa pascendum carne leonem
Iam domitum : constat leviori belua sumptu
Nimirum, et capiunt plus intestina poetae.
Contentus fama iaceat Lucanus in hortis
Marmoreis : at Serrano tenuique Saleio   80
Gloria quantalibet quid erit, si gloria tantum est?
Curritur ad vocem iucundam et carmen amicae
Thebaidos, laetam cum fecit Statius urbem
Promisitque diem : tanta dulcedine captos
Afficit ille animos, tantaque libidine volgi   85
Auditur; sed cum fregit subsellia versu,
Esurit, intactam Paridi nisi vendit Agaven.
Ille et militiae multis largitur honorem,
Semenstri digitos vatum circumligat auro.
Quod non dant proceres, dabit histrio : tu Camerinos   90
Et Baream, tu nobilium magna atria curas?
Praefectos Pelopea facit, Philomela tribunos.
Haud tamen invideas vati, quem pulpita pascunt.
Quis tibi Maecenas, quis nunc erit aut Proculeius
Aut Fabius? quis Cotta iterum, quis Lentulus alter?   95
Tunc par ingenio pretium; tunc utile multis
Pallere et vinum toto nescire Decembri.
    Vester porro labor fecundior, historiarum
  Scriptores? perit hic plus temporis atque olei plus;
Nullo quippe modo millensima pagina surgit   100

_____

    99. perit *P*, petit ω.

Omnibus et crescit multa damnosa papyro;
Sic ingens rerum numerus iubet atque operum lex.
Quae tamen inde seges? terrae quis fructus apertae?
Quis dabit historico quantum daret acta legenti?
—"Sed genus ignavum, quod lecto gaudet et umbra."—105
Dic igitur quid causidicis civilia praestent
Officia et magno comites in fasce libelli.
Ipsi magna sonant, sed tum, cum creditor audit,
Praecipue, vel si tetigit latus acrior illo,
Qui venit ad dubium grandi cum codice nomen.   110
Tunc immensa cavi spirant mendacia folles
Conspuiturque sinus : veram deprendere messem
Si libet, hinc centum patrimonia causidicorum,
Parte alia solum russati pone Lacernae.
Consedere duces : surgis tu pallidus Aiax,   115
Dicturus dubia pro libertate, bubulco
Iudice.   Rumpe miser tensum iecur, ut tibi lasso
Figantur virides, scalarum gloria, palmae ;
Quod vocis pretium? siccus petasunculus et vas
Pelamydum, aut veteres, Maurorum epimenia, bulbi, 120
Aut vinum Tiberi devectum, quinque lagonae,
Si quater egisti.   Si contigit aureus unus,
Inde cadunt partes ex foedere pragmaticorum.
Aemilio dabitur quantum licet, et melius nos
Egimus; huius enim stat currus aheneus, alti   125
Quadriiuges in vestibulis, atque ipse feroci
Bellatore sedens curvatum hastile minatur
Eminus et statua meditatur proelia lusca.
Sic Pedo conturbat, Matho deficit; exitus hic est
Tongilii, magno cum rhinocerote lavari   130

---

109. *damnabat Iahn.*   114. lacernae *P*, lacertae *ω*.   115. surgis *pω*,
surdis (?) *P*.   124. quanti *Iahn ;* petit *ω*.   128. statuam *P*.   130. Ton-
gilii *Iahn*, tongili *P*, tongilli *pω*.

Qui solet et vexat lutulenta balnea turba
Perque forum iuvenes longo premit assere Maedos,
Empturus pueros, argentum, murrina, villas;
Spondet enim Tyrio stlataria purpura filo.
Et tamen est illis hoc utile; purpura vendit   135
Causidicum, vendunt amethystina; convenit illis
Et strepitu et facie maioris vivere census.
Sed finem inpensae non servat prodiga Roma.
Fidimus eloquio?   Ciceroni nemo ducentos
Nunc dederit nummos, nisi fulserit anulus ingens.   140
Respicit haec primum, qui litigat, an tibi servi
Octo, decem comites, an post te sella, togati
Ante pedes.   Ideo conducta Paulus agebat
Sardonyche, atque ideo pluris quam Gallus agebat,
Quam Basilus.   Rara in tenui facundia panno.   145
Quando licet Basilo flentem producere matrem?
Quis bene dicentem Basilum ferat? accipiat te
Gallia vel potius nutricula causidicorum
Africa, si placuit mercedem ponere linguae.
    Declamare doces? O ferrea pectora Vetti,   150
Cui perimit saevos classis numerosa tyrannos!
Nam quaecumque sedens modo legerat, haec eadem stans
Perferet atque eadem cantabit versibus isdem;
Occidit miseros crambe repetita magistros.
Quis color et quod sit causae genus atque ubi summa   155
Quaestio, quae veniant diversae forte sagittae,
Nosse volunt omnes, mercedem solvere nemo.—
" Mercedem appellas? quid enim scio? "—" Culpa docentis
Scilicet arguitur, quod laevae parte mamillae

---

136. illis *pω, om P.*   145. clara *P.*   149. ponere *P,* imponere *ω.*
151. cui *Iahn,* cum *Pω.*   153. idem *Iahn.*   157. volunt *pω,* velunt *P,*
velint *Pithoeus.*   159. leve (= laevae) *P.*

Nil salit Arcadico iuveni, cuius mihi sexta   160
Quaque die miserum dirus caput Hannibal implet;
Quidquid id est, de quo deliberat, an petat urbem
A Cannis, an post nimbos et fulmina cautus
Circumagat madidas a tempestate cohortes.
Quantum vis stipulare et protinus accipe, quod do   165
Ut totiens illum pater audiat."—Haec alii sex
Vel plures uno conclamant ore sophistae,
Et veras agitant lites, raptore relicto;
Fusa venena silent, malus ingratusque maritus,
Et quae iam veteres sanant mortaria caecos.   170
Ergo sibi dabit ipse rudem, si nostra movebunt
Consilia, et vitae diversum iter ingredietur,
Ad pugnam qui rhetorica descendit ab umbra,
Summula ne pereat, qua vilis tessera venit
Frumenti; quippe haec merces lautissima.   Tempta, 175
Chrysogonus quanti doceat vel Polio quanti
Lautorum pueros : artem scindes Theodori.
Balnea sescentis et pluris porticus, in qua
Gestetur dominus, quotiens pluit; anne serenum
Expectet spargatque luto iumenta recenti?   180
Hic potius, namque hic mundae nitet ungula mulae.
Parte alia longis Numidarum fulta columnis
Surgat et algentem rapiat cenatio solem.
Quanticumque domus, veniet qui fercula docte
Componat; veniet qui pulmentaria condit.   185
Hos inter sumptus sestertia Quintiliano,
Ut multum, duo sufficient: res nulla minoris
Constabit patri, quam filius.—" Unde igitur tot

---

165. accipe *pω*, accipere *P ;* quid do *P*, quod do *pω*, qui do *Ribbeck*.
174. summula *ω*, summavia *P.*   177. scindes *Iahn*, scindens *PSω.*   181.
delebat Heinrich.   185. componit *s*, condit *Pω*, condiat *Lachmann.*

Quintilianus habet saltus?"—Exempla novorum
Fatorum transi: felix et pulcer et acer,   190
Felix et sapiens et nobilis et generosus,
Adpositam nigrae lunam subtexit alutae;
Felix orator quoque maximus et iaculator;
Et si perfrixit, cantat bene.   Distat enim, quae
Sidera te excipiant modo primos incipientem   195
Edere vagitus et adhuc a matre rubentem.
Si Fortuna volet, fies de rhetore consul;
Si volet haec eadem, fies de consule rhetor.
Ventidius quid enim? quid Tullius? anne aliud quam
Sidus et occulti miranda potentia fati?   200 .
Servis regna dabunt, captivis fata triumphum;
Felix ille tamen corvo quoque rarior albo.
Paenituit multos vanae sterilisque cathedrae,
Sicut Thrasymachi probat exitus atque Secundi
Carrinatis: et hunc inopem vidistis, Athenae,   205
Nil praeter gelidas ausae conferre cicutas.
Di, maiorum umbris tenuem et sine pondere terram,
Spirantisque crocos et in urna perpetuum ver,
Qui praeceptorem sancti voluere parentis
Esse loco!   Metuens virgae iam grandis Achilles   210
Cantabat patriis in montibus et cui non tunc
Eliceret risum citharoedi cauda magistri;
Sed Rufum atque alios caedit sua quemque iuventus,
Rufum, quem totiens Ciceronem Alloboga dixit.
   Quis gremio Celadi doctique Palaemonis adfert,   215
Quantum grammaticus meruit labor? et tamen ex hoc
Quodcumque est—minus est autem quam rhetoris aera—
Discipuli custos praemordet acoenonoetus;

---

192. *damnarat Iahn,* alutes *P.*   198. fies *pω,* fiet *P.*   204. Tharsy-
machi *Ritschl.*   208. spirantes *pω,* spirandis *P.*   217. autem *pω,* om. *P.*

Et qui dispensat, frangit sibi.   Cede, Palaemon,
Et patere inde aliquid decrescere, non aliter quam   220
Institor hibernae tegetis niveique cadurci ;
Dummodo non pereat, mediae quod noctis ab hora
Sedisti, qua nemo faber, qua nemo sederet
Qui docet obliquo lanam deducere ferro ;
Dummodo non pereat, totidem olfecisse lucernas,   225
Quot stabant pueri, cum totus decolor esset
Flaccus et haereret nigro fuligo Maroni.
Rara tamen merces, quae cognitione tribuni
Non egeat.   Sed vos saevas imponite leges,
Ut praeceptori verborum regula constet,   230
Ut legat historias, auctores noverit omnes
Tamquam ungues digitosque suos ; ut forte rogatus,
Dum petit aut thermas aut Phoebi balnea, dicat
Nutricem Anchisae, nomen patriamque novercae
Anchemoli ; dicat, quot Acestes vixerit annis,   235
Quot Siculi Phrygibus vini donaverit urnas.
Exigite, ut mores teneros ceu pollice ducat,
Ut si quis cera voltum facit ; exigite, ut sit
Et pater ipsius coetus.   239
" Haec," inquit, " curas, et cum se verterit annus,   242
Accipe victori populus quod postulat aurum."

---

219. frangat *Ps*, franget *s*, frangit *s*.   229. salvas *P*.   232. ut forte
P, sit forte *p*.   235. Anchemoli *s*, Archemori *PSω*; annis *P*, annos *ω*.
236. Siculi *valesius*, Siculis *P*, Siculus *ω*.   242. curas et *Pω*, cura sed *vel*
cures et *s*.   243. postulaturum *P*.

Atrium.

SATURA VIII.

STEMMATA quid faciunt? quid prodest, Pontice, longo
Sanguine censeri, pictos ostendere vultus
Maiorum, et stantis in curribus Aemilianos,
Et Curios iam dimidios, umerosque minorem
Corvinum, et Galbam auriculis nasoque carentem?　　5
Quis fructus, generis tabula iactare capaci
Corvinum, posthac multa contingere virga
Fumosos equitum cum dictatore magistros,
Si coram Lepidis male vivitur? effigies quo
Tot bellatorum, si luditur alea pernox　　　　　　10
Ante Numantinos? si dormire incipis ortu
Luciferi, quo signa duces et castra movebant?
Cur Allobrogicis et magna gaudeat ara
Natus in Herculeo Fabius lare, si cupidus, si

　　4-8. *delebat Ribbeck.* 5-6. *delebat Hermann.* 6-8. *delebat Weidner.*
7. *om. ω, damnarat Iahn.*

Vanus et Euganea quantumvis mollior agna?   15
Si tenerum attritus Catinensi pumice lumbum
Squalentis traducit avos, emptorque veneni
Frangenda miseram funestat imagine gentem?
Tota licet veteres exornent undique cerae
Atria, nobilitas sola est atque unica virtus.   20
Paulus vel Cossus vel Drusus moribus esto;
Hos ante effigies maiorum pone tuorum;
Praecedant ipsas illi te consule virgas.
Prima mihi debes animi bona; sanctus haberi
Iustitiaeque tenax factis dictisque mereris?   25
Agnosco procerem: salve, Gaetulice, seu tu
Silanus; quocumque alio de sanguine, rarus
Civis et egregius patriae contingis ovanti.
Exclamare libet, populus quod clamat Osiri
Invento.   Quis enim generosum dixerit hunc, qui   30
Indignus genere et praeclaro nomine tantum
Insignis? nanum cuiusdam Atlanta vocamus,
Aethiopem Cycnum, pravam extortamque puellam
Europen; canibus pigris scabieque vetusta
Levibus et siccae lambentibus ora lucernae   35
Nomen erit pardus, tigris, leo, si quid adhuc est
Quod fremat in terris violentius.   Ergo cavebis
Et metues, ne tu sic Creticus aut Camerinus.
    His ego quem monui? tecum est mihi sermo, Rubelli
Blande.   Tumes alto Drusorum stemmate, tamquam   40
Feceris ipse aliquid, propter quod nobilis esses,
Ut te conciperet, quae sanguine fulget Iuli,
Non quae ventoso conducta sub aggere texit.
" Vos humiles," inquis, " volgi pars ultima nostri,

---

33. pravam *Ps*, parvam *ω*.   38. sic *Iunius*, si *P*, sis *ω*.   39. quem
pω, quae *P*.   40. Blande *PSω*, Plante *Lipsius;* stemmate *P*, sanguine *ω*.

Quorum nemo queat patriam monstrare parentis :   45
Ast ego Cecropides."—Vivas et originis huius
Gaudia longa feras! tamen ima plebe Quiritem
Facundum invenies; solet hic defendere causas
Nobilis indocti; veniet de plebe togata
Qui iuris nodos et legum aenigmata solvat.   50
Hic petit Euphraten iuvenis domitique Batavi
Custodes aquilas, armis industrius : at tu
Nil nisi Cecropides truncoque simillimus Hermae.
Nullo quippe alio vincis discrimine, quam quod
Illi marmoreum caput est, tua vivit imago.   55
Dic mihi, Teucrorum proles, animalia muta
Quis generosa putet, nisi fortia.   Nempe volucrem
Sic laudamus equum, facili cui plurima palma
Fervet et exultat rauco victoria circo.
Nobilis hic, quocumque venit de gramine, cuius   60
Clara fuga ante alios et primus in aequore pulvis;
Sed venale pecus Coryphaei posteritas et
Hirpini, si rara iugo victoria sedit.
Nil ibi maiorum respectus, gratia nulla
Umbrarum; dominos pretiis mutare iubentur   65
Exiguis, trito ducunt epiraedia collo
Segnipedes dignique molam versare nepotes.
· Ergo, ut miremur te, non tua, primum aliquid da
Quod possim titulis incidere praeter honores,
Quos illis damus ac dedimus, quibus omnia debes.   70
    Haec satis ad iuvenem, quem nobis fama superbum
Tradit et inflatum plenumque Nerone propinquo;
Rarus enim ferme sensus communis in illa

---

49. veniat *P corr. p.*   51. hinc *Weidner.*   61. pulvis *pω Servius,* cuius *P.*   66. trito *s,* et trito *P,* tritoque *ω*; ducunt *P* (?), trahunt *ω.* 67. nepotes *P,* nepotis *pω.*   68. primum *Pω,* privum *Salmasius.*

Fortuna; sed te censeri laude tuorum,
Pontice, noluerim sic ut nihil ipse futurae   75
Laudis agas. Miserum est aliorum incumbere famae,
Ne conlapsa ruant subductis tecta columnis.
Stratus humi palmes viduas desiderat ulmos.
Esto bonus miles, tutor bonus, arbiter idem
Integer; ambiguae si quando citabere testis   80
Incertaeque rei, Phalaris licet imperet ut sis
Falsus et admoto dictet periuria tauro,
Summum crede nefas animam praeferre pudori
Et propter vitam vivendi perdere causas.
Dignus morte perit, cenet licet ostrea centum   85
Gaurana et Cosmi toto mergatur aheno.
Expectata diu tandem provincia cum te
Rectorem accipiat, pone irae frena modumque,
Pone et avaritiae, miserere inopum sociorum:
Ossa vides regum vacuis exucta medullis.   90
Respice quid moneant leges, quid curia mandet,
Praemia quanta bonos maneant, quam fulmine iusto
Et Capito et Numitor ruerint, damnante senatu,
Piratae Cilicum.   Sed quid damnatio confert?
Praeconem, Chaerippe, tuis circumspice pannis,   95
Cum Pansa eripiat, quidquid tibi Natta reliquit,
Iamque tace; furor est post omnia perdere naulum.
Non idem gemitus olim neque vulnus erat par
Damnorum, sociis florentibus et modo victis.
Plena domus tunc omnis, et ingens stabat acervus   100
Nummorum, Spartana chlamys, conchylia Coa,
Et cum Parrhasii tabulis signisque Myronis
Phidiacum vivebat ebur, nec non Polycliti

---

88. accipiat *P*, accipiet *ω*.   90. regum *ω*, rerum *P*.   97. naulum *pω*,
na * lu *P*, naulon *s*.

Multus ubique labor; rarae sine Mentore mensae.
Inde Dolabella atque istinc Antonius, inde   105
Sacrilegus Verres referebant navibus altis
Occulta spolia et plures de pace triumphos.
Nunc sociis iuga pauca boum, grex parvus equarum,
Et pater armenti capto eripietur agello,
Ipsi deinde Lares, si quod spectabile signum,   110
Si quis in aedicula deus unicus; haec etenim sunt
Pro summis, nam sunt haec maxima. Despicias tu
Forsitan inbellis Rhodios unctamque Corinthon:
Despicias merito; quid resinata iuventus
Cruraque totius facient tibi levia gentis?   115
Horrida vitanda est Hispania, Gallicus axis
Illyricumque latus; parce et messoribus illis,
Qui saturant urbem circo scaenaeque vacantem.
Quanta autem inde feres tam dirae praemia culpae,
Cum tenuis nuper Marius discinxerit Afros?   120
Curandum in primis ne magna iniuria fiat
Fortibus et miseris. Tollas licet omne quod usquam est
Auri atque argenti, scutum gladiumque relinques
Et iaculum et galeam: spoliatis arma supersunt.
Quod modo proposui, non est sententia; verum est;   125
Credite me vobis folium recitare Sibyllae.
Si tibi sancta cohors comitum, si nemo tribunal
Vendit acersecomes, si nullum in coniuge crimen,
Nec per conventus et cuncta per oppida curvis
Unguibus ire parat nummos raptura Celaeno: 130
Tu licet a Pico numeres genus, altaque si te
Nomina delectant, omnem Titanida pugnam

---

105. adque stinc cantonius *P*, atque hinc Antonius *ω*, atque dehinc
Lachmann. 109. eripietur *pω*, eripi . . . *P*, eripiatur *s.* 112. iam
coniecit Buecheler. 122. usquam *ω*, umquam *P.* 123. relinqu . . . *P*,
relinquas *S.* 124. *delebat Lachmann.* 131. tu *PSs*, tum *p*, tunc *ω*.

Inter maiores ipsumque Promethea ponas:
De quocumque voles proavum tibi sumito libro.
Quod si praecipitem rapit ambitio atque libido,   135
Si frangis virgas sociorum in sanguine, si te
Delectant hebetes lasso lictore secures:
Incipit ipsorum contra te stare parentum
Nobilitas claramque facem praeferre pudendis.
Omne animi vitium tanto conspectius in se   140
Crimen habet, quanto maior qui peccat habetur.
Quo mihi te solitum falsas signare tabellas
In templis, quae fecit avus, statuamque parentis
Ante triumphalem? quo, si nocturnus adulter
Tempora Santonico velas adoperta cucullo?   145
    Praeter maiorum cineres atque ossa volucri
Carpento rapitur pinguis Lateranus, et ipse,
Ipse rotam astringit sufflamine mulio consul,
Nocte quidem; sed Luna videt, sed sidera testes
Intendunt oculos.   Finitum tempus honoris   150
Cum fuerit, clara Lateranus luce flagellum
Sumet et occursum numquam trepidabit amici
Iam senis, ac virga prior annuet atque maniplos
Solvet et infundet iumentis hordea lassis.
Interea, dum lanatas robumque iuvencum   155
More Numae caedit Iovis ante altaria, iurat
Solam Eponam et facies olida ad praesepia pictas.
Sed cum pervigiles placet instaurare popinas,
Obvius adsiduo Syrophoenix unctus amomo
Currit, Idumaeae Syrophoenix incola portae   160
Hospitis adfectu dominum regemque salutat,

---

148. sufflamine mulio *S ad florilegium S. Galli grammaticus G. L. K.*
VI, *p. 231*, multo sufflamine *P* (*immo p*) ω.   155. rob*um S florilegium*,
torvum *pω, erasum in P, scriptum erat ut videtur robum.*   159. unctus
Ps, udus *pω*.   160. *damnarat Iahn.*

Et cum venali Cyanis succincta lagona.
Defensor culpae dicet mihi : " Fecimus et nos
Haec iuvenes."—Esto ; desisti nempe, nec ultra
Fovisti errorem.   Breve sit, quod turpiter audes ;   165
Quaedam cum prima resecentur crimina barba ;
Indulge veniam pueris : Lateranus ad illos
Thermarum calices inscriptaque lintea vadit
Maturus bello, Armeniae Syriaeque tuendis
Amnibus et Rheno atque Histro ; praestare Neronem 170
Securum valet haec aetas.   Mitte Ostia, Caesar,
Mitte, sed in magna legatum quaere popina ;
Invenies aliquo cum percussore iacentem,
Permixtum nautis et furibus ac fugitivis,
Inter carnifices et fabros sandapilarum   175
Et resupinati cessantia tympana Galli.
Aequa ibi libertas, communia pocula, lectus
Non alius cuiquam, nec mensa remotior ulli.
Quid facias talem sortitus, Pontice, servum ?
Nempe in Lucanos aut Tusca ergastula mittas.   180
At vos, Troiugenae, vobis ignoscitis et, quae
Turpia cerdoni, Volesos Brutumque decebunt.
    Quid, si numquam adeo foedis adeoque pudendis
Utimur exemplis ut non peiora supersint ?
Consumptis opibus vocem, Damasippe, locasti   185
Sipario, clamosum ageres ut Phasma Catulli.
Laureolum velox etiam bene Lentulus egit,
Iudice me dignus vera cruce.   Nec tamen ipsi
Ignoscas populo : populi frons durior huius,
Qui sedet et spectat triscurria patriciorum,   190
Planipedes audit Fabios, ridere potest qui
Mamercorum alapas.   Quanti sua funera vendant,

Quid refert? vendunt nullo cogente Nerone,
Nec dubitant celsi praetoris vendere ludis.
Finge tamen gladios inde atque hinc pulpita poni,   195
Quid satius? mortem sic quisquam exhorruit, ut sit
Zelotypus Thymeles, stupidi collega Corinthi?
Res haud mira tamen, citharoedo principe, mimus
Nobilis.   Haec ultra quid erit nisi ludus? et illic
Dedecus urbis habes, nec murmillonis in armis,   200
Nec clipeo Gracchum pugnantem aut falce supina—
Damnat enim tales habitus, et damnat et odit,
Nec galea faciem abscondit:—movet ecce tridentem
Postquam vibrata pendentia retia dextra
Nequiquam effudit, nudum ad spectacula vultum   205
Erigit, et tota fugit agnoscendus harena.
Credamus tunicae, de faucibus aurea cum se
Porrigat et longo iactetur spira galero.
Ergo ignominiam graviorem pertulit omni
Vulnere cum Graccho iussus pugnare secutor.   210
    Libera si dentur populo suffragia, quis tam
Perditus ut dubitet Senecam praeferre Neroni,
Cuius supplicio non debuit una parari
Simia nec serpens unus nec culleus unus?
Par Agamemnonidae crimen, sed causa facit rem   215
Dissimilem: quippe ille deis auctoribus ultor
Patris erat caesi media inter pocula; sed nec
Electrae iugulo se polluit aut Spartani
Sanguine coniugii, nullis aconita propinquis
Miscuit, in scaena numquam cantavit Orestes,   220
Troica non scripsit.   Quid enim Verginius armis
Debuit ulcisci magis, aut cum Vindice Galba,

---

194. *delebat Ruperti.*   202. *delebant Ruperti, Heinrich;* et *pω,* sed *P,*
sed — abscondit *delebat Hermann.*   204. vibrata *pω,* bibrata *P,* librata
s, Macleane.

5

Quod Nero tam saeva crudaque tyrannide fecit?
Haec opera atque hae sunt generosi principis artes,
Gaudentis foedo peregrina ad pulpita cantu   225
Prostitui Graiaeque apium meruisse coronae.
Maiorum effigies habeant insignia vocis,
Ante pedes Domiti longum tu pone Thyestae
Syrma vel Antigonae personam vel Melanippae,
Et de marmoreo citharam suspende colosso.   230
Quid, Catilina, tuis natalibus atque Cethegi
Inveniet quisquam sublimius? arma tamen vos
Nocturna et flammas domibus templisque paratis,
Ut Bracatorum pueri Senonumque minores,
Ausi quod liceat tunica punire molesta.   235
Sed vigilat consul vexillaque vestra coercet:
Hic novus Arpinas, ignobilis et modo Romae
Municipalis eques, galeatum ponit ubique
Praesidium attonitis et in omni gente laborat.
Tantum igitur muros intra toga contulit illi   240
Nominis ac tituli, quantum non Leucade, quantum
Thessaliae campis Octavius abstulit udo
Caedibus adsiduis gladio; sed Roma parentem,
Roma patrem patriae Ciceronem libera dixit.
Arpinas alius Volscorum in monte solebat   245
Poscere mercedes, alieno lassus aratro;
Nodosam post haec frangebat vertice vitem,
Si lentus pigra muniret castra dolabra.
Hic tamen et Cimbros et summa pericula rerum
Excipit, et solus trepidantem protegit urbem;   250
Atque ideo, postquam ad Cimbros stragemque volabant,

---

223. quod *Madvig*, quid *Pω*. 226. Graiaeque *pω*, grataeque *P*. 229.
seu *Iahn*, aut *Hermann ante* personam; *Buecheler* vel *post* p. *addidit*.
239. gente *pω*, monte *et* ponte *S*, *erasum* in *P*, inermi mente *Weidner*.
241. non *pω*, in *P*, vix *Hermann*, unda *Weidner*.

Qui numquam attigerant maiora cadavera corvi,
Nobilis ornatur lauru collega secunda.
Plebeiae Deciorum animae, plebeia fuerunt
Nomina; pro totis legionibus hi tamen et pro   255
Omnibus auxiliis atque omni pube Latina
Sufficiunt dis infernis terraeque parenti;
Pluris enim Decii, quam quae servantur ab illis.
Ancilla natus trabeam et diadema Quirini
Et fasces meruit, regum ultimus ille bonorum: 260
Prodita laxabant portarum claustra tyrannis
Exulibus iuvenes ipsius consulis et quos
Magnum aliquid dubia pro libertate deceret,
Quod miraretur cum Coclite Mucius et quae
Imperii fines Tiberinum virgo natavit.   265
Occulta ad patres produxit crimina servus,
Matronis lugendus; at illos verbera iustis
Adficiunt poenis et legum prima securis.
   Malo pater tibi sit Thersites, dummodo tu sis
Aeacidae similis Vulcanique arma capessas,   270
Quam te Thersitae similem producat Achilles.
Et tamen, ut longe repetas longeque revolvas
Nomen, ab infami gentem deducis asylo;
Maiorum primus, quisquis fuit ille, tuorum
Aut pastor fuit aut illud quod dicere nolo.   275

The Roman circus

SATURA X.

OMNIBUS in terris, quae sunt a Gadibus usque
Auroram et Gangen, pauci dinoscere possunt
Vera bona atque illis multum diversa, remota
Erroris nebula.   Quid enim ratione timemus
Aut cupimus? quid tam dextro pede concipis ut te   5
Conatus non paeniteat votique peracti?
Evertere domos totas optantibus ipsis
Di faciles; nocitura toga, nocitura petuntur
Militia; torrens dicendi copia multis
Et sua mortifera est facundia; viribus ille   10
Confisus periit admirandisque lacertis.
Sed plures nimia congesta pecunia cura
Strangulat et cuncta exuperans patrimonia census,
Quanto delphinis ballaena Britannica maior.
Temporibus diris igitur iussuque Neronis   15
Longinum et magnos Senecae praedivitis hortos
Clausit et egregias Lateranorum obsidet aedes
Tota cohors: rarus venit in cenacula miles.
Pauca licet portes argenti vascula puri,
Nocte iter ingressus gladium contumque timebis   20

Et motae ad lunam trepidabis harundinis umbram:
Cantabit vacuus coram latrone viator.
Prima fere vota et cunctis notissima templis
Divitiae, crescant ut opes, ut maxima toto
Nostra sit arca foro. Sed nulla aconita bibuntur   25
Fictilibus; tunc illa time, cum pocula sumes
Gemmata et lato Setinum ardebit in auro.
Iamne igitur laudas, quod de sapientibus alter
Ridebat, quotiens de limine moverat unum
Protuleratque pedem, flebat contrarius auctor?   30
Sed facilis cuivis rigidi censura cachinni:
Mirandum est, unde ille oculis suffecerit umor.
Perpetuo risu pulmonem agitare solebat
Democritus, quamquam non essent urbibus illis
Praetextae, trabeae, fasces, lectica, tribunal.   35
Quid, si vidisset praetorem curribus altis
Extantem et medii sublimem pulvere circi
In tunica Iovis et pictae Sarrana ferentem
Ex umeris aulaea togae magnaeque coronae
Tantum orbem, quanto cervix non sufficit ulla?   40
Quippe tenet sudans hanc publicus et, sibi consul
Ne placeat, curru servus portatur eodem.
Da nunc et volucrem, sceptro quae surgit eburno,
Illinc cornicines, hinc praecedentia longi
Agminis officia et niveos ad frena Quirites,   45
Defossa in loculos quos sportula fecit amicos.
Tum quoque materiam risus invenit ad omnis
Occursus hominum, cuius prudentia monstrat
Summos posse viros et magna exempla daturos

---

21. umbram ω, umbras *s*, umbra *P*. 30. auctor *Ps*, alter ω. 31.
cuivis *pω*, cuius *P*. 35. praetexta et rabeae *P*, practexta trabeae *florilc-*
gium S. Galli, praetexta et trabeae *p*. 46. loculos *P*, loculis ω.

Vervecum in patria crassoque sub aere nasci.   50
Ridebat curas, nec non et gaudia vulgi,
Interdum et lacrimas, cum Fortunae ipse minaci
Mandaret laqueum mediumque ostenderet unguem.
Ergo supervacua aut vel perniciosa petuntur,
Propter quae fas est genua incerare deorum.   55
     Quosdam praecipitat subiecta potentia magnae
Invidiae; mergit longa atque insignis honorum
Pagina. Descendunt statuae restemque sequuntur,
Ipsas deinde rotas bigarum inpacta securis
Caedit et inmeritis franguntur crura caballis: 60
Iam strident ignes, iam follibus atque caminis
Ardet adoratum populo caput et crepat ingens
Seianus; deinde ex facie toto orbe secunda
Fiunt urceoli, pelves, sartago, matellae.
Pone domi laurus, duc in Capitolia magnum   65
Cretatumque bovem: Seianus ducitur unco
Spectandus; gaudent omnes: " Quae labra, quis illi
Vultus erat! numquam, si quid mihi credis, amavi
Hunc hominem! sed quo cecidit sub crimine? quisnam
Delator? quibus indicibus, quo teste probavit? "   70
" Nil horum: verbosa et grandis epistula venit
A Capreis."—" Bene habet; nil plus interrogo."—Sed quid
Turba Remi? Sequitur Fortunam ut semper et odit
Damnatos; idem populus, si Nortia Tusco
Favisset, si oppressa foret secura senectus   75
Principis, hac ipsa Seianum diceret hora
Augustum. Iam pridem, ex quo suffragia nulli
Vendimus, effudit curas; nam qui dabat olim
Imperium, fasces, legiones, omnia, nunc se

---

54. aut *Pω*, vel *Doederlein*, ut *Munro*, aut ne p. petantur *Lachmann*, quae *Buecheler*. 64. matellae *P*, patellae *s*. 70. indicibus *Pω*, indiciis *s*.

Continet atque duas tantum res anxius optat,   80
Panem et circenses.—" Perituros audio multos."
" Nil dubium, magna est fornacula ; pallidulus mi
Bruttidius meus ad Martis fuit obvius aram."
" Quam timeo victus ne poenas exigat Aiax
Ut male defensus ! curramus praecipites et,   85
Dum iacet in ripa, calcemus Caesaris hostem.
Sed videant servi, ne quis neget et pavidum in ius
Cervice obstricta dominum trahat."—Hi sermones
Tunc de Seiano, secreta haec murmura vulgi.
Visne salutari sicut Seianus ? habere   90
Tantundem atque illi summas donare curules,
Illum exercitibus praeponere ? tutor haberi
Principis augusta Caprearum in rupe sedentis
Cum grege Chaldaeo ? vis certe pila, cohortes,
Egregios equites et castra domestica ? quidni   95
Haec cupias ? et qui nolunt occidere quemquam,
Posse volunt.   Sed quae praeclara et prospera tanti
Ut rebus laetis par sit mensura malorum ?
Huius, qui trahitur, praetextam sumere mavis,
An Fidenarum Gabiorumque esse potestas   100
Et de mensura ius dicere, vasa minora
Frangere pannosus vacuis aedilis Ulubris ?
Ergo quid optandum foret, ignorasse fateris
Seianum ; nam qui nimios optabat honores
Et nimias poscebat opes, numerosa parabat   105
Excelsae turris tabulata, unde altior esset
Casus et impulsae praeceps immane ruinae.
Quid Crassos, quid Pompeios evertit, et illum,
Ad sua qui domitos deduxit flagra Quirites ?
Summus nempe locus nulla non arte petitus,   110

---

82. pallidulus mi *pω*, palli.lus mihi *P*.   93. augusta *Ps*, angusta *s*.

Auriga.

Magnaque numinibus vota exaudita malignis.
Ad generum Cereris sine caede ac vulnere pauci
Descendunt reges et sicca morte tyranni.
    Eloquium aut famam Demosthenis aut Ciceronis
Incipit optare et totis quinquatribus optat,   115
Quisquis adhuc uno parcam colit asse Minervam,
Quem sequitur custos angustae vernula capsae.
Eloquio sed uterque perit orator; utrumque
Largus et exundans leto dedit ingenii fons.
Ingenio manus est et cervix caesa; nec umquam   120
Sanguine causidici maduerunt rostra pusilli.
"O fortunatam natam me consule Romam!"—
Antoni gladios potuit contemnere, si sic
Omnia dixisset. Ridenda poemata malo,
Quam te conspicuae, divina Philippica, famae,   125
Volveris a prima quae proxima. Saevus et illum
Exitus eripuit, quem mirabantur Athenae
Torrentem et pleni moderantem frena theatri.
Dis ille adversis genitus fatoque sinistro,
Quem pater ardentis massae fuligine lippus   130
A carbone et forcipibus gladiosque parante
Incude et luteo Vulcano ad rhetora misit.
    Bellorum exuviae, truncis adfixa tropaeis
Lorica et fracta de casside buccula pendens
Et curtum temone iugum victaeque triremis   135
Aplustre et summo tristis captivus in arcu
Humanis maiora bonis creduntur. Ad hoc se
Romanus Graiusque et barbarus induperator
Erexit: causas discriminis atque laboris
Inde habuit. Tanto maior famae sitis est, quam   140
Virtutis. Quis enim virtutem amplectitur ipsam,

114. aut famam *P*, ac famam *pω*. 116. parcam *P*, partam *pω*.

Praemia si tollas? patriam tamen obruit olim
Gloria paucorum et laudis titulique cupido
Haesuri saxis cinerum custodibus, ad quae
Discutienda valent sterilis mala robora fici,   145
Quandoquidem data sunt ipsis quoque fata sepulcris.
Expende Hannibalem: quot libras in duce summo
Invenies? hic est, quem non capit Africa Mauro
Percussa Oceano Niloque admota tepenti,
Rursus ad Aethiopum populos altosque elephantos.   150
Additur imperiis Hispania, Pyrenaeum
Transilit; opposuit natura Alpemque nivemque:
Diducit scopulos et montem rumpit aceto.
Iam tenet Italiam; tamen ultra pergere tendit:
"Actum," inquit, "nihil est, nisi Poeno milite portas 155
Frangimus et media vexillum pono Subura."
O qualis facies et quali digna tabella,
Cum Gaetula ducem portaret belua luscum!
Exitus ergo quis est? O gloria! vincitur idem
Nempe et in exilium praeceps fugit atque ibi magnus 160
Mirandusque cliens sedet ad praetoria regis,
Donec Bithyno libeat vigilare tyranno.
Finem animae, quae res humanas miscuit olim,
Non gladii, non saxa dabunt, nec tela, sed ille
Cannarum vindex et tanti sanguinis ultor   165
Anulus.   I demens et saevas curre per Alpes,
Ut pueris placeas et declamatio fias!
Unus Pellaeo iuveni non sufficit orbis;
Aestuat infelix angusto limite mundi,
Ut Gyari clausus scopulis parvaque Seripho: 170
Cum tamen a figulis munitam intraverit urbem,
Sarcophago contentus erit.   Mors sola fatetur

---

145. fici *Ps*, ficus *ω*.   150. altos *Ps*, alios *ω*.

Quantula sint hominum corpuscula. Creditur olim
Velificatus Athos et quidquid Graecia mendax
Audet in historia, constratum classibus isdem   175
Suppositumque rotis solidum mare; credimus altos
Defecisse amnes epotaque flumina Medo
Prandente, et madidis cantat quae Sostratus alis.
Ille tamen qualis rediit Salamine relicta,
In Corum atque Eurum solitus saevire flagellis   180
Barbarus, Aeolio numquam hoc in carcere passos,
Ipsum conpedibus qui vinxerat Ennosigaeum?
Mitius id sane, quod non et stigmate dignum
Credidit. Huic quisquam vellet servire deorum!
Sed qualis rediit? nempe una nave, cruentis   185
Fluctibus ac tarda per densa cadavera prora.
Has totiens optata exegit gloria poenas!
   "Da spatium vitae, multos da, Iuppiter, annos!"
Hoc recto vultu, solum hoc et pallidus optas.
Sed quam continuis et quantis longa senectus   190
Plena malis! deformem et taetrum ante omnia vultum
Dissimilemque sui, deformem, pro cute pellem
Pendentisque genas et talis aspice rugas,
Quales, umbriferos ubi pandit Thabraca saltus,
In vetula scalpit iam mater simia bucca.   195
Plurima sunt iuvenum discrimina; pulchrior ille
Hoc, atque ille alio, multum hic robustior illo:
Una senum facies, cum voce trementia membra
Et iam leve caput madidique infantia nasi,
Frangendus misero gingiva panis inermi.   200
Usque adeo gravis uxori natisque sibique,
Ut captatori moveat fastidia Cosso.

---

175. constratum *pω*, contractum *P.*   189. *delebat Heinrich,* hoc recto
ω, hoc alto recto *P.*   197. ille *om. P.*

Non eadem vini atque cibi, torpente palato,
Gaudia.   204

       Aspice partis   209
Nunc damnum alterius; nam quae cantante voluptas, 210
Sit licet eximius, citharoedo sive Seleuco,
Et quibus aurata mos est fulgere lacerna?
Quid refert magni sedeat qua parte theatri,
Qui vix cornicines exaudiet atque tubarum
Concentus? clamore opus est, ut sentiat auris,   215
Quem dicat venisse puer, quot nuntiet horas.
Praeterea minimus gelido iam in corpore sanguis
Febre calet sola: circumsilit agmine facto
Morborum omne genus; quorum si nomina quaeras,   219
Percurram citius quot villas possideat nunc,   225
Quo tondente gravis iuveni mihi barba sonabat.
Ille umero, hic lumbis, hic coxa debilis; ambos
Perdidit ille oculos et luscis invidet; huius
Pallida labra cibum accipiunt digitis alienis,
Ipse ad conspectum cenae diducere rictum   230
Suetus hiat tantum, ceu pullus hirundinis, ad quem
Ore volat pleno mater ieiuna.   Sed omni
Membrorum damno maior dementia, quae nec
Nomina servorum nec vultum agnoscit amici,
Cum quo praeterita cenavit nocte, nec illos,   235
Quos genuit, quos eduxit.   Nam codice saevo
Heredes vetat esse suos, bona tota feruntur
Ad Phialen.   238
Ut vigeant sensus animi, ducenda tamen sunt   240
Funera natorum, rogus aspiciendus amatae
Coniugis et fratris plenaeque sororibus urnae.

---

211. sive Seleuco *P*, sitve Seleucus *ω*.   217. in *om. s.*   232. mater
ieiuna *pω*, materiae luna *P*.   240. sunt *pω*, sint *P*.

Haec data poena diu viventibus, ut renovata
Semper clade domus multis in luctibus inque
Perpetuo maerore et nigra veste senescant. 245
Rex Pylius, magno si quidquam credis Homero,
Exemplum vitae fuit a cornice secundae.
Felix himirum, qui tot per saecula mortem
Distulit atque suos iam dextra computat annos,
Quique novum totiens mustum bibit. Oro, parumper 250
Attendas, quantum de legibus ipse queratur
Fatorum et nimio de stamine, cum videt acris
Antilochi barbam ardentem, cum quaerit ab omni
Quisquis adest socius, cur haec in tempora duret,
Quod facinus dignum tam longo admiserit aevo. 255
Haec eadem Peleus, raptum cum luget Achillem,
Atque alius, cui fas Ithacum lugere natantem.
Incolumi Troia Priamus venisset ad umbras
Assaraci magnis sollemnibus, Hectore funus
Portante ac reliquis fratrum cervicibus inter 260
Iliadum lacrimas, ut primos edere planctus
Cassandra inciperet scissaque Polyxena palla,
Si foret exstinctus diverso tempore, quo non
Coeperat audaces Paris aedificare carinas.
Longa dies igitur quid contulit? omnia vidit 265
Eversa et flammis Asiam ferroque cadentem.
Tunc miles tremulus posita tulit arma tiara
Et ruit ante aram summi Iovis, ut vetulus bos,
Qui domini cultris tenue et miserabile collum
Praebet, ab ingrato iam fastiditus aratro. 270
Exitus ille utcumque hominis, sed torva canino
Latravit rictu, quae post hunc vixerat, uxor.

---

243. viventibus *Pω*, viventi est *Weidner*. 245. senescant *pω*, senescat *P*. 259. magni *P*. 263. quo non *P*, quo iam *ω*.

Festino ad nostros et regem transeo Ponti
Et Croesum, quem vox iusti facunda Solonis
Respicere ad longae iussit spatia ultima vitae.   275
Exilium et carcer Minturnarumque paludes
Et mendicatus victa Carthagine panis
Hinc causas habuere. Quid illo cive tulisset
Natura in terris, quid Roma beatius umquam,
Si circumducto captivorum agmine et omni   280
Bellorum pompa animam exhalasset opimam,
Cum de Teutonico vellet descendere curru?
Provida Pompeio dederat Campania febres
Optandas, sed multae urbes et publica vota
Vicerunt; igitur fortuna ipsius et urbis   285
Servatum victo caput abstulit. Hoc cruciatu
Lentulus, hac poena caruit ceciditque Cethegus
Integer, et iacuit Catilina cadavere toto.   288
    "Nil ergo optabunt homines?"—Si consilium vis,   346
Permittes ipsis expendere numinibus quid
Conveniat nobis rebusque sit utile nostris.
Nam pro iucundis aptissima quaeque dabunt di.
Carior est illis homo, quam sibi. Nos animorum   350
Impulsu et caeca magnaque cupidine ducti
Coniugium petimus partumque uxoris; at illis
Notum qui pueri qualisque futura sit uxor.
Ut tamen et poscas aliquid voveasque sacellis
Exta et candiduli divina tomacula porci,   355
Orandum est ut sit mens sana in corpore sano.
Fortem posce animum, mortis terrore carentem,
Qui spatium vitae extremum inter munera ponat
Naturae, qui ferre queat quoscumque labores,
Nesciat irasci, cupiat nihil et potiores   360

---

359. dolores *Ruperti, Leid. Hosius.*

Herculis aerumnas credat saevosque labores
Et Venere et cenis et pluma Sardanapalli.
Monstro quod ipse tibi possis dare ; semita certe
Tranquillae per virtutem patet unica vitae.
Nullum numen habes, si sit prudentia ; nos te 365
Nos facimus, Fortuna, deam caeloque locamus.

---

365. habes *Pω*, abest *p*.

Reading from Homer.

SATURA XI.

ATTICUS eximie si cenat, lautus habetur;
Si Rutilus, demens.   Quid enim maiore cachinno
Excipitur vulgi, quam pauper Apicius? omnes
Convictus, thermae, stationes, omne theatrum
De Rutilo.   Nam dum valida ac iuvenalia membra   5
Sufficiunt galeae, dumque ardet sanguine, fertur,
Non cogente quidem, sed nec prohibente tribuno,
Scripturus leges et regia verba lanistae.
Multos porro vides, quos saepe elusus ad ipsum
Creditor introitum solet expectare macelli,   10
Et quibus in solo vivendi causa palato est.
Egregius cenat meliusque miserrimus horum
Et cito casurus iam perlucente ruina.
Interea gustus elementa per omnia quaerunt,
Numquam animo pretiis opstantibus; interius si   15
Attendas, magis illa iuvant, quae pluris ementur.

---

3. omnis *P rasa* i.   6. ardet *Guietus*, ardenti *P*, ardens *pω*, ardent
Barthius.   16. ementur *P*, emuntur *pω*.

Ergo haud difficile est perituram arcessere summam,
Lancibus oppositis vel matris imagine fracta,
Et quadringentis nummis condire gulosum
Fictile: sic veniunt ad miscillanea ludi. 20
Refert ergo, quis haec eadem paret: in Rutilo nam
Luxuria est, in Ventidio laudabile nomen
Sumit et a censu famam trahit. Illum ego iure
Despiciam, qui scit quanto sublimior Atlas
Omnibus in Libya sit montibus, hic tamen idem 25
Ignoret quantum ferrata distet ab arca
Sacculus. E caelo descendit γνῶθι σεαυτόν,
Figendum et memori tractandum pectore, sive
Coniugium quaeras vel sacri in parte senatus
Esse velis; neque enim loricam poscit Achillis 30
Thersites, in qua se traducebat Ulixes;
Ancipitem seu tu magno discrimine causam
Protegere adfectas, te consule, dic tibi qui sis,
Orator vehemens, an Curtius et Matho buccae.
Noscenda est mensura sui spectandaque rebus 35
In summis minimisque, etiam cum piscis emetur;
Ne mullum cupias, cum sit tibi gobio tantum
In loculis. Quis enim te deficiente crumina
Et crescente gula manet exitus, aere paterno
Ac rebus mersis in ventrem, faenoris atque 40
Argenti gravis et pecorum agrorumque capacem?
Talibus a dominis post cuncta novissimus exit
Anulus, et digito mendicat Pollio nudo.
Non praematuri cineres nec funus acerbum
Luxuriae, sed morte magis metuenda senectus. 45
Hi plerumque gradus: conducta pecunia Romae
Et coram dominis consumitur; inde ubi paulum

---

35. suis *P*. 38. c . . . ina *P*, crumena *pω*, culina *s*.

6

Nescio quid superest et pallet faenoris auctor,
Qui vertere solum, Baias et ad ostrea currunt.
Cedere namque foro iam non est deterius quam   50
Esquilias a ferventi migrare Subura.
Ille dolor solus patriam fugientibus, illa
Maestitia est, caruisse anno circensibus uno.
Sanguinis in facie non haeret gutta; morantur
Pauci ridiculum effugientem ex urbe pudorem.   55
   Experiere hodie, numquid pulcherrima dictu,
Persice, non praestem vita vel moribus et re,
Si laudem siliquas occultus ganeo, pultes
Coram aliis dictem puero, sed in aure placentas.
Nam cum sis conviva mihi promissus, habebis   60
Evandrum, venies Tirynthius aut minor illo
Hospes, et ipse tamen contingens sanguine caelum:
Alter aquis, alter flammis ad sidera missus.
Fercula nunc audi nullis ornata macellis.
De Tiburtino veniet pinguissimus agro   65
Haedulus et toto grege mollior, inscius herbae,
Necdum ausus virgas humilis mordere salicti,
Qui plus lactis habet quam sanguinis, et montani
Asparagi, posito quos legit vilica fuso;
Grandia praeterea tortoque calentia faeno   70
Ova adsunt ipsis cum matribus, et servatae
Parte anni, quales fuerant in vitibus, uvae,
Signinum Syriumque pirum, de corbibus isdem
Aemula Picenis et odoris mala recentis,
Nec metuenda tibi, siccatum frigore postquam   75
Autumnum et crudi posuere pericula suci.
Haec olim nostri iam luxuriosa senatus

---

55. effugientem *Pω*, et fugientem *s Priscian.*   57. vel *pω*, . . . *P*, nec
s.   58. si *P*, sed *pω.*   63. missis *P*.

Cena fuit: Curius, parvo quae legerat horto,
Ipse focis brevibus ponebat holuscula, quae nunc
Squalidus in magna fastidit compede fossor,   80
Qui meminit, calidae sapiat quid vulva popinae.
Sicci terga suis, rara pendentia crate,
Moris erat quondam festis servare diebus
Et natalicium cognatis ponere lardum,
Accedente nova, si quam dabat hostia, carne.   85
Cognatorum aliquis, titulo ter consulis atque
Castrorum imperiis et dictatoris honore
Functus, ad has epulas solito maturius ibat,
Erectum domito referens a monte ligonem.
Cum tremerent autem Fabios durumque Catonem   90
Et Scauros et Fabricium, postremo severos
Censoris mores etiam collega timeret,
Nemo inter curas et seria duxit habendam,
Qualis in Oceano fluctu testudo nataret,
Clarum Troiugenis factura et nobile fulcrum;   95
Sed nudo latere et parvis frons aerea lectis
Vile coronati caput ostendebat aselli,
Ad quod lascivi ludebant ruris alumni.
Tales ergo cibi, qualis domus atque supellex.
Tunc rudis et Graias mirari nescius artes   100
Urbibus eversis praedarum in parte reperta
Magnorum artificum frangebat pocula miles,
Ut phaleris gauderet equus caelataque cassis
Romuleae simulacra ferae mansuescere iussae
Imperii fato, geminos sub rupe Quirinos,   105
Ac nudam effigiem clipeo venientis et hasta

---

81. sapiat quid *pω*, sapiat qui *P*.   91. Fabricium *P*, Fabricios *ω*,
postremo *P*, rigidique *ω*.   93. habendam *P*, habendum *pω*.   94. oceano
s, oceana *P*, oceani *pω*.   99. *delebat Heinrich*.   100. rudis *pω*, ruris *P*.

Pendentisque dei perituro ostenderet hosti.
Ponebant igitur Tusco farrata catino;
Argenti quod erat, solis fulgebat in armis.
Omnia tunc, quibus invideas, si lividulus sis.   110
Templorum quoque maiestas praesentior et vox
Nocte fere media mediamque audita per urbem,
Litore ab Oceani Gallis venientibus et dis
Officium vatis peragentibus; his monuit nos,
Hanc rebus Latiis curam praestare solebat   115
Fictilis et nullo violatus Iuppiter auro.
Illa domi natas nostraque ex arbore mensas
Tempora viderunt; hos lignum stabat ad usus,
Annosam si forte nucem deiecerat Eurus.
At nunc divitibus cenandi nulla voluptas,   120
Nil rhombus, nil damma sapit, putere videntur
Unguenta atque rosae, latos nisi sustinet orbes
Grande ebur et magno sublimis pardus hiatu,
Dentibus ex illis, quos mittit porta Syenes
Et Mauri celeres et Mauro obscurior Indus,   125
Et quos deposuit Nabataeo belua saltu,
Iam nimios capitique graves.   Hinc surgit orexis,
Hinc stomacho vires; nam pes argenteus illis,
Anulus in digito quod ferreus.   Ergo superbum
Convivam caveo, qui me sibi comparet et res   130
Despicit exiguas.   Adeo nulla uncia nobis
Est eboris, nec tessellae, nec calculus ex hac
Materia quin ipsa manubria cultellorum
Ossea; non tamen his ulla umquam obsonia fiunt
Rancidula, aut ideo peior gallina secatur.   135
Sed nec structor erit, cui cedere debeat omnis

---

109. *om. s.*   110. tunc in quibus *P rasa* in.   118. hos *ω*, hoc *P*.
130. comparet *PS*, comparat *ω*.   136. cedere *pω*, credere *P*.

Pergula, discipulus Trypheri doctoris, apud quem
Sumine cum magno lepus atque aper et pygargus
Et Scythicae volucres et phoenicopterus ingens
Et Gaetulus oryx hebeti lautissima ferro   140
Caeditur et tota sonat ulmea cena Subura.
Nec frustum capreae subducere nec latus Afrae
Novit avis noster, tirunculus ac rudis omni
Tempore et exiguae furtis inbutus ofellae.
Plebeios calices et paucis assibus emptos   145
Porriget incultus puer atque a frigore tutus;
Non Phryx aut Lycius, non a mangone petitus
Quisquam erit: in magno cum posces, posce Latine.
Idem habitus cunctis, tonsi rectique capilli
Atque hodie tantum propter convivia pexi.   150
Pastoris duri hic est filius, ille bubulci.
Suspirat longo non visam tempore matrem,
Et casulam et notos tristis desiderat haedos,
Ingenui vultus puer ingenuique pudoris,
Quales esse decet, quos ardens purpura vestit.   155
Hic tibi vina dabit diffusa in montibus illis,   159
A quibus ipse venit, quorum sub vertice lusit;   160
Namque una atque eadem est vini patria atque ministri. 161
Nostra dabunt alios hodie convivia ludos: 179
Conditor Iliados cantabitur atque Maronis   180
Altisoni dubiam facientia carmina palmam.
Quid refert, tales versus qua voce legantur?
    Sed nunc dilatis averte negotia curis
Et gratam requiem dona tibi: quando licebat
Per totum cessare diem? non faenoris ulla   185

---

142. capreae $p\omega S$, caprae P.   147. non — magno *delebat Guietus*.
148. in magno PSs, et magno ω.   161. *delebat Markland*.   180. condi-
tor $p\omega$, condi . . . tur P, conducitur S.   184. licebit $p\omega$, licebat P.

Mentio.   186
Protinus ante meum quidquid dolet exue limen;   190
Pone domum et servos et quidquid frangitur illis
Aut perit; ingratos ante omnia pone sodales.
Interea Megalesiacae spectacula mappae,
Idaeum sollemne, colunt, similisque triumpho
Praeda caballorum praetor sedet ac, mihi pace   195
Immensae nimiaeque licet si dicere plebis,
Totam hodie Romam circus capit et fragor aurem
Percutit, eventum viridis quo colligo panni;
Nam si deficeret, maestam attonitamque videres
Hanc urbem, veluti Cannarum in pulvere victis   200
Consulibus.   Spectent iuvenes, quos clamor et audax
Sponsio, quos cultae decet adsedisse puellae;
Nostra bibat vernum contracta cuticula solem
Effugiatque togam.   Iam nunc in balnea salva
Fronte licet vadas, quamquam solida hora supersit   205
Ad sextam.   Facere hoc non possis quinque diebus
Continuis, quia sunt talis quoque taedia vitae
Magna; voluptates commendat rarior usus.

---

208. rarior *pω*, parior *P*.

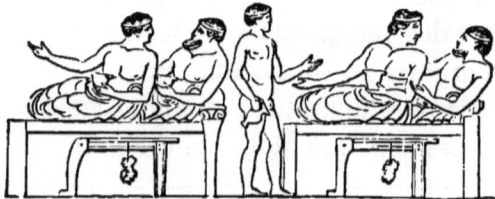

Bas-relief: Rowers in an Attic trireme.

SATURA XII.

Natali, Corvine, die mihi dulcior haec lux,
Qua festus promissa deis animalia caespes
Expectat. Niveam reginae ducimus agnam;
Par vellus dabitur pugnanti Gorgone Maura;
Sed procul extensum petulans quatit hostia funem   5
Tarpeio servata Iovi frontemque coruscat;
Quippe ferox vitulus, templis maturus et arae
Spargendusque mero, quem iam pudet ubera matris
Ducere, qui vexat nascenti robora cornu.
Si res ampla domi similisque affectibus esset,   10
Pinguior Hispulla traheretur taurus et ipsa
Mole piger, nec finitima nutritus in herba,
Laeta sed ostendens Clitumni pascua sanguis
Iret et a grandi cervix ferienda ministro,
Ob reditum trepidantis adhuc horrendaque passi   15
Nuper et incolumem sese mirantis amici.
Nam praeter pelagi casus et fulminis ictus

---

14. iret *Pω*, Umber *Weidner.*

Evasit.   Densae caelum abscondere tenebrae
Nube una, subitusque antemnas inpulit ignis,
Cum se quisque illo percussum crederet, et mox   20
Attonitus nullum conferri posse putaret
Naufragium velis ardentibus.   Omnia fiunt
Talia, tam graviter, si quando poetica surgit
Tempestas.   Genus ecce aliud discriminis; audi
Et miserere iterum, quamquam sint cetera sortis   25
Eiusdem, pars dira quidem, sed cognita multis
Et quam votiva testantur fana tabella
Plurima; pictores quis nescit ab Iside pasci?
Accidit et nostro similis fortuna Catullo.
Cum plenus fluctu medius foret alveus, et iam   30
Alternum puppis latus evertentibus undis,
Arbori incertae nullam prudentia cani
Rectoris conferret opem, decidere iactu
Coepit cum ventis.   34
"Fundite, quae mea sunt," dicebat, "cuncta," Catullus, 37
Praecipitare volens etiam pulcherrima, vestem
Purpuream, teneris quoque Maecenatibus aptam,
Atque alias, quarum generosi graminis ipsum   40
Infecit natura pecus, sed et egregius fons
Viribus occultis et Baeticus adiuvat aer.
Ille nec argentum dubitabat mittere, lances
Parthenio factas, urnae cratera capacem
Et dignum sitiente Pholo vel coniuge Fusci;   45
Adde et bascaudas et mille escaria, multum
Caelati, biberat quo callidus emptor Olynthi.
Sed quis nunc alius, qua mundi parte quis audet

---

23. si *Pω*, quam *Schurzfleisch*.   29. *damnarat Iahn*.   32. arbori *Lachmann*, arboris *Pω*, aequoris (incerti) *Iacobs*, arbitrio incerto *Bezzenberger*, arboris — nutu *et (33)* non ferret *Weidner*.   47. quo *pω*, quod *P*; callidus *s*, pallidus *P*.

Argento praeferre caput rebusque salutem?
Non propter vitam faciunt patrimonia quidam,   50
Sed vitio caeci propter patrimonia vivunt.
Iactatur rerum utilium pars maxima, sed nec
Damna levant; tunc adversis urguentibus illuc
Reccidit ut malum ferro summitteret, ac se
Explicat angustum: discriminis ultima, quando   55
Praesidia adferimus navem factura minorem.
I nunc et ventis animam committe, dolato
Confisus ligno, digitis a morte remotus
Quattuor aut septem, si sit latissima taeda;
Mox cum reticulis et pane et ventre lagonae   60
Aspice sumendas in tempestate secures.
Sed postquam iacuit planum mare, tempora postquam
Prospera vectoris fatumque valentius Euro
Et pelago, postquam Parcae meliora benigna
Pensa manu ducunt hilares et staminis albi   65
Lanificae, modica nec multum fortior aura
Ventus adest, inopi miserabilis arte cucurrit
Vestibus extentis et, quod superaverat unum,
Velo prora suo.   Iam deficientibus Austris
Spes vitae cum sole redit; tunc gratus Iulo   70
Atque, novercali sedes praelata Lavino,
Conspicitur sublimis apex, cui candida nomen
Scrofa dedit, laetis Phrygibus miserabile sumen,
Et numquam visis triginta clara mamillis.
Tandem intrat positas inclusa per aequora moles   75
Tyrrhenamque pharon porrectaque bracchia rursum,
Quae pelago occurrunt medio longeque relinquunt

50, 51. *delebat Bentley.*   54. recidit *P,* decidit *ω.*   61. aspice *Pω,*
respice *Iahn.*   71. Lavinio *A. de Roog,* Lavino *Pω.*   73. miserabile *PS,*
mirabile *ωS.*

Italiam; non sic igitur mirabere portus,
Quos natura dedit; sed trunca puppe magister
Interiora petit Baianae pervia cumbae,   80
Tuti stagna sinus.   Gaudent ibi vertice raso
Garrula securi narrare pericula nautae.
 Ite igitur, pueri, linguis animisque faventes,
Sertaque delubris et farra inponite cultris
Ac mollis ornatc focos glebamque virentem!   85
Iam sequar et sacro, quod praestat, rite peracto
Inde domum repetam, graciles ubi parva coronas
Accipiunt fragili simulacra nitentia cera.
Hic nostrum placabo Iovem Laribusque paternis
Tura dabo atque omnis violae iactabo colores.   90
Cuncta nitent; longos erexit ianua ramos
Et matutinis operatur festa lucernis.
Nec suspecta tibi sint haec, Corvine.   Catullus,
Pro cuius reditu tot pono altaria, parvos
Tres habet heredes.   Libet expectare, quis aegram   95
Et claudentem oculos gallinam inpendat amico
Tam sterili; verum haec nimia est inpensa; coturnix
Nulla umquam pro patre cadet.   Sentire calorem
Si coepit locuples Gallitta et Pacius orbi,
Legitime fixis vestitur tota libellis   100
Porticus, existunt qui promittant hecatomben;
Quatenus hic non sunt nec venales elephanti,
Nec Latio aut usquam sub nostro sidere talis
Belua concipitur, sed furva gente petita
Arboribus Rutulis et Turni pascitur agro,   105
Caesaris armentum, nulli servire paratum
Privato; siquidem Tyrio parere solebant

---

81. ibi *Ps*, ubi ω.   93. ne *Lachmann;* tibi *pω*, ibi *P*.   100. libellis
Ps, tabcllis *s*.

Hannibali et nostris ducibus regique Molosso
Horum maiores ac dorso ferre cohortes
Partem aliquam belli et euntem in proelia turrem.   110
Nulla igitur mora per Novium, mora nulla per Histrum
Pacuvium, quin illud ebur ducatur ad aras
Et cadat ante Lares Gallittae victima, sola
Tantis digna deis et captatoribus horum.
Alter enim, si concedas, mactare vovebit   115
De grege servorum magna et pulcherrima quaeque
Corpora, vel pueris et frontibus ancillarum
Inponet vittas, et si qua est nubilis illi
Iphigenia domi, dabit hanc altaribus, etsi
Non sperat tragicae furtiva piacula cervae.   120
Laudo meum civem, nec comparo testamento
Mille rates; nam si Libitinam evaserit aeger,
Delebit tabulas, inclusus carcere nassae,
Post meritum sane mirandum, atque omnia soli
Forsan Pacuvio breviter dabit, ille superbus   125
Incedet victis rivalibus.   Ergo vides quam
Grande operae pretium faciat iugulata Mycenis.
Vivat Pacuvius, quaeso, vel Nestora totum;
Possideat, quantum rapuit Nero; montibus aurum
Exaequet; nec amet quemquam, nec ametur ab ullo.   130

---

116. et *pω*, ut *P*, aut *s*.   128. tantum *s*.

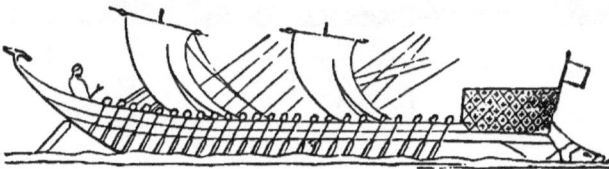

Jupiter.

Jupiter Ammon.

SATURA XIII.

Exemplo quodcumque malo committitur, ipsi
Displicet auctori.   Prima est haec ultio, quod se
Iudice nemo nocens absolvitur, inproba quamvis
Gratia fallaci praetoris vicerit urna.
Quid sentire putas omnis, Calvine, recenti   5
De scelere et fidei violatae crimine? sed nec
Tam tenuis census tibi contigit ut mediocris
Iacturae te mergat onus, nec rara videmus,
Quae pateris; casus multis hic cognitus ac iam
Tritus et e medio Fortunae ductus acervo.   10
Ponamus nimios gemitus; flagrantior aequo
Non debet dolor esse viri, nec vulnere maior.
Tu quamvis levium minimam exiguamque malorum
Particulam vix ferre potes, spumantibus ardens
Visceribus, sacrum tibi quod non reddat amicus   15
Depositum.   Stupet haec, qui iam post terga reliquit
Sexaginta annos, Fonteio consule natus?
An nihil in melius tot rerum proficit usu?
Magna quidem, sacris quae dat praecepta libellis,

---

4. fallaci *Ps*, fallacis *pω*.   5. omnes *Pω*, homines *Ribbeck*.   6. fidei
pω, fide *P*.   12. viri *pω*, veri *P*.   18. usu *Pω*, usus *S*.

Victrix Fortunae sapientia; ducimus autem   20
Hos quoque felices, qui ferre incommoda vitae
Nec iactare iugum vita didicere magistra.
Quae tam festa dies ut cesset prodere furem,
Perfidiam, fraudes, atque omni ex crimine lucrum
Quaesitum et partos gladio vel pyxide nummos?   25
Rari quippe boni, numero vix sunt totidem quot
Thebarum portae vel divitis ostia Nili.
Nunc aetas agitur peioraque saecula ferri
Temporibus, quorum sceleri non invenit ipsa
Nomen et a nullo posuit natura metallo;   30
Nos hominum divumque fidem clamore ciemus,
Quanto Faesidium laudat vocalis agentem
Sportula. Dic, senior bulla dignissime, nescis
Quas habeat veneres aliena pecunia? nescis
Quem tua simplicitas risum vulgo moveat, cum   35
Exigis a quoquam ne peieret et putet ullis
Esse aliquod numen templis araeque rubenti?
Quondam hoc indigenae vivebant more, priusquam
Sumeret agrestem posito diademate falcem
Saturnus fugiens, tunc, cum virguncula Iuno   40
Et privatus adhuc Idaeis Iuppiter antris.
Nulla super nubes convivia caelicolarum,
Nec puer Iliacus, formonsa nec Herculis uxor
Ad cyathos, et iam siccato nectare tergens
Bracchia Vulcanus Liparaea nigra taberna.   45
Prandebat sibi quisque deus, nec turba deorum
Talis ut est hodie, contentaque sidera paucis
Numinibus miserum urguebant Atlanta minori
Pondere. Nondum aliquis sortitus triste profundi

---

26. numero vix sunt *pω*, numerus vix est *s*, numerum si * totidem *P*.
28. nunc *P*, nona *pω*, nova *s*.

Imperium aut Sicula torvus cum coniuge Pluton,   50
Nec rota, nec Furiae, nec saxum aut vulturis atri
Poena; sed infernis hilares sine regibus umbrae.
Inprobitas illo fuit admirabilis aevo,
Credebant quo grande nefas et morte piandum,
Si iuvenis vetulo non adsurrexerat et si   55
Barbato cuicumque puer, licet ipse videret
Plura domi fraga et maiores glandis acervos.
Tam venerabile erat praecedere quattuor annis,
Primaque par adeo sacrae lanugo senectae!
Nunc, si depositum non infitietur amicus,   60
Si reddat veterem cum tota aerugine follem,
Prodigiosa fides et Tuscis digna libellis,
Quaeque coronata lustrari debeat agna.
Egregium sanctumque virum si cerno, bimembri
Hoc monstrum puero et miranti sub aratro   65
Piscibus inventis et fetae comparo mulae,
Sollicitus, tamquam lapides effuderit imber
Examenque apium longa consederit uva
Culmine delubri, tamquam in mare fluxerit amnis
Gurgitibus miris et lactis vertice torrens.   70
    Intercepta decem quereris sestertia fraude
Sacrilega? quid si bis centum perdidit alter
Hoc arcana modo? maiorem tertius illa
Summam, quam patulae vix ceperat angulus arcae?
Tam facile et pronum est superos contemnere testes,   75
Si mortalis idem nemo sciat!   Aspice quanta
Voce neget, quae sit ficti constantia vultus:
Per Solis radios Tarpeiaque fulmina iurat
Et Martis frameam et Cirrhaei spicula vatis,

---

58. tum *Iahn.* 65. et *P*, vel *p*, aut *s*; miranti *ps*, mirandis *Ps*, mi-
rantis *s*. 70. miniis *Porson.*

Per calamos venatricis pharetramque puellae,   80
Perque tuum, pater Aegaei Neptune, tridentem;
Addit et Herculeos arcus hastamque Minervae,
Quidquid habent telorum armamentaria caeli.
Si vero et pater est, " Comedam," inquit, " flebile nati
Sinciput elixi Pharioque madentis aceto."   85
  Sunt in Fortunae qui casibus omnia ponant
Et nullo credant mundum rectore moveri,
Natura volvente vices et lucis et anni,
Atque ideo intrepidi quaecumque altaria tangunt.
Est alius metuens ne crimen poena sequatur;   90
Hic putat esse deos et peierat, atque ita secum:
" Decernat, quodcumque volet, de corpore nostro
Isis et irato feriat mea lumina sistro,
Dummodo vel caecus teneam quos abnego nummos.
Et phthisis et vomicae putres et dimidium crus   95
Sunt tanti.   Pauper locupletem optare podagram
Nec dubitet Ladas, si non eget Anticyra nec
Archigene; quid enim velocis gloria plantae
Praestat et esuriens Pisaeae ramus olivae?
Ut sit magna, tamen certe lenta ira deorum est: 100
Si curant igitur cunctos punire nocentes,
Quando ad me venient?   Sed et exorabile numen
Fortasse experiar; solet his ignoscere; multi
Committunt eadem diverso crimina fato;
Ille crucem sceleris pretium tulit, hic diadema."   105
Sic animum dirae trepidum formidine culpae
Confirmat; tunc te sacra ad delubra vocantem
Praecedit, trahere immo ultro ac vexare paratus.
Nam cum magna malae superest audacia causae,

---

90. *damnarat Jahn.*   107. confirmat *Ss*, confirmant *Pω*; ad *pω*,
ac *Ps.*

Creditur a multis fiducia. Mimum agit ille, 110
Urbani qualem fugitivus scurra Catulli.
Tu miser exclamas, ut Stentora vincere possis,
Vel potius quantum Gradivus Homericus: "Audis,
Iuppiter, haec, nec labra moves, cum mittere vocem
Debueris vel marmoreus vel aheneus? aut cur 115
In carbone tuo charta pia tura soluta
Ponimus et sectum vituli iecur albaque porci
Omenta? Ut video, nullum discrimen habendum est
Effigies inter vestras statuamque Vagelli."
Accipe, quae contra valeat solacia ferre 120
Et qui nec Cynicos, nec Stoica dogmata legit
A Cynicis tunica distantia, non Epicurum
Suspicit exigui laetum plantaribus horti.
Curentur dubii medicis maioribus aegri,
Tu venam vel discipulo committe Philippi. 125
Si nullum in terris tam detestabile factum
Ostendis, taceo, nec pugnis caedere pectus
Te veto nec plana faciem contundere palma;
Quandoquidem accepto claudenda est ianua damno,
Et maiore domus gemitu, maiore tumultu 130
Planguntur nummi, quam funera. Nemo dolorem
Fingit in hoc casu, vestem diducere summam
Contentus, vexare oculos umore coacto:
Ploratur lacrimis amissa pecunia veris.
Sed si cuncta vides simili fora plena querella, 135
Si deciens lectis diversa parte tabellis
Vana supervacui dicunt chirographa ligni,
Arguit ipsorum quos littera gemmaque princeps
Sardonychum, loculis quae custoditur eburnis:
Ten', O delicias! extra communia censes 140

132. diducere *P*, deducere ω.

7

Ponendum, quia tu gallinae filius albae,
Nos viles pulli, nati infelicibus ovis?
Rem pateris modicam et mediocri bile ferendam,
Si flectas oculos maiora ad crimina.   Confer
Conductum latronem, incendia sulpure coepta   145
Atque dolo, primos cum ianua colligit ignes;
Confer et hos, veteris qui tollunt grandia templi
Pocula adorandae robiginis et populorum
Dona vel antiquo positas a rege coronas.
Haec ibi si non sunt, minor extat sacrilegus, qui   150
Radat inaurati femur Herculis et faciem ipsam
Neptuni, qui bratteolam de Castore ducat;
An dubitet, solitus totum conflare Tonantem?
Confer et artifices mercatoremque veneni,
Et deducendum corio bovis in mare, cum quo   155
Clauditur adversis innoxia simia fatis.
Haec quota pars scelerum, quae custos Gallicus urbis
Usque a lucifero, donec lux occidat, audit?
Humani generis mores tibi nosse volenti
Sufficit una domus; paucos consume dies, et   160
Dicere te miserum, postquam illinc veneris, aude.
Quis tumidum guttur miratur in Alpibus? aut quis
In Meroe crasso maiorem infante mamillam?
Caerula quis stupuit Germani lumina, flavam
Caesariem et madido torquentem cornua cirro?   165
Nempe quod haec illis natura est omnibus una.
Ad subitas Thracum volucres nubemque sonoram
Pygmaeus parvis currit bellator in armis,
Mox impar hosti raptusque per aera curvis
Unguibus a saeva fertur grue.   Si videas hoc   170
Gentibus in nostris, risu quatiare; sed illic,

---

141. quia *Pω*, quid? *Heinrich.*   147. veteres *P.*

Quamquam eadem adsidue spectentur proelia, ridet
Nemo, ubi tota cohors pede non est altior uno.
  " Nullane peiuri capitis fraudisque nefandae
Poena erit?"—Abreptum crede hunc graviore catena 175
Protinus et nostro—quid plus velit ira?—necari
Arbitrio; manet illa tamen iactura, nec umquam
Depositum tibi sospes erit, sed corpore trunco
Invidiosa dabit minimus solacia sanguis.—
" At vindicta bonum vita iucundius ipsa."—   180
Nempe hoc indocti, quorum praecordia nullis
Interdum aut levibus videas flagrantia causis :
Quantulacumque adeo est occasio, sufficit irae.
Chrysippus non dicet idem nec mite Thaletis
Ingenium dulcique senex vicinus Hymetto,   185
Qui partem acceptae saeva inter vincla cicutae
Accusatori nollet dare.   Plurima felix
Paulatim vitia atque errores exuit, omnes
Prima docet rectum sapientia; quippe minuti
Semper et infirmi est animi exiguique voluptas   190
Ultio : continuo sic collige, quod vindicta
Nemo magis gaudet, quam femina.   Cur tamen hos tu
Evasisse putes, quos diri conscia facti
Mens habet attonitos et surdo verbere caedit
Occultum quatiente animo tortore flagellum?   195
Poena autem vehemens ac multo saevior illis,
Quas et Caedicius gravis invenit et Rhadamanthus,
Nocte dieque suum gestare in pectore testem.
Spartano cuidam respondit Pythia vates,
Haud inpunitum quondam fore, quod dubitaret   200
Depositum retinere et fraudem iure tueri

---

174. peiuri *PS*.   183. *damnarat Iahn*.   187. Plurima — sapientia
delebat Guietus.   188. exuit, omnes *Buecheler*, exuit omnes, *alii*.

Iurando; quaerebat enim quae numinis esset
Mens, et an hoc illi facinus suaderet Apollo.
Reddidit ergo metu, non moribus; et tamen omnem
Vocem adyti dignam templo veramque probavit,   205
Extinctus tota pariter cum prole domoque
Et quamvis longa deductis gente propinquis.
Has patitur poenas peccandi sola voluntas;
Nam scelus intra se tacitum qui cogitat ullum,
Facti crimen habet: cedo, si conata peregit!   210
Perpetua anxietas nec mensae tempore cessat,
Faucibus ut morbo siccis interque molares
Difficili crescente cibo; sed vina misellus
Expuit, Albani veteris pretiosa senectus
Displicet; ostendas melius, densissima ruga   215
Cogitur in frontem, velut acri ducta Falerno.
Nocte brevem si forte indulsit cura soporem
Et toto versata toro iam membra quiescunt,
Continuo templum et violati numinis aras
Et, quod praecipuis mentem sudoribus urguet,   220
Te videt in somnis; tua sacra et maior imago
Humana turbat pavidum cogitque fateri.
Hi sunt, qui trepidant et ad omnia fulgura pallent,
Cum tonat, exanimes, primo quoque murmure caeli;
Non quasi fortuitus nec ventorum rabie, sed   225
Iratus cadat in terras et iudicet ignis.
Illa nihil nocuit: cura graviore timetur
Proxima tempestas, velut hoc dilata sereno.
Praeterea, lateris vigili cum febre dolorem
Si coepere pati, missum ad sua corpora morbum   230
Infesto credunt a numine; saxa deorum

---

208. sola ω, saeva *P;* voluptas *P.* 213. sed vina *PSω,* Setina *Here-lius.* 226. iudicet *Pω,* vindicet *s.*

Haec et tela putant. Pecudem spondere sacello
Balantem et Laribus cristam promittere galli
Non audent; quid enim sperare nocentibus aegris
Concessum? vel quae non dignior hostia vita? 235
Mobilis et varia est ferme natura malorum.
Cum scelus admittunt, superest constantia; quod fas
Atque nefas tandem incipiunt sentire, peractis
Criminibus. Tamen ad mores natura recurrit
Damnatos, fixa et mutari nescia. Nam quis 240
Peccandi finem posuit sibi? quando recepit
Eiectum semel attrita de fronte ruborem?
Quisnam hominum est quem tu contentum videris uno
Flagitio? dabit in laqueum vestigia noster
Perfidus et nigri patietur carceris uncum 245
Aut maris Aegaei rupem scopulosque frequentes
Exulibus magnis. Poena gaudebis amara
Nominis invisi, tandemque fatebere laetus,
Nec surdum nec Tiresian quemquam esse deorum.

236. *damnarat Iahn ;* fermentatura *P.* 237. quod *Pω,* quid *s.*

The Emperor Claudius.

SATURA XIV.

PLURIMA sunt, Fuscine, et fama digna sinistra
Et nitidis maculam haesuram figentia rebus,
Quae monstrant ipsi pueris traduntque parentes.
Si damnosa senem iuvat alea, ludit et heres
Bullatus parvoque eadem movet arma fritillo.   5
Nec melius de se cuiquam sperare propinquo
Concedet iuvenis, qui radere tubera terrae,
Boletum condire et eodem iure natantis
Mergere ficedulas didicit, nebulone parente
Et cana monstrante gula.   Cum septimus annus   10
Transierit puerum, nondum omni dente renato,
Barbatos licet admoveas mille inde magistros,
Hinc totidem, cupiet lauto cenare paratu
Semper et a magna non degenerare culina.
Mitem animum et mores modicis erroribus aequos   15
Praecipit, atque animas servorum et corpora nostra

9. ficellas *Lachmann.*   11. puerum *P*, puero *ω*.   16. utque *Buecheler.*

Materia constare putat paribusque elementis,
An saevire docet Rutilus, qui gaudet acerbo
Plagarum strepitu et nullam Sirena flagellis
Comparat, Antiphates trepidi laris ac Polyphemus,   20
Tunc felix, quotiens aliquis tortore vocato
Uritur ardenti duo propter lintea ferro?
Quid suadet iuveni laetus stridore catenae,
Quem mire adficiunt inscripti, ergastula, carcer?   24
Sic natura iubet: velocius et citius nos   31
Corrumpunt vitiorum exempla domestica, magnis
Cum subeunt animos auctoribus.   Unus et alter
Forsitan haec spernant iuvenes, quibus arte benigna
Et meliore luto finxit praecordia Titan;   35
Sed reliquos fugienda patrum vestigia ducunt
Et monstrata diu veteris trahit orbita culpae.
Abstineas igitur damnandis; huius enim vel
Una potens ratio est, ne crimina nostra sequantur
Ex nobis geniti, quoniam dociles imitandis   40
Turpibus ac pravis omnes sumus; et Catilinam
Quocumque in populo videas, quocumque sub axe,
Sed nec Brutus erit, Bruti nec avunculus umquam.
Nil dictu foedum visuque haec limina tangat,
Intra quae pater est.   45
Maxima debetur puero reverentia.   Si quid   47
Turpe paras, ne tu pueri contempseris annos;
Sed peccaturo obstet tibi filius infans.
Nam si quid dignum censoris fecerit ira   50
Quandoque et similem tibi se non corpore tantum
Nec vultu dederit, morum quoque filius et qui

---

17. putet *Buecheler*.   24. scripta *P*, inscripta *ω*, inscripti, *Weidner*.
33. subeunt *P*, subeant *ω*; animos *pω*, animis *P*.   34. spernant *pω*,
sperant *PS*, spernent *s*, spernunt *s*.   43. umquam *P*, usquam *pω*.   45.
pater *Ps*, puer *s*.   48. ne *s*, nec *Pω*.

Omnia deterius tua per vestigia peccet,
Corripies nimirum et castigabis acerbo
Clamore ac post haec tabulas mutare parabis.   55
Unde tibi frontem libertatemque parentis,
Cum facias peiora senex, vacuumque cerebro
Iam pridem caput hoc ventosa cucurbita quaerat?
    Hospite venturo, cessabit nemo tuorum.
"Verre pavimentum, nitidas ostende columnas,   60
Arida cum tota descendat aranea tela,
Hic leve argentum, vasa aspera tergeat alter":
Vox domini furit instantis virgamque tenentis.
Ergo miser trepidas, ne stercore foeda canino
Atria displiceant oculis venientis amici,   65
Ne perfusa luto sit porticus; et tamen uno
Semodio scobis haec emendat servulus unus:
Illud non agitas, ut sanctam filius omni
Aspiciat sine labe domum vitioque carentem?
Gratum est, quod patriae civem populoque dedisti,   70
Si facis ut'patriae sit idoneus, utilis agris,
Utilis et bellorum et pacis rebus agendis.
Plurimum enim intererit, quibus artibus et quibus hunc tu
Moribus instituas.   Serpente ciconia pullos
Nutrit et inventa per devia rura lacerta: 75
Illi eadem sumptis quaerunt animalia pinnis.
Vultur iumento et canibus crucibusque relictis
Ad fetus properat partemque cadaveris adfert:
Hic est ergo cibus magni quoque vulturis et se
Pascentis, propria cum iam facit arbore nidos.   80
Sed leporem aut capream famulae Iovis et generosae
In saltu venantur aves, hinc praeda cubili
Ponitur: inde autem cum se matura levarit

---

82. haec *Lachmann*.   83. levarit *s*, levaret *P*, levavit *Priscian*, levabit *ω*.

Progenies stimulante fame, festinat ad illam
Quam primum praedam rupto gustaverat ovo.   85
  Aedificator erat Cretonius et modo curvo
Litore Caietae, summa nunc Tiburis arce,
Nunc Praenestinis in montibus alta parabat
Culmina villarum, Graecis longeque petitis
Marmoribus vincens Fortunae atque Herculis aedem,   90
Ut spado vincebat Capitolia nostra Posides.
Dum sic ergo habitat Cretonius, imminuit rem,
Fregit opes; nec parva tamen mensura relictae
Partis erat: totam hanc turbavit filius amens,
Dum meliore novas attollit marmore villas.   95
  Quidam sortiti metuentem sabbata patrem
Nil praeter nubes et caeli numen adorant,
Nec distare putant humana carne suillam,
Qua pater abstinuit.
Romanas autem soliti contemnere leges   100
Iudaicum ediscunt et servant ac metuunt ius,
Tradidit arcano quodcumque volumine Moyses,
Non monstrare vias eadem nisi sacra colenti,
Quaesitum ad fontem solos deducere verpos.
Sed pater in causa, cui septima quaeque fuit lux   105
Ignava et partem vitae non attigit ullam.
  Sponte tamen iuvenes imitantur cetera: solam
Inviti quoque avaritiam exercere iubentur.
Fallit enim vitium specie virtutis et umbra,
Cum sit triste habitu vultuque et veste severum   110
Nec dubie tamquam frugi laudetur avarus,
Tamquam parcus homo et rerum tutela suarum
Certa magis, quam si fortunas servet easdem
Hesperidum serpens aut Ponticus.   Adde quod hunc, de

---

91. Posides *pω*, possideus *P*.   111. laudetur *P*, laudatur *ω*.   113. quasi *P*.

Quo loquor, egregium populus putat adquirendi   115
Artificem; quippe his crescunt patrimonia fabris;
Sed crescunt quocumque modo, maioraque fiunt
Incude adsidua semperque ardente camino.
Et pater ergo animi felices credit avaros,
Qui miratur opes, qui nulla exempla beati   120
Pauperis esse putat, iuvenes hortatur, ut illa
Ire via pergant et eidem incumbere sectae.
Sunt quaedam vitiorum elementa: his protinus illos
Inbuit et cogit minimas ediscere sordes,
Mox adquirendi docet insatiabile votum.   125
Servorum ventres modio castigat iniquo,
Ipse quoque esuriens; neque enim omnia sustinet umquam
Mucida caerulei panis consumere frusta,
Hesternum solitus medio servare minutal   ·
Septembri, nec non differre in tempora cenae   130
Alterius conchem aestivam cum parte lacerti
Signatam vel dimidio putrique siluro,
Filaque sectivi numerata includere porri:
Invitatus ad haec aliquis de ponte negabit.
Sed quo divitias haec per tormenta coactas,   135
Cum furor haud dubius, cum sit manifesta phrenesis,
Ut locuples moriaris, egentis vivere fato?
Interea pleno cum turget sacculus ore,
Crescit amor nummi, quantum ipsa pecunia crevit,
Et minus hanc optat qui non habet. Ergo paratur   140
Altera villa tibi, cum rus non sufficit unum,
Et proferre libet fines, maiorque videtur
Et melior vicina seges: mercaris et hanc et
Arbusta et densa montem qui canet oliva.

---

117. *damnarat Iahn.*   119. felices *P*, felicis *pω*.   120. cum — cum
Weidner.   121. illam *ω*.   122. viam *ω*.   125. *damnarat Iahn.*   128.
frusta *pω*, frustra *P*.   131. aestivam *P*, aestivi *pω*.

Quorum si pretio dominus non vincitur ullo,   145
Nocte boves macri lassoque famelica collo
Iumenta ad virides huius mittentur aristas;
Nec prius inde domum, quam tota novalia saevos
In ventres abeant, ut credas falcibus actum.
Dicere vix possis, quam multi talia plorent,   150
Et quot venales iniuria fecerit agros.
Sed qui sermones, quam foede bucina famae!—
"Quid nocet haec?" inquit; "tunicam mihi malo lupini,
Quam si me toto laudet vicinia pago
Exigui ruris paucissima farra secantem."—   155
Scilicet et morbis et debilitate carebis,
Et luctum et curam effugies, et tempora vitae
Longa tibi posthac fato meliore dabuntur,
Si tantum culti solus possederis agri,
Quantum sub Tatio populus Romanus arabat.   160
Mox etiam fractis aetate ac Punica passis
Proelia vel Pyrrhum immanem gladiosque Molossos
Tandem pro multis vix iugera bina dabantur
Vulneribus: merces haec sanguinis atque laboris
Nullis visa umquam meritis minor, aut ingratae   165
Curta fides patriae.   Saturabat glebula talis
Patrem ipsum turbamque casae, qua feta iacebat
Uxor et infantes ludebant quattuor, unus
Vernula, tres domini; sed magnis fratribus horum
A scrobe vel sulco redeuntibus altera cena   170
Amplior et grandes fumabant pultibus ollae.
Nunc modus hic agri nostro non sufficit horto.
Inde fere scelerum causae; nec plura venena
Miscuit aut ferro grassatur saepius ullum
Humanae mentis vitium, quam saeva cupido   175

---

147. mitentur (mittentur) *Ps*, mittuntur *ω*.   152. foede *P*, foedae *ω*.

Immodici census. Nam dives qui fieri vult,
Et cito vult fieri ; sed quae reverentia legum,
Quis metus aut pudor est umquam properantis avari ?
" Vivite contenti casulis et collibus istis,
O pueri !" Marsus dicebat et Hernicus olim   180
Vestinusque senex : " panem quaeramus aratro,
Qui satis est mensis ; laudant hoc numina ruris,
Quorum ope et auxilio gratae post munus aristae
Contingunt homini veteris fastidia quercus.
Nil vetitum fecisse volet, quem non pudet alto   185
Per glaciem perone tegi, qui summovet Euros
Pellibus inversis ; peregrina ignotaque nobis
Ad scelus atque nefas, quaecumque est, purpura ducit."
     Haec illi veteres praecepta minoribus : at nunc
Post finem autumni media de nocte supinum   190
Clamosus iuvenem pater excitat : " Accipe ceras,
Scribe, puer, vigila, causas age, perlege rubras
Maiorum leges aut vitem posce libello.
Sed caput intactum buxo naresque pilosas
Adnotet et grandes miretur Laelius alas.   195
Dirue Maurorum attegias, castella Brigantum,
Ut locupletem aquilam tibi sexagesimus annus
Adferat ; aut, longos castrorum ferre labores
Si piget et trepidum solvunt tibi cornua ventrem
Cum lituis audita, pares quod vendere possis   200
Pluris dimidio, nec te fastidia mercis
Ullius subeant ablegandae Tiberim ultra,
Neu credas ponendum aliquid discriminis inter
Unguenta et corium. Lucri bonus est odor ex re
Qualibet. Illa tuo sententia semper in ore   205
Versetur, dis atque ipso Iove digna poeta :

---

182. ruris *pω*, roris *P*.   199. trepidum *Ps*, trepido *pω*.

' Unde habeas quaerit nemo, sed oportet habere ' : ”
Hoc monstrant vetulae pueris repentibus assae,
Hoc discunt omnes ante alpha et beta puellae.
Talibus instantem monitis quemcumque parentem   210
Sic possem adfari : “ Dic, O vanissime, quis te
Festinare iubet ? meliorem praesto magistro
Discipulum.   Securus abi ; vinceris, ut Aiax
Praeteriit Telamonem, ut Pelea vicit Achilles.
Parcendum est teneris, nondum implevere medullas ;   215
Naturae mala nequitia est.   Cum pectere barbam
Coeperit et longi mucronem admittere cultri,
Falsus erit testis, vendet periuria summa
Exigua et Cereris tangens aramque pedemque.
Elatam iam crede nurum, si limina vestra   220
Mortifera cum dote subit : quibus illa premetur
Per somnum digitis ! nam quae terraque marique
Adquirenda putas, brevior via conferet illi :
Nullus enim magni sceleris labor.   ' Haec ego numquam
Mandavi,' dices olim, ' nec talia suasi.'   225
Mentis causa malae tamen est et origo penes te.
Nam quisquis magni census praecepit amorem,
Et laevo monitu pueros producit avaros,
Et qui per fraudes patrimonia conduplicare,
Dat libertatem et totas effundit habenas   230
Curriculo ; quem si revoces, subsistere nescit
Et te contempto rapitur metisque relictis.
Nemo satis credit tantum delinquere, quantum
Permittas ; adeo indulgent sibi latius ipsi.
Cum dicis iuveni stultum qui donet amico,   235

208, 209. *damnarat Iahn.*   216. naturae *Pω*, maturae *s*; nequitia
est cum *P*, nequitiae cum *pω*, nequitiae ast cum *s*.   217. longi *pω*, longe
P.   229. *damnarat Iahn ;* conduplicandi *Weidner.*

Qui paupertatem levet attollatque propinqui,
Et spoliare doces et circumscribere et omni
Crimine divitias adquirere, quarum amor in te
Quantus erat patriae Deciorum in pectore, quantum
Dilexit Thebas, si Graecia vera, Menoeceus;   240
In quorum sulcis legiones dentibus anguis
Cum clipeis nascuntur et horrida bella capessunt
Continuo, tamquam et tubicen surrexerit una.
Ergo ignem, cuius scintillas ipse dedisti,
Flagrantem late et rapientem cuncta videbis;   245
Nec tibi parcetur misero, trepidumque magistrum
In cavea magno fremitu leo tollet alumnus.
Nota mathematicis genesis tua; sed grave tardas
Expectare colus: morieris stamine nondum
Abrupto.   Iam nunc obstas et vota moraris,   250
Iam torquet iuvenem longa et cervina senectus.
Ocius Archigenen quaere atque eme quod Mithridates
Composuit, si vis aliam decerpere ficum
Atque alias tractare rosas.   Medicamen habendum est,
Sorbere ante cibum quod debeat et pater et rex."   255
    Monstro voluptatem egregiam, cui nulla theatra,
Nulla aequare queas praetoris pulpita lauti,
Si spectes, quanto capitis discrimine constent
Incrementa domus, aerata multus in arca
Fiscus et ad vigilem ponendi Castora nummi,   260
Ex quo Mars Ultor galeam quoque perdidit et res
Non potuit servare suas.   Ergo omnia Florae
Et Cereris licet et Cybeles aulaea relinquas;
Tanto maiores humana negotia ludi.
An magis oblectant animum iactata petauro   265

---

241. quorum *Pω*, quarum *s*.   255. sorbere ante *pω*, sorbere et ante
Ps.

Corpora quique solet rectum descendere funem,
Quam tu, Corycia semper qui puppe moraris
Atque habitas, Coro semper tollendus et Austro,
Perditus ac vilis sacci mercator olentis,
Qui gaudes pingue antiquae de litore Cretae   270
Passum et municipes Iovis advexisse lagonas?
Hic tamen ancipiti figens vestigia planta
Victum illa mercede parat brumamque famemque
Illa reste cavet: tu propter mille talenta
Et centum villas temerarius. Aspice portus   275
Et plenum magnis trabibus mare: plus hominum est iam
In pelago; veniet classis, quocumque vocarit
Spes lucri, nec Carpathium Gaetulaque tantum
Aequora transiliet, sed longe Calpe relicta
Audiet Herculeo stridentem gurgite solem.   280
Grande operae pretium est ut tenso folle reverti
Inde domum possis, tumidaque superbus aluta
Oceani monstra et iuvenes vidisse marinos.
Non unus mentes agitat furor: ille sororis
In manibus vultu Eumenidum terretur et igni,   285
Hic bove percusso mugire Agamemnona credit
Aut Ithacum; parcat tunicis licet atque lacernis,
Curatoris eget, qui navem mercibus implet
Ad summum latus et tabula distinguitur unda,
Cum sit causa mali tanti et discriminis huius   290
Concisum argentum in titulos faciesque minutas.
Occurrunt nubes et fulgura: " Solvite funem,"
Frumenti dominus clamat piperisve coempti:
" Nil color hic caeli, nil fascia nigra minatur;
Aestivum tonat."—Infelix hac forsitan ipsa   295
Nocte cadit fractis trabibus, fluctuque premetur

---

285. torretur *p*. 296. cadit *P*, cadet *ω*.

Obrutus et zonam laeva morsuque tenebit.
Sed cuius votis modo non suffecerat aurum,
Quod Tagus et rutila volvit Pactolus harena,
Frigida sufficient velantis inguina panni   300
Exiguusque cibus, mersa rate naufragus assem
Dum rogat et picta se tempestate tuetur.
   Tantis parta malis cura maiore metuque
Servantur.   Misera est magni custodia census!
Dispositis praedives amis vigilare cohortem   305
Servorum noctu Licinus iubet, attonitus pro
Electro signisque suis Phrygiaque columna
Atque ebore et lata testudine.   Dolia nudi
Non ardent Cynici; si fregeris, altera fiet
Cras domus, atque eadem plumbo commissa manebit. 310
Sensit Alexander, testa cum vidit in illa
Magnum habitatorem, quanto felicior hic qui
Nil cuperet, quam qui totum sibi posceret orbem,
Passurus gestis aequanda pericula rebus.
Nullum numen habes, si sit prudentia; nos te,   315
Nos facimus, Fortuna, deam.   Mensura tamen quae
Sufficiat census, si quis me consulat, edam :
In quantum sitis atque fames et frigora poscunt,
Quantum, Epicure, tibi parvis suffecit in hortis,
Quantum Socratici ceperunt ante penates.   320
Numquam aliud natura, aliud sapientia dicit.
Acribus exemplis videor te cludere? misce
Ergo aliquid nostris de moribus, effice summam,
Bis septem ordinibus quam lex dignatur Othonis.
Haec quoque si rugam trahit extenditque labellum,   325
Sume duos equites, fac tertia quadringenta.
Si nondum implevi gremium, si panditur ultra,

---

315. habes *Pω*, abest *ʃ*.   319. suffccit *pω*, sufficit *P*.

Nec Croesi fortuna umquam nec Persica regna
Sufficient animo nec divitiae Narcissi,
Indulsit Caesar cui Claudius omnia, cuius   330
Paruit imperiis uxorem occidere iussus.

The Nile.

SATURA XV.

Quis nescit, Volusi Bithynice, qualia demens
Aegyptos portenta colat? crocodilon adorat
Pars haec, illa pavet saturam serpentibus ibin.
Effigies sacri nitet aurea cercopitheci,
Dimidio magicae resonant ubi Memnone chordae   5
Atque vetus Thebe centum iacet obruta portis.
Illic aeluros, hic piscem fluminis, illic
Oppida tota canem venerantur, nemo Dianam.
Porrum et caepe nefas violare et frangere morsu :
O sanctas gentes, quibus haec nascuntur in hortis   10
Numina!   Lanatis animalibus abstinet omnis
Mensa, nefas illic fetum iugulare capellae :

---

7. aeluros *Brodaeus,* aeruleos *P,* cacruleos *ω.*

Carnibus humanis vesci licet. Attonito cum
Tale super cenam facinus narraret Ulixes
Alcinoo, bilem aut risum fortasse quibusdam   15
Moverat, ut mendax aretalogus: " In mare nemo
Hunc abicit, saeva dignum veraque Charybdi,
Fingentem immanes Laestrygonas atque Cyclopas?
Nam citius Scyllam vel concurrentia saxa
Cyaneis, plenos et tempestatibus utres   20
Crediderim, aut tenui percussum verbere Circes
Et cum remigibus grunnisse Elpenora porcis:
Tam vacui capitis populum Phaeaca putavit? "—
Sic aliquis merito nondum ebrius et minimum qui
De Corcyraea temetum duxerat urna;   25
Solus enim haec Ithacus nullo sub teste canebat.
Nos miranda quidem, sed nuper consule Iunco
Gesta super calidae referemus moenia Copti,
Nos vulgi scelus et cunctis graviora cothurnis.
Nam scelus, a Pyrrha quamquam omnia syrmata volvas, 30
Nullus apud tragicos populus facit. Accipe, nostro
Dira quod exemplum feritas produxerit aevo.
   Inter finitimos vetus atque antiqua simultas,
Immortale odium et numquam sanabile vulnus
Ardet adhuc, Ombos et Tentyra. Summus utrimque   35
Inde furor volgo, quod numina vicinorum
Odit uterque locus, cum solos credat habendos
Esse deos, quos ipse colit. Sed tempore festo
Alterius populi rapienda occasio cunctis
Visa inimicorum primoribus ac ducibus, ne   40
Laetum hilaremque diem, ne magnae gaudia cenae
Sentirent, positis ad templa et compita mensis
Pervigilique toro, quem nocte ac luce iacentem

---

26. haec *s*, hic *P*. hoc *ω*.

Septimus interdum sol invenit. Horrida sane
Aegyptos, sed luxuria, quantum ipse notavi,   45
Barbara famoso non cedit turba Canopo.
Adde quod et facilis victoria de madidis et
Blaesis atque mero titubantibus. Inde virorum
Saltatus nigro tibicine, qualiacumque
Unguenta et flores multaeque in fronte coronae;   50
Hinc ieiunum odium. Sed iurgia prima sonare
Incipiunt animis ardentibus, haec tuba rixae;
Dein clamore pari concurritur, et vice teli
Saevit nuda manus; paucae sine vulnere malae,
Vix cuiquam aut nulli toto certamine nasus   55
Integer, aspiceres iam cuncta per agmina vultus
Dimidios, alias facies et hiantia ruptis
Ossa genis, plenos oculorum sanguine pugnos.
Ludere se credunt ipsi tamen et puerilis
Exercere acies, quod nulla cadavera calcent;   60
Et sane quo tot rixantis milia turbae,
Si vivunt omnes? ergo acrior impetus, et iam
Saxa inclinatis per humum quaesita lacertis
Incipiunt torquere, domestica seditioni
Tela, nec hunc lapidem, qualis et Turnus et Aiax,   65
Vel quo Tydides percussit pondere coxam
Aeneae, sed quem valeant emittere dextrae
Illis dissimiles et nostro tempore natae.
Nam genus hoc vivo iam decrescebat Homero;
Terra malos homines nunc educat atque pusillos.   70
Ergo deus, quicumque aspexit, ridet et odit.
    A deverticulo repetatur fabula. Postquam,
Subsidiis aucti, pars altera promere ferrum
Audet et infestis pugnam instaurare sagittis:

---

45. Aegyptos *P*, Aegyptus *ω*.

Terga fuga celeri praestant, instantibus Ombis,   · 75
Qui vicina colunt umbrosae Tentyra palmae.
Labitur hinc quidam, nimia formidine cursum
Praecipitans, capiturque. Ast illum in plurima sectum
Frusta et particulas, ut multis mortuus unus
Sufficeret, totum corrosis ossibus edit   80
Victrix turba, nec ardenti decoxit aheno
Aut veribus; longum usque adeo tardumque putavit
Expectare focos, contenta cadavere crudo.
Hic gaudere libet quod non violaverit ignem,
Quem summa caeli raptum de parte Prometheus   85
Donavit terris; elemento gratulor et te
Exultare reor. Sed qui mordere cadaver
Sustinuit, nil umquam hac carne libentius edit;
Nam scelere in tanto ne quaeras et dubites an
Prima voluptatem gula senserit; ultimus autem   90
Qui stetit, absumpto iam toto corpore, ductis
Per terram digitis aliquid de sanguine gustat.
Vascones, haec fama est, alimentis talibus olim
Produxere animas: sed res diversa, sed illic
Fortunae invidia est bellorumque ultima, casus   95
Extremi, longae dira obsidionis egestas.
Huius enim, quod nunc agitur, miserabile debet
Exemplum esse cibi; sicut modo dicta mihi gens
Post omnes herbas, post cuncta animalia, quidquid
Cogebat vacui ventris furor, hostibus ipsis   100
Pallorem ac maciem et tenues miserantibus artus,
Membra aliena fame lacerabant, esse parati
Et sua. Quisnam hominum veniam dare, quisve deorum,

---

75. fugat celeri *P*, fuga sceleri *p*, fugae *s*; praestant instantibus
Ombis *Mercerus*, praestan . . . *P*, praestantibus omnibus instant *pω*.
93. alimentis *pω*, elementis *P*.   97, 98. *delebat Guiterus.*

Urbibus abnueret dira atque immania passis,
Et quibus illorum poterant ignoscere manes,   105
Quorum corporibus vescebantur?   Melius nos
Zenonis praecepta monent; nec enim omnia quidam
Pro vita facienda putant : sed Cantaber unde
Stoicus, antiqui praesertim aetate Metelli?
Nunc totus Graias nostrasque habet orbis Athenas,   110
Gallia causidicos docuit facunda Britannos,
De conducendo loquitur iam rhetore Thyle.
Nobilis ille tamen populus, quem diximus, et par
Virtute atque fide, sed maior clade, Zacynthos,
Tale quid excusat : Maeotide saevior ara   115
Aegyptos.   Quippe illa nefandi Taurica sacri
Inventrix homines—ut iam, quae carmina tradunt,
Digna fide credas—tantum immolat, ulterius nil
Aut gravius cultro timet hostia : quis modo casus
Inpulit hos? quae tanta fames infestaque vallo   120
Arma coegerunt tam detestabile monstrum
Audere? anne aliam, terra Memphitide sicca,
Invidiam facerent nolenti surgere Nilo?
Qua nec terribiles Cimbri nec Brittones umquam
Sauromataeque truces aut immanes Agathyrsi,   125
Hac saevit rabie inbelle et inutile vulgus,
Parvula fictilibus solitum dare vela phaselis
Et brevibus pictae remis incumbere testae.
Nec poenam sceleri invenies, nec digna parabis
Supplicia his populis, in quorum mente pares sunt   130
Et similes ira atque fames.   Mollissima corda
Humano generi dare se natura fatetur,
Quae lacrimas dedit; haec nostri pars optima sensus.

---

104. urbibus *Ps*, viribus *pω*, ventribus *Valesius*.   107. quidam *P*,
quaedam *pω*.   114. Zacynthos *P*, Saguntus *ω*.

Plorare ergo iubet causam dicentis amici
Squaloremque rei, pupillum ad iura vocantem   135
Circumscriptorem, cuius manantia fletu
Ora puellares faciunt incerta capilli.
Naturae imperio gemimus, cum funus adultae
Virginis occurrit vel terra clauditur infans
Et minor igne rogi; quis enim bonus et face dignus   140
Arcana, qualem Cereris vult esse sacerdos,
Ulla aliena sibi credit mala? Separat hoc nos
A grege mutorum, atque ideo venerabile soli
Sortiti ingenium, divinorumque capaces,
Atque exercendis capiendisque artibus apti   145
Sensum a caelesti demissum traximus arce,
Cuius egent prona et terram spectantia. Mundi
Principio indulsit communis conditor illis
Tantum animas, nobis animum quoque, mutuus ut nos
Adfectus petere auxilium et praestare iuberet,   150
Dispersos trahere in populum, migrare vetusto
De nemore et proavis habitatas linquere silvas,
Aedificare domos, laribus coniungere nostris
Tectum aliud, tutos vicino limine somnos
Ut collata daret fiducia, protegere armis   155
Lapsum aut ingenti nutantem vulnere civem,
Communi dare signa tuba, defendier isdem
Turribus atque una portarum clave teneri.
Sed iam serpentum maior concordia; parcit
Cognatis maculis similis fera: quando leoni   160
Fortior eripuit vitam leo? quo nemore umquam
Expiravit aper maioris dentibus apri?
Indica tigris agit rabida cum tigride pacem
Perpetuam, saevis inter se convenit ursis:

---

134. causam dicentis *Pω*, casum lugentis *s*.   142. credit *Ps*, credat *pω*.

Ast homini ferrum letale incude nefanda   165
Produxisse parum est, cum rastra et sarcula tantum
Adsueti coquere et marris ac vomere lassi
Nescierint primi gladios extendere fabri.
Aspicimus populos, quorum non sufficit irae
Occidisse aliquem, sed pectora, bracchia, vultum   170
Crediderint genus esse cibi; quid diceret ergo
Vel quo non fugeret, si nunc haec monstra videret,
Pythagoras, cunctis animalibus abstinuit qui
Tamquam homine, et ventri indulsit non omne legumen?

174. homine *pω*, homini *P*.

Ruins of a Roman camp in Servia.

SATURA XVI.

Quis numerare queat felicis praemia, Galli,
Militiae? nam si subeuntur prospera castra,
Me pavidum excipiat tironem porta secundo
Sidere. Plus etenim fati valet hora benigni,
Quam si nos Veneris commendet epistula Marti   5
Et Samia genetrix quae delectatur harena.
   Commoda tractemus primum communia, quorum
Haud minimum illud erit, ne te pulsare togatus
Audeat, immo etsi pulsetur, dissimulet, nec
Audeat excussos praetori ostendere dentes   10
Et nigram in facie tumidis livoribus offam
Atque oculum medico nil promittente relictum.
Bardaicus iudex datur haec punire volenti,
Calceus et grandes magna ad subsellia surae,
Legibus antiquis castrorum et more Camilli   15
Servato, miles ne vallum litiget extra
Et procul a signis. Iustissima centurionum
Cognitio est igitur de milite, nec mihi derit

---

   1. Galli *P*, Galle *pω*. 2. nam si *Pω*, quod si *Priscian, ante 3 lacunam statuerat Iahn.* 12. oculum *P*, oculos *ω*; relictos *pω*, relictum *om. P*.

Ultio, si iustae defertur causa querellae;
Tota tamen chors est inimica, omnesque manipli   20
Consensu magno efficiunt, curabilis ut sit
Vindicta et gravior quam iniuria.   Dignum erit ergo
Declamatoris mulino corde Vagelli,
Cum duo crura habeas, offendere tot caligas, tot
Milia clavorum.   Quis tam procul absit ab urbe   25
Praeterea, quis tam Pylades, molem aggeris ultra
Ut veniat? lacrimae siccentur protinus, et se
Excusaturos non sollicitemus amicos.
" Da testem," iudex cum dixerit, audeat ille
Nescio quis, pugnos qui vidit, dicere " Vidi ":   30
Et credam dignum barba dignumque capillis
Maiorum.   Citius falsum producere testem
Contra paganum possis, quam vera loquentem
Contra fortunam armati contraque pudorem.
     Praemia nunc alia atque alia emolumenta notemus   35
Sacramentorum.   Convallem ruris aviti
Improbus aut campum mihi si vicinus ademit,
Et sacrum effodit medio de limite saxum,
Quod mea cum patulo coluit puls annua libo,
Debitor aut sumptos pergit non reddere nummos,   40
Vana supervacui dicens chirographa ligni :
Expectandus erit qui lites inchoet annus
Totius populi; sed tunc quoque mille ferenda
Taedia, mille morae : totiens subsellia tantum
Sternuntur; iam facundo ponente lacernas   45
Caedicio, parati
Digredimur, lentaque fori pugnamus, harena.
Ast illis, quos arma tegunt et balteus ambit,
Quod placitum est ipsis praestatur tempus agendi,

---

20. tamen cohors *P*, cohors tamen *ω*.   24. caligas tot *s*, caligatos *Ps*.

Nec res atteritur longo sufflamine litis. 50
Solis praeterea testandi militibus ius
Vivo patre datur; nam, quae sunt parta labore
Militiae, placuit non esse in corpore census,
Omne tenet cuius regimen pater. Ergo Coranum,
Signorum comitem castrorumque aera merentem, 55
Quamvis iam tremulus captat pater. Hunc favor aequus
Provehit et pulchro reddit sua dona labori.
Ipsius certe ducis hoc referre videtur,
Ut, qui fortis erit, sit felicissimus idem,
Ut laeti phaleris omnes et torquibus omnes 60

---

56. favor *Ruperti*, labor *Pω*.

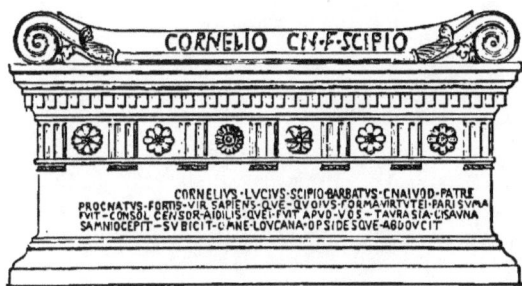

CORNELIO CN·F·SCIPIO

CORNELIVS·LVCIVS·SCIPIO·BARBATVS·CNAIVOD·PATRE
PROCNATVS·FORTIS·VIR SAPIENS·QVE-QVOIVS·FORMA·VIRTVTEI·PARISVMA
FVIT-CONSOL CENSOR·AIDILIS·QVEI·FVIT APVD·VOS-TAVRASIA·CISAVNA
SAMNIOCEPIT-SVBICIT·OMNE·LOVCANA·OPSIDESQVE·ABDOVCIT

NOTES.

NOTES.

SATIRE I.

THE STATE OF THE TIMES.

Introduction.—The reference to the trial of Marius Priscus (line 49) shows that the satire was not written before 100 A. D.

Juvenal first gives his reasons for writing. He is tired of hearing wearisome accounts of mythological commonplaces, and will take his revenge by giving his tormentors something to listen to. He then explains why he chooses the field of satire: the corruption of the times, when luxury and wealth rule society, forces an earnest man to deal with the present rather than the past. He will take human life with all its passions as his theme; these passions were never more openly displayed than at this time in Rome, when gambling, gluttony, and avarice are at their height. The subject may demand more audacity than he possesses, but, if he dare not deal with the living, he may at least attack the vices of the generation just passed away.

1. **Auditor tantum,** *a mere listener.* The practice of giving readings from one's own poems (introduced by Asinius Pollio about 100 B. C.) had become very common and, to most people, very disagreeable. The younger Pliny, however, seems to have enjoyed it. Cf. Plin. Ep. I, 13.

Reponam, *pay back*—i. e., write something of my own for others to listen to.

2. **Rauci,** from so much reading aloud.

Theseide—i. e., the story of Theseus, as the *Aeneid* was the story of Aeneas. Mythology and hero-stories furnished a rich field for the society poet.

3. **Ergo,** *then*, as often.

Togatas (*fabulas*). The principal forms of Roman drama were: *togatae*, comedies on Roman subjects, in which the characters wore the *toga;* *palliatae*, comedies dealing with Greek life, in which the Greek garment, the *pallium*, was worn; *praetextae*, tragedies, so called from the *toga praetexta*.

4. Ingens Telephus. The adjective probably refers to the length of the poem. Telephus was king of Mysia, wounded by Achilles's spear. Cf. Hor. A. P. 96.

5. Summi. There is some doubt about the meaning; probably *summi* here = *extremi*—i. e., the margin up to the very last part of the book was full.

6. In tergo. Roman books were usually composed of sheets of papyrus or parchment. It was customary to write on only one side of each sheet. Cf. Fig. 1.

FIG. 1.—Roman reading.

7. Lucus Martis. Several such groves are mentioned by the ancients; this may be any one of them.

8. Antrum Vulcani. Vergil VIII, 422, calls Lipara, one of the Aeolian islands, north of Sicily, *Vulcani domus*.

9. Agant and the following verbs are subjunctive in indirect questions, objects of *clamant*.

10. Aeacus, Minos, and Rhadamanthus were the judges of the dead.

Alius, Jason, who went in search of the golden fleece. Cf. Ov. Met. VII, 1 ff.

11. Monychus, in the contest between the Centaurs and the Lapithae. Cf. Ov. Met. XII, 510 ff.

12. Frontonis, some rich patron of literature ; perhaps Ti. Catius Fronto, who defended Marius Priscus. Cf. line 49.

Marmora convulsa, a strong expression of the effect produced by the vigorous reading. Cf. VII, 86, *fregit subsellia versu.*

13. Adsiduo lectore, almost = *the assiduity of the reader ;* the ablative of the agent properly requires the preposition *ab ;* in such cases as this the stress is laid on the quality expressed by the adjective, not on the person.

14. Cf. Hor. Ep. II. 1, 117. *Scribimus indocti doctique poemata passim.*

15. Et nos, etc. *I, too, have flinched from the rod, and written compositions,* i. e.—in these times a common-school education seems to be the only requisite for a poet; that I have had: why should not I write poems as well as others ?

16. Consilium, etc. School themes were often on subjects drawn from history. This was an address to Sulla advising his abdication.

Altum, used as an adverb. Cf. Pope's *" Drink deep, or taste not the Pierian spring."*

18. Vatibus, used contemptuously, *" bards."* The dative is indirect object. " Verbs compounded with certain prepositions take the dative" only because the combination modifies the original meaning in such a way that the resulting verbal phrase (verb + preposition) requires an *indirect* object.

Periturae—i. e., sure to be spoiled by some one.

19. Having justified his *writing,* Juvenal proceeds to justify his writing *satire.*

20. Auruncae alumnus. Lucilius, the early Roman satirist, was born at Suessa Aurunca in Campania, 148 B. C. Cf. Hor. Sat. I, 10, 56–74 ; II, 1, 30 ff.

21. Si vacat—i. e., *si vacui estis, if you are at leisure.*

25. Quo tondente, ablative absolute, translate, *under whose shears.*

Gravis, his beard was *gravis* because it brought a certain amount of *gravitas, dignity.*

Mihi iuveni, a sort of dative of reference. This line occurs again X, 226.

26. Pars refers to *Crispinus.*

Verna Canopi, *born and bred at Canopus,* not necessarily a house slave. Canopus was a city of Egypt, near Alexandria, noted for its profligacy.

27. Crispinus is said to have come to Rome as a fish-peddler, and to have been made an *eques* by Domitian.

Umero revocante, he gave a lazy shrug of the shoulder to prevent his cloak from slipping off.

9

28. Aestivum aurum. The ultra-fashionable Romans had lighter finger-rings for summer.

30. Saturam. Juvenal seems to use the word with something of the idea of our *satire;* originally it meant *medley*, and was derived from *lanx satura*, a basket of first fruit-offerings.

32. Causidici, *pettifogger.* Matho seems to have been well known. Juvenal mentions him in two other places, and Martial often.

Lectica. Cf. Fig. 2.

Fig. 2.—Lectica.

33. Delator. The trade of informer was very profitable as well as very disreputable. Cf. Tac. Hist. IV, 42.

35. Massa. Baebius Massa was procurator of Africa in 70 A. D. He was accused of extortion (*repetundarum*), after his proconsulate in Baetica, by Herennius Senecio and the younger Pliny.

36. Carus. Mettius Carus was another infamous informer; he secured the condemnation of Herennius Senecio in 73 A. D. Cf. Plin. Ep. I, 5, 8; VII, 19, 5. Thymele was an actress, Latinus an actor.

45. Iecur. The ancients localized various passions in different organs of the body, for which physiological justification is not wanting. Translate *heart.* Cf. Hor. Odes I, 13, 4.

46. Gregibus. An intentionally undignified word, almost = "*gangs.*"

48. Infamia. Either general = *disgrace*, or special = ἀτιμία, *loss of civil rights.*

49. Ab octava—i. e., he began his feasting at the unseemly hour of two o'clock in the afternoon.

Marius (*Priscus*) was accused for his extortion in Africa, by Pliny and Tacitus, in 100 A. D. He was condemned, but had stolen enough to pay his fine and live in luxury besides. The province gained its case, but very little else.

51. Venusina lucerna. Horace was born at *Venusia*, 65 B. C. Cf. Hor. Sat. II, 1, 34.

Lucerna, perhaps, as most editors think, means "midnight oil"; it may, however, as the Scholiast suggests, refer to the light shed by the lamp of genius.

52. Agitem, *drive at, pursue.*

Heracleas (*fabulas*). The plural makes it general.

53. Labyrinthi mugitum—i. e., the Minotaur.

54. Puero, *Icarus.* The preposition is not used, because the unfortunate boy was not an active agent in the matter.

Fabrum, *Daedalus.*

58. Curam, *charge, control.*

59. Caret follows the perfect *donavit* naturally, since it denotes a present state resulting from past action.

60. Pervolat, *flies along.*

61. Flaminiam (*viam*). The great north road leading from Rome over the *pons Mulvius* to Ariminum.

Automedon, the charioteer of Achilles. The young man drives his own chariot. So in the modern tally-ho.

62. Lacernatae, *in a man's cloak.*

Se iactaret. *Se iactare* = *to brag, boast, show off.*

63. Ceras. The Romans often took notes for temporary use on wax-coated tablets, writing with a pointed ivory *stylus.* Cf. Figs. 3 and 4.

64. Iam sexta cervice. He already has six slaves to bear his litter, soon he may have eight.

FIG. 3.
Stylus.

65. Hinc atque inde = *hinc atque hinc, on this side and that.*

Nuda, *open.*

66. Referens, *recalling.*

Maecenate supino. Maecenas, the friend and patron of Horace, had a reputation for effeminacy, which is referred to in the adjective *supino.*

67. Falso. *Signator* retains sufficient verbal force to admit the use of the adverb.

68. Uda, to prevent it from clinging to the wax.

69. Calenum (*vinum*), wine from Cales in Campania.

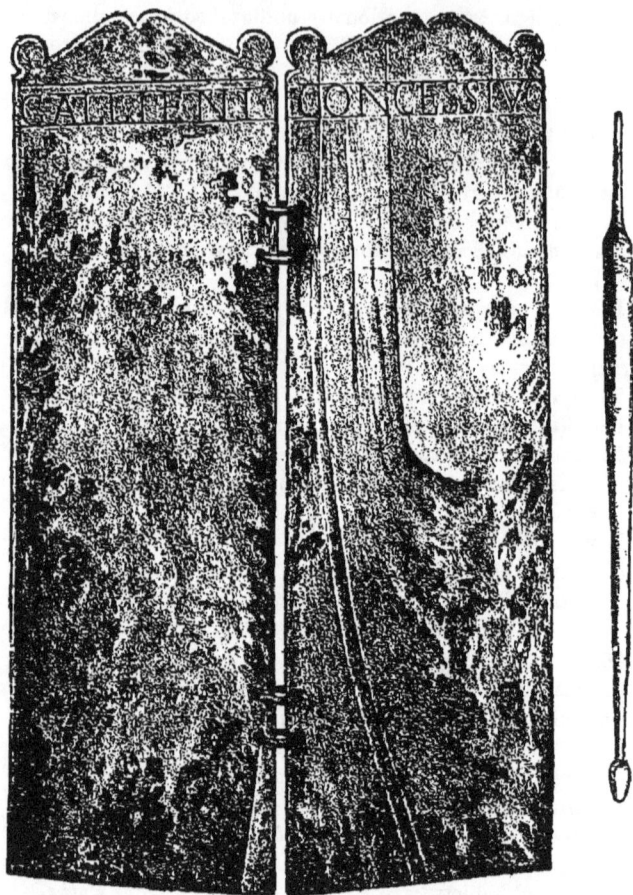

FIG. 4.—Writing tablets.

70. Sitiente is probably ablative absolute with *eo* understood, while *viro* is dative. The explanation seems harsh but unavoidable. Note that the quantity of the *i* in *viro* prevents it from being mistaken for a form of *virus*.

71. Locusta was a famous professional poisoner who killed Claudius to please Agrippina, and Britannicus to please Nero.

Propinquas, *neighbors.*

72. Per famam et populum, *through* (and so in defiance of) *the talk of the people.*

Nigros, from the effect of the poison.

Efferre has the special sense, *to carry out the bodies of the dead.* Cf. Nepos. Arist. 3, 2.

73. **Gyaris,** a small desolate island near Andros, one of the Cyclades, to which criminals were transported.

75. **Criminibus,** usually *accusations,* here probably *crimes.*

Debent, the subject is to be supplied.

Praetoria, *palaces,* originally the tents of the commander.

76. **Caprum**—i. e., the ornaments on the silver-ware, among which fig-ures of animals were common. Cf. Fig. 5.

79. **Indignatio.** The *o* in such words shows a gradual tendency to become short.

80. **Cluvienus** is un-known, probably some poor poet of the time, with whom Juvenal, with assumed modesty, com-pares himself.

FIG. 5.—Bronze jugs.

81. **Deucalion.** For an account of the flood from which Deucalion and Pyrrha alone were saved, cf. Ov. Met. I, 260.

Nimbis—i. e., the rains.

83. The legend was that, after the destruction of the inhabitants of the earth by the flood, a new race was created from the stones upon the mountain-side.

86. **Discursus,** restless running to and fro.

Farrago, *medley,* literally mixed fodder given to cattle. Cf. *far* and *farina.*

88. **Sinus.** The fold of the toga, used as a pocket, was called *sinus.* Cf. Fig. 6. This is probably what is meant here. Others take *sinus* to mean *sail,* others *gulf;* of these the former seems less well suited to the meaning of *patuit;* the latter is inapplicable; avarice does not throw things into an abyss, but draws them into its own keeping.

Alea, supply *habuit.* Such omissions are common in conversational style. Translate *when was gambling so bold?*

89. **Neque,** *nec* is much more usual in post-Augustan poets. Juvenal has it 160 times, *neque* only 7.

Itur, "*on va, they go.*"

91. **Dispensatore.** In the battles of the gaming-table the steward took charge of the sinews of war—i. e., furnished the money.

92. Sestertia centum, about $4,000. H. 647, III.

93. Reddere = *to give back*, then *to give what is due*, so here. It does not mean that the master gambles away all his property and then pledges his slave's clothing, but that his losses are so great that he can not properly clothe his servants.

94. Quis totidem, etc. Avarice, recklessness, and luxury all go together. The rich men of the day dined on seven courses, but alone. What a contrast to the frugal meals of the ancients, where the patron was surrounded by his clients, whose relation to him was one of honorable dependence!

95. Sportula. In early times the clients dined with their patron (*cena recta*); later a basket of food, a "dole," was given

FIG. 6.—Toga with sinns.

to each client at the door; finally, a sum of money was substituted.

96. Turbae togatae. There is a certain irony in the combination of these two words, "*a dress-coat mob.*"

97. Ille. Like our emphatic *he*, the master.

99. A praecone. A regular list of those to whom the *sportula* was due was kept to avoid repeaters and substitutes.

100. Troiugenas, members of the oldest Roman families. Many *gentes* traced their origin from Trojan heroes; so the Julian gens from *Iulus.*

Et ipsi, *they too, even they.*

101. Da praetori, etc. There seem to have been two classes of these respectable beggars, the impoverished aristocrats and the wealthy upstarts. The *praetor* and the *tribunus* belong to the former, the *libertinus* to the latter.

104. Quod refers to the statement concerning his birthplace.

Fenestrae. Holes for ear-rings, marking his Eastern origin.

105. Licet, *although.*

Tabernae, *shops.* Cf. Fig. 7, a bas-relief representation of a cutler's shop.

106. Quadringenta (*sestertia*). The *census equester* was 400,000 sesterces.

Quid confert, etc., what does equestrian rank amount to, if a member of one of the old families like Corvinus has to hire himself out as a shepherd?

FIG. 7.—Taberna.

107. Laurenti. Laurentum was near the coast of Latium, between Ostia and Lavinium. Cf. Livy I, 1.

108. Conductas. *Conducere* is used in two senses : *conducere rem utendam* means to pay for the use of a thing, *conducere rem faciendam* means to receive pay for taking care of a thing.

109. Pallante et Licinis. For the plural, cf. line 52. Pallas and Licinus were freedmen proverbial for their wealth. The former was a favorite of the Emperor Claudius and a brother of the Felix mentioned in the Acts of the Apostles. The latter was one of Augustus's favorites.

110. Sacro honori, the tribuneship, which was a sacred office, in that the incumbent was secure from arrest.

111. Pedibus albis. This is usually explained by reference to some supposed custom of marking the feet of slaves with chalk. May it not mean barefooted?

113. Etsi, etc. It is a wonder that, among the host of temples erected to all sorts of divinities, we have not dedicated one to the real god of our idolatry, the "almighty dollar."

114. Habitat, used intransitively.

116. Quae, referring to *Concordia*, is the subject of *crepitat*.

Salutato nido refers to the noise of the birds that had built their nests in the ruins of the temple.

117. Summus honor—i. e., the *consul*, so men of rank and position.

119. Comites, etc., the rest of us, we poor men who depend on the *sportula* for the necessaries of life, are naturally reduced to such tricks as those described below.

120. Densissima lectica, *crowds of litters*. The singular is used collectively. Cf. *plurima rosa*.

Centum quadrantes, the usual amount of the *sportula*, about 25 cents.

125. Galla mea est. One man brings his wife, that he may secure a double amount ; another brings an empty sedan-chair. If the *praeco* has his suspicions, the man puts on a bold front and calls out to the supposed occupant to show herself; as she remains invisible, he excuses her, on the ground that she is probably asleep, and begs the clerk not to disturb her.

126. Quiescet. The future denotes probability, as often in German.

127. Pulchro, ironical, *fine*.

128. Iuris. The use of the genitive with such adjectives as *peritus*, is increasingly common in post-Augustan writers. There was a statue of Apollo near the law-courts, hence his supposed skill in law.

130. Nescio quis, *some — or other*.

Arabarches, an Egyptian title, used here in contempt.

133. Vota, *hopes ;* so Horace, *Hoc erat in votis.* Sat. II, 6, 1.

134. Miseris, dative of "apparent agent." Really a dative of interest like any other.

136. Rex horum, the patron.

Toris. *Torus*, properly a cushion placed on the couch, came to be applied to the couch itself. Cf. Fig. 8.

137. Orbibus. The collection of round tables made from a single section of rare wood, was a fashionable folly of the time. Cf. Becker, Gallus II, 302, ff.

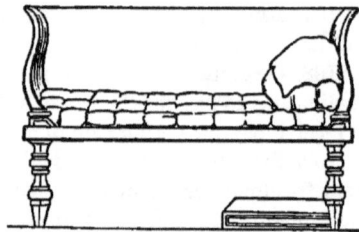

FIG. 8.—Torus.

139. Nullus iam, etc. The race of parasites, poor but agreeable table companions, is gradually disappearing (and a good thing too), for who could bear, etc. Others take this to be a remark of the rich man : "At all events we shall get rid of parasites."

142. Amictus, accusative plural.

145. Nec tristis—i. e., by no means sad.

146. Ducitur funus. One of the many specialized uses of *ducere*.

Iratis amicis, because, dying intestate, the rich man had left them no legacies. Another dative of apparent agent.

149. Omne in praecipiti, etc. Vice has reached its climax, subject for satire is ready, one has only to spread one's sails.

153. Simplicitas, *boldness, frankness.* The following lines are quoted as an example of the boldness of ancient satire.

154. Refert. Note the difference between *rĕfert* and *refĕrt* — e. g., line 118.

155. Pone Tigellinum, etc., *put Tigellinus into your verses*—i. e., try such satire in these times—and you will find your punishment ready. The punishment here described is said to have been inflicted on many of the early Christians. The victim was surrounded with pitch (*taeda*), his chin supported by a stake (*fixo pectore*), and he was then burned. The body would be drawn away through the sand of the arena.

157. Deducis must be for the future tense. Others read *deducit*, supplying *quae* referring to *taeda* above as its subject.

158. Qui dedit, etc. Juvenal asks, "Shall all these crimes go on unrebuked?"

Vehatur is subjunctive in a deliberative question.

159. Illinc— i. e., from his *lectica*.

160. Contra = *obviam.*

161. Accusator, etc. Merely saying, "*That is the man*," will cause you to be looked on as his accuser.

FIG. 9.—Tomb of Caecilia Metella.

162. Aenean. You may safely pit Aeneas against Rutulus, or write of Achilles or Hylas, but beware of rousing men's wrath and tears by touching on the sins of the day. We are reminded of a modern clergyman who desired to spare the feelings of his hearers, and so preached on the terrible depravity of cannibalism.

164. Hylas was the favorite of Hercules; going to draw water, he was seized and carried off by the nymphs.

168. Inde irae et lacrimae. Terence's *hinc illae lacrimae* (And. I, 126) had become proverbial.

169. Duelli. *Duellum* is the older form of *bellum*, as *duonus* of *bonus*. Cf. *duo* and *bis*.

170. Experiar. Juvenal answers, "I will try then what I may be allowed to say about the dead whose tombs line the highways." The most imposing monuments of the dead were built beside the Appian, Flaminian,

Fig. 10.—Restoration of tombs on the Appian Way.

and Latin roads. The laws of the twelve tables forbade interments within the city. The tomb of Caecilia Metella, on the Appian, is shown in Fig. 9. Fig. 10 is an attempt to reproduce the original appearance of the tombs on the Appian road.

171. Notice the singular *cinis*, where we use the plural; Juvenal has *cineres* in XI, 44.

SATIRE III.

THE DISADVANTAGES OF LIFE AT ROME.

INTRODUCTION.—Juvenal tells us that as Umbricius, one of his friends, who has decided to leave Rome and find a home at Cumae, is waiting for the cart that is to carry his goods to his new dwelling-place, they walk together to a spot just outside the walls, and there Umbricius tells him why the great city has become unbearable to him. There is no room for honest men where all success is the reward of wrong-doing. Rome has become the paradise of servile, versatile, conscienceless Greeks, who are ready to assume every *rôle*, even that of the professional philosopher, and are equally unscrupulous in all. Nor is there room at Rome for a poor man. He is ill-treated and despised, and is likely to be driven to dishonesty by the ostentation and display that society forces upon him. The dangers of the city are described, and it is shown that they press most heavily on him who can not purchase safety. The fire that ruins the poor man is a source of gain to the rich; the poor man must be jostled in the crowd and risk his life among the loaded wagons, while the rich man is borne aloft out of reach of danger in his luxurious litter.

The subject is not exhausted, but the wagon has come, the driver calls, and Umbricius bids Juvenal good-by.

1. **Confusus,** *disturbed.*
2. **Laudo,** its object is readily supplied from *amici.*
Cumis. *Cumae* was an old Greek settlement, whence the Romans derived their alphabet. It was a few miles north of modern Naples, and was at this time almost deserted, *vacuis.*
3. **Destinet.** The subjunctive marks the thought as that of *Umbricius* (l. 21). H. 516, II, or (better) Madvig 357, a.
Sybillae. The cave of the Sybil, which is still shown, was near *Cumae.* Cf. Verg. Aen. VI, 18; *Cumaea Sybilla.* It was from her that Tarquin was said to have purchased the Sybilline books.
4. **Baiarum.** *Baiae* was a fashionable resort near *Cumae.*
Amoeni secessus. Appositional genitive. Cf. *urbs Romae* and, in English, *the city of London.* H. 396, VI.
5. **Prochytam.** A rocky desert island (*Procida*) off the coast between *Naples* and *Cumae.*
Suburae. The crowded, noisy part of Rome, between the Viminal and Esquiline Hills. Juvenal speaks as if all Rome were one Subura. For the dative, cf. I, 18, note.
6. **Ut non—credas,** negative result clause.
7. **Lapsus tectorum.** Cf. ll. 190-196. The buildings at Rome were often

carried to a great height, owing to the cost of land, and the upper stories were usually of wood. *Tectum (tego)* means *covering, roof, building.*

8. Saevae. Cf. *iniquae,* I. 30.

9. As if such recitations formed the climax of horrors. Cf. VIII, 221. The name of the month was changed from *Sextilis* in honor of the emperor.

10. Domus—i. e., his family and possessions.

Raeda. A four-wheeled travel-ing-carriage. The word is said to be Celtic. Cf. Fig. 11. The pres-ent tense with *dum* is regular in narrative.

11. Ad, *at* or *near.*

Arcus, the arches of the aqueduct that passed over the *porta Capena,* hence *madida.* The *via Appia* began at this gate.

12. Constituebat. *Constituo, to make an appointment,* is used either with the dative, as here, or with *cum* and the ablative.

Fig. 11.—Raeda.

Amicae. *Egeria,* Liv. I, 21. For the case, cf. note on I, 18.

14. Quorum depends on *supellex ; cophinus faenumque* are in the pred-icate.

15. I. e., what was formerly a holy place has become a mere source of income. *Mercedem pendere = to pay rent.*

16. Camenis, the Roman national Muses, *Egeria, Carmenta, Antevorta,* and *Postvorta.*

17. Speluncas, *grottoes,* here artificial.

18. Veris—i. e., *speluncis.*

20. Ingenuum tofum, *the natural stone* (tufa).

23. Res, *property.*

Here, in the time of Augustus *heri* was the regular form. Cf. *vesperi, vespere ; mani, mane.*

Eadem (*res*) is the subject of *deteret.* More usual is *res deteritur.*

24. Exiguis, neuter plural, *the trifling* (*remnants*) ; it seems to be dative, though best translated *from.*

25. Exuit alas. Daedalus flew north from Crete and alighted at Cumae. Verg. Aen. VI, 14 ff. *Exuo* is the regular word for taking off garments, the opposite is *induo.*

27. Lachesi. The individual duties of the Fates were not always clearly defined. Properly Lachesis decided the length of each human life. Clotho spun the thread, and Atropos cut it off.

28. **Subeunte,** *supporting.*

29. **Artorius et Catulus.** Typical rascals; personally unknown.

31. **Quis facile est aedem conducere,** etc.—ı. e., the whole tribe of contractors, men who could make money out of anything, from building a temple to removing sewage.

Quis, dative.

Conducere means to take a contract for. Cf. note I, 108.

Flumina, portus—i. e., for such things as building dams and dredging harbors.

32. **Busta,** *the funeral pyre.* *Buro = uro,* whence *comburo ;* cf. combustion. Cremation must have been common in Rome before 450 B. C., for the laws of the Twelve Tables forbid it within the city.

33. **Caput,** from meaning *head,* comes to mean *body, life, person.*

Domina—sub hasta. This seems to refer to a custom of fixing a spear above the slave auction-block, as a sign of conquest.

Venale, *to be sold, for sale.*

34. **Hi,** subject of *edunt.*

35. **Buccae** is in apposition with *hi ; blowers, bawlers.*

36. **Munera,** *the public shows.* These were often provided by private citizens as a means of establishing popularity. The person that provided for the expenses was called *editor muneris.*

37. **Occidunt (quem vulgus, pollice verso, jubet).** When a gladiator was beaten, the people called for his death *verso pollice ;* if they thought he had deserved by his bravery to have his life spared, they gave the sign *presso pollice.* Just what the two terms mean is unknown; *pollicem vertere* is usually considered to be to turn the thumb up, but the whole matter is in doubt. The *editor* was the interpreter of public opinion.

Populariter, *to please the people.*

38. **Et cur non omnia ?**—i. e., why should they not do everything?

40. The success of such men is merely the sport of Fortune, who raises them at her caprice.

42. **Poscere,** *call for*—i. e., ask to read.

Motus astrorum, etc.—i. e., I have no knowledge of fortune-telling.

44. **Ranarum,** etc. Poison was prepared from the entrails of a venomous species of frog. Cf. I, 70.

47. **Tamquam manous,** etc.—i. e., as I am neither able nor willing to help men steal, they think of me as maimed, a useless trunk with a withered right hand. The members of a provincial governor's *cohors* were called his *comites.*

48. **Exstinctae dextrae,** genitive of quality.

49. **Conscius,** *accomplice.*

50. **Aestuat.** In classical Latin the subjunctive is used in such cases.

52. **Secreti honesti,** *an honorable secret.*

Fecit; *fecerit* would be more exact.

53. Verri. Verres is taken as the type of an extortionate governor. He was propraetor of Sicily 73–70 B. C.

Vult; the subject is the same as that of *erit.*

54. Tanti, *of so much value.* Probably a locative. Cf. Roby II, lvii.

Non, rarely, as here, used for *ne.* Hor. A. P. 460.

Opaci, *shaded.*

55. Tagi, the river Tagus was said to contain golden sand.

56. Careas, sumas, and **timearis,** are subjunctives in clauses of result.

Ponenda = *deponenda.*

60. Opstabit, notice the form; *obstat* occurs in lines 164, 194, 243.

61. Quamvis; in classical Latin *quamquam* would be used.

Quota, *how small.*

Achaei, predicate nominative.

62. The stream of Oriental influence has been flowing into Rome for a long time.

FIG. 12.—Sambuca.   FIG. 13.—Tympanum.

63. Chordas obliquas; the *sambuca,* a sort of harp, is meant. Cf. Fig. 12.

64. Nec non = *et.*

Gentilia, *national;* for the *tympanum,* cf. Fig. 13.

67. Rusticus ille, etc.—i. e., the old Roman peasant has degenerated into a servile imitator of the Greeks.

Trechedipna. The meaning is uncertain, probably a sort of Greek shoe.

68. Niceteria, *wrestling prizes.*

69. Sicyone, on the Gulf of Corinth.

Amydone, in Macedonia, on the river Axius.

70. Trallibus aut Alabandis; these towns were in Caria.

71. Esquilias, the *Esquiline.*

Dictum a vimine collem is, of course, the *Viminal.*

72. Viscera, *the vitals;* they worm themselves into positions of confidence, and finally supplant their masters.

73. Here follows a description of Greek character and attainments. It is painful to reflect, in this connection, that the Americans have been called the Greeks of modern times, for the three characteristics to which Juvenal gives prominence are—elegance being sacrificed to force—" smartness," "impudence," and "the gift of gab."

74. Isaeo, a famous rhetorician whom the younger Pliny praises highly. Pl. Ep. II, 3.

Ede, *tell.*

75. Hominem, *character.*

76. Aliptes, *an anointer, a trainer.*

77. Schoenobates, *funambulus =* a rope-dancer. Cf. Fig. 14.

Omnia novit Graeculus esuriens— i. e., "your Greek can do anything to earn a living."

78. Miseris; most editions have *iusseris.*

80. Qui sumpsit pinnas, *Daedalus.*

FIG. 14.—Funambulus.

81. Conchylia, *purple cloaks,* so *luxury.*

Prior signabit—i. e., take precedence in signing wills, etc.

82. Toro meliore—i. e., a higher place at the table.

83. Pruna et cottona; both plums and figs came from Syria.

84. Usque adeo nihil est, quod, *is it so absolutely nothing that; usque adeo* is literally *even up to that*—i. e., *to such a degree.*

85. Baca Sabina, the olive.

86. Quid quod, *what of the fact that?*

88. Invalidi is used as a noun and depends on *collum.*

Collum and cervix are purposely compared.

89. Herculis depends on *cervicibus.*

Antaeum. Hercules overcame him only by holding him up from the earth, whence he derived his strength.

92. *We too may praise these same things.*

98. Antiochus, etc. The best actors excite no wonder in Greece (*illic*), for the whole people is born to dissimulation.

102. Brumae, for *brevimae;* so, *the shortest day;* so, *winter.*

103. Endromidem, a thick, heavy cloak. Cf. Osric, in Hamlet V, 2.

104. Omni; Weidner reads *omnis,* and compares Hor. Odes III, 30, 6: *Non omnis moriar.*

105. Aliena sumere vultum, etc.; to make his face a mirror to reflect other men's moods.

106. Iactare manus—i e., to make gestures of admiration.

114. The meaning seems to be: Since I have begun to talk of the Greeks, let me tell you what their learning, their philosophy, does; I might go into details about their schools (*gymnasia*), but pass that by and listen to the practical effect of their vaunted philosophy.

115. Abollae. The *abolla* was a cloak much affected by the professional philosophers. It is shown in Fig. 15.

116. Stoicus | P. Egnatius Celer accused Barea, his pupil, of treason.

117. Nutritus, *educated.*

118. Gorgonei caballi. Pegasus, who sprang from the Gorgon's blood, is said to have dropped a feather from his wing in flying over Tarsus. Note that *caballus* is the Low-Latin word whence the French *cheval* is derived.

120. Protogenes, etc., *some Greek flatterer.*

121. Gentis vitio—i. e., in accordance with the selfish practice of his race.

122. Solus habet, *keeps him for himself.*

Facilem, *receptive.*

125. Minor, *of less account.*

Iactura, *the tossing aside, throwing overboard.*

126. Officium, *service.*

Fig. 15.
Abolla.

Ne nobis blandiar, *not to flatter ourselves, to speak the plain truth.*

127. *What good does it do a poor man if he takes pains to put on his toga and hurry off before daylight to pay his visit of ceremony to some rich, childless widow, when he has a prætor as his rival?* Legacy-hunting became a regular business during the empire, and as such little attentions as morning-calls were highly valued, the legacy-hunters made a point of being at hand as early as possible.

129. Orbis. *Orbus* means either *without parents*, or, as here, *without children.* The cognate English word *orphan* has been restricted to the former meaning.

137. The character of even a Nasīca, a Numa, or a Metellus, would be no recommendation nowadays. The first question would be, "How much is he worth?"

Hospes numinis Idaei. When the statue of Cybele was to be brought to Rome, 204 b. c., the oracle declared that it must be intrusted to the most virtuous man in the state. The senate awarded the honor to P. Scipio Nasica, who thus became the host of the divinity.

139. When the temple of Vesta was burned, 241 b. c., L. Caecilius Metellus rescued the palladium of Minerva.

141. Pascit | *pascere* is the technical term for keeping slaves or cattle.

142. Paropside, *side dish*, *entrée.*

143. Cf. Hor. Sat. I, 1, 62.

144. Licet, *although.*

Samothracum, genitive. The Samothracian gods were the *Cabiri;* their worship was very mysterious.

145. Nostrorum (*deorum*).

146. Dis ignoscentibus ipsis; the very gods pardon perjury in a poor man, for they know that his case is desperate.

147. Quid quod, cf. 1. 86.

148. Hic idem, *this same man.*

150. Consuto vulnere, ablative absolute.

151. Non una, *many a.*

153. Inquit; the subject is probably the *designator,* whose duty it was to see that the distinction of rank was observed.

155. Ouius res legi non sufficit. After the time of Augustus, a fortune of 400,000 sesterces was necessary to entitle one to equestrian rank, and to a seat among the knights in the theatre. Cf. 1, 106, and line 159.

FIG. 16.—Pinnirapus.

158. Pinnirapi. The gladiators had various modes of combat; the *pinnirapus* achieved victory when he seized the *pinna* or crest from his adversary's helmet. Cf. Fig. 16.

Lanistae, a trainer of gladiators. Cf. Fig. 17, which shows the *retiarius* (on the left), the *secutor,* and the *lanista.*

159. Othoni. The law of Otho (*lex Roscia*), passed 67 B. C., provided that the first fourteen rows of seats in the theatre should be reserved for the knights.

160. Hic, here at Rome.

Censu minor, *of small means.* Possibly Juvenal wrote "*censu minore.*"

161. Sarcinulis, *dowry,* literally *baggage.*

Inpar — i. e., whose property is unequal to hers.

FIG. 17.—Retiarius, secutor, and lanista.

162. Aedilibus, dative. The aediles had the care of the city, and often asked counsel of private citizens.

163. **Debuerant.** Notice the tense.

Olim is often used in the silver age for *iam dudum.*

Tenues, *of slender fortune.*

165. **Res angusta domi,** a proverbial phrase for poverty.

Illis, dative.

166. **Conatus,** *the effort.*

Magno (*pretio*), ablative of price (instrumental).

167. **Frugi,** an "indeclinable adjective," really the dative of *frux,* originally used as predicative dative. Cf. Roby II, xliv.

168. Fashion makes simple living still more difficult. One is ashamed of earthenware at Rome, but in the country it is no disgrace.

170. **Veneto**—i. e., such as the Veneti use.

Cucullo, *hood, cloak.*

Fɪɢ. 18.—Theatre at Aspendos.

171. The wearing of so expensive a garment as the toga is only a Roman fashion.

172. Even when the glory of festal days is celebrated in the grassy theatre. The country theatre was usually an open space, where the audience might find seats on the slope of the hill-side.

174. **Notum exodium,** the old familiar play, given every year.

176. **Formidat,** *trembles at.*

177. **Similes** modifies *orchestram* and *populum.*

178. Orchestram. The *orchestra* in the Greek theatre was the place occupied by the chorus; in the Roman theatre, where there was no chorus, it was devoted to the seats of the senators and men of highest rank. Cf. Fig. 18.

Clari velamen honoris, *as the mark of distinguished honor*—i. e., as the garb of their great office.

180. Hic, *here, at Rome.*

Habitus nitor, *the splendor of dress.*

181. Arca, ablative of separation.

184. Cossum, unknown.

185. Clauso labello—i. e., even if he does not say a word to you.

Veiento, nominative. He was one of the *delatores.*

186. One rich man celebrates the day when his favorite (son?) first shaves his beard, another when his hair is cut; the slaves all have cakes for sale which the visitor is obliged to buy. A delicate way of feeing the servants.

187. Accipe, etc.; take one, since you must, and let it serve as yeast to stir your indignation.

188. Praestare, *to furnish, pay.*

189. Peculia. A slave could hold no property without the permission of his master, if allowed to retain his earnings, they were called *peculium.*

190. Gelida Praeneste, *cool Praeneste.* It was about 23 miles east of Rome. Cf. Hor. Od. III, 4, 22.

Ruinam, *ruina* was the special term for the fall of a building.

191. Volsiniis, in Etruria, about 70 miles from Rome.

192. Simplicibus Gabiis. Between Rome and Praeneste. Possibly there is a reference to the simplicity of the inhabitants when they were duped by Sextus Tarquinius. Cf. Livy I, 53 f.

Proni Tiburis. Tibur was on a hill sloping down to the Anio, 16 miles from Rome. Horace often refers to it.

193. Tenui tibicine, *by a slender prop.*

194. Sui, partitive genitive.

196. Securos—i. e., *nos, the inhabitants.*

FIG. 19.—Abacus.

198. A description of such an *incendium.* The name *Ucalegon* is borrowed from Vergil's account of the burning of Troy. Aen. II, 311.

199. **Tabulata tertia,** *the third story.*

Tibi, ethical dative.

200. **Trepidatur,** *the commotion begins.*

203. **Codro,** unknown.

Procula. Probably the name of a dwarf well known at the time.

204. **Abaci,** a sort of marble-topped sideboard. Cf. Fig. 19.

Nec non et, the *nec non* = *et,* the *et* is correlative with the *et* of the next line.

205. **Chiro**—i. e., a statue of the centaur *Chiron.* Cf. Fig. 35.

207. **Divina carmina,** probably the poems of Homer.

Opici, the Greek word for *Osci = barbarians.*

208. **Illud totum nihil,** *all that nothing.*

210. If fire deprives a poor man of his all, none helps him, he is left to starve; but if a rich man's house burns, every one is anxious to help repair the loss.

212. **Asturici,** unknown; he is called Persicus below, line 221.

Horrida mater—i. e., the matrons appear with disheveled hair, as on occasions of public mourning.

213. **Pullati,** in the *pulla vestis,* a dark-gray mourning-garment.

Vadimonia, *the sessions of the court.*

216. **Signa,** *statues; nuda* marks them as Greek.

217. **Euphranoris et Polycliti;** the former was a sculptor at Athens in the time of Alexander, the latter came from Argos in the time of Pericles.

218. **Phaecasiatorum;** this is Roth's reading, adopted by Mayor. The φαικάσιον was a white shoe worn by Greek priests. Here the epithet is transferred to the gods. In the reading, "*haec Asianorum,*" *haec* is usually explained as nom. sg. fem.; but Weidner calls it neut. pl.

219. **Mediamque Minervam,** *and among them* (*a statue of*) *Minerva;* others, less correctly, I think, take it to mean a bust of Minerva.

221. **Orborum,** cf. note, line 129. His childlessness makes him the object of special attentions.

222. **Suspectus, tamquam,** *suspected of,* a common use of *tamquam* in the silver age.

223. **Avelli** has the force of the middle voice.

Circensibus. The public shows were used to keep the lower classes amused and contented. Napoleon III tried the same plan in Paris. The most important of the Roman games were the *ludi magni,* held in April. Cf. X, 81.

Sorae, Fabrateriae, Frusinone; these were small towns in Latium. Notice that the first two are locatives, the third locative ablative.

225. **Quanti.** The antecedent *tanti* is omitted. So-called genitive of price or value. Probably a locative construction.

Conducis, *hire.* Cf. I, 108.

226. **Puteusque brevis,** *a shallow well, needing no rope.*

229. Pythagoreis. They were vegetarians, probably owing to their belief in the transmigration of souls.

231. It is something to feel that you actually *own* any part of the world, even if it be but a single lizard.

232. Plurimus, *very many a.*

Vigilando, *from lying awake.* Notice the quantity of the *o*, and cf. I, 6S.

234. Meritoria, *lodgings.*

235. Magnis opibus, ablative of means; if one owns a large house and sleeps in the middle of it, he may avoid the noise.

236. Caput morbi, *the source of disease.*

237. Convicia mandrae, the quarreling and mutual abuse of the drovers, when there was a "block" in the street.

238. Druso. *Tiberius Claudius Drusus* (the Emperor Claudius) was famous for his sleepiness, as are the animals referred to in *vitulis marinis.*

239. Officium, *duty,* such as making a call, or attending a recitation.

240. Super ora—i. e., above the heads of the common people.

Liburno—i. e., a Liburnian slave. Cf. I, 64. This reading is better than *liburna.* The absence of the preposition may be explained, as in I, 54.

241. Obiter, *on the way.*

243. Ante, adverb.

245. Assere, *the pole* (perhaps of a litter).

247. Pinguia crura luto. Notice the omission of the verb; common in Juvenal.

248. Digito; *digitus* is used of either a finger or a toe.

Clavus; soldiers wore "hob-nailed" shoes.

249. The crowd going to the *sportula* adds another element of confusion. Above it is spoken of as a sum of money; here it seems to be actual food, which was taken away in a portable kitchen kept warm for the purpose; hence *fumo.*

251. Corbulo, unknown, probably some proverbially strong man; possibly Nero's famous general, Cn. Domitius Corbulo, whom Tacitus calls *corpore ingens.*

253. Cursu ventilat ignem, *fans the fire by his running.*

254. Coruscat, *sways.*

257. Saxa Ligustica—i. e., from the Ligurian quarries.

258. Axis, the subject of *procubuit,* is drawn into the relative clause.

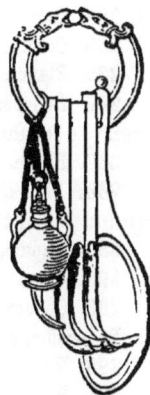

Fig. 20.
Oil flask and strigils.

261. More animae, *like a breath.*

Domus, *the household.*

263. Striglibus; the *strigilis* was a sort of flesh-scraper used after the bath.

Guto, *oil-flask.* Dative. Cf. Fig. 20, which shows the oil flask and several strigils.

265. Novicius, *a new-comer;* cf. Eng., *novice.*

266. Porthmea, *the ferryman*—i. e., Charon.

Nec sperat; if the body were unburied, the soul must wait a hundred years on the bank of the Styx.

Caenosi gurgitis—i. e., the Styx. *Caenosus* is also written *cenosus* and *coenosus.*

Alnum, the boat.

267. Trientem, a copper coin, one third of an *as,* Charon's fee, which was placed between the lips of the dead.

269. Spatium, *distance.*

270. Fenestris. Notice the (poetical) omission of the preposition *de.*

272. Silicem, *the pavement.*

Haberi, *to be held, considered.*

274. Intestatus, *without making your will.*

Adeo—i. e., so true is it that there are.

275. Vigiles, windows where people are awake.

277. Contentae agrees with *fenestrae.*

279. Dat poenas, etc., he pays for the lack of his usual amusement by suffering such a night as Achilles mourning for the death of his friend Patroclus.

281. This line is rejected by several editors. If genuine, it seems better to consider it as a continuation of Umbricius's speech rather than an interruption by Juvenal.

282. Inprobus, *hot-headed, reckless.*

283. Coccina laena; the purple cloak marks him as rich and powerful.

285. Flammarum, partitive genitive.

286. Deducere, *escort.* Used of clients accompanying their patron to or from the forum.

287. Filum, *wick.*

288. This description of the bullying attack upon an inoffensive stranger reminds us of the "Mohawks" of London in the time of Addison.

289. Vapulo, *take the blows.*

292. Aceto, vinegar and water was a common drink of the poorer classes.

296. Quaero. Notice the tense, and cf. Eng., "*When do you go away?*"

Proseucha, a Jewish house of prayer. Used in contempt.

298. Vadimonia faciunt, *bring a complaint.*

301. Paucis, *a few, some.*

Reverti, commonly used as a deponent verb; as usual in deponent verbs, the force of the middle voice is evident.

302. Metuas, *you may fear, you have to fear.*

Spoliet; subjunctive in a relative clause of purpose.

303. Derit = *deerit.* **Omnis** agrees with *compago,* which is the subject of *siluit.*

305. Agit rem, *plies his trade;* *subitus* contrasts the highwayman's method with that of the thief.

307. The Pontine marshes in Latium, and the Gallinarian forests in Campania, were favorite lurking-grounds for robbers, who, when they were driven thence, flocked to Rome, as if to "preserves" where game was abundant.

309. Catenae; some verb, as *conficiuntur,* is understood. The regular order would be *qua fornace, qua incude, non graves catenae ?*

310. Maximus in vinclis, etc.—i. e., so much iron is used to furnish chains.

311. Vomer. Cf. Fig. 21.

312. Proavorum atavos; the ascending order of ancestors was *pater, avus, proavus, abavus, atavus, tritavus.*

313. Sub regibus atque tribunis—i. e., in regal and republican times, before the empire.

314. Uno, *a single*—i. e., the Mamertine prison at the

Fig. 21.—Vomer.

foot of the Capitoline, said to have been built by Ancus Martius. Jugurtha and Cethegus were imprisoned there.

315. Poteram, *I was able, I might have.*

317. Iandudum, often written *iam dudum.*

318. Adnuit, from meaning *to nod,* comes to mean *to give a sign, to motion.*

319. Tuo Aquino; this is taken to mean that Juvenal was born at Aquinum. **Refici** depends on *properantem.*

320. Helvinam; the force of this epithet as applied to Ceres is unknown. Helvia was the name of a Roman gens, by whom a temple to Ceres may have been built at Aquinum.

321. Converte, *call.*

Ni pudet illas, *unless they are ashamed of me.*

322. Caligatus, with a countryman's heavy shoes, such as he would wear at Cumae.

SATIRE IV.

INTRODUCTION.—(The lines omitted at the beginning have no essential connection with the rest.)

This satire describes the degradation of the senate. A fisherman catches a remarkably fine fish, and, knowing that it is likely to be confiscated, makes a virtue of necessity and presents it to the Emperor Domitian. The emperor summons the senate from Rome to his Alban villa to consult as to the disposition of the fish. Various senators are described, and each sketch is a masterpiece. The council is dismissed after this weighty matter is decided. Juvenal expresses the wish that Domitian had spent all his time in the luxury and frivolity that this incident illustrates instead of venting his cruelty upon the best men of the state.

37. **Iam** modifies *semianimum.*

Laceraret. Domitian was like a tiger tearing the half-dead world.

Flavius ultimus, *the last of the Flavians* (Vespasián, Titus, Domitian), T. Domitianus Flavius Nero. From all accounts he seems to have been a cruel, hypocritical, cunning, cowardly scoundrel.

38. **Calvo.** Domitian's vanity made his baldness a serious grief to him.

39. **Adriaci spatium admirabile rhombi.** *Adriaci* is an adjective modifying *rhombi.* The whole expression = *rhombus ingens.* Cf. *Crispi iucunda senectus,* l. 81 ; *Montani venter,* l. 107.

40. **Ancon.** *Ancona* (in Picenum) was settled by Dorians from Sicily.

41. **Sinus.** The full expression would be *incidit in sinus retis eosque implevit.*

Haeserat, *had stuck, had been caught.*

Illis, ablative with the comparative.

42. **Maeotica**—i. e., in the sea of Azov, formerly called Lake Maeotis.

46. **Pontifici summo.** All the emperors had the title, *pontifex maximus.*

Proponere, *offer for sale.*

47. **Et,** *even.*

48. **Protinus,** *straightway.*

49. **Agerent cum remige nudo,** *would bring a charge against the poverty-stricken fisherman.*

51. **Vivaria,** object of *depastum* (= *fed upon*).

53. **Palfurio—Armillato.** They seem to have been expounders of the law.

55. **Fisci.** The *fiscus* was the private treasury of the emperor, as distinguished from the *aerarium* or state treasury.

57. **Autumno,** ablative absolute with *cedente.*

Quartanam, a mild form of fever.

58. **Recentem,** *fresh ;* predicate adjective.

59. **Hic,** the fisherman.

Auster, the southwest wind would spoil the fish.

60. **Lacus.** There are two small lakes at the foot of the Alban hills.

Quamquam ; the use of *quamquam* without a finite verb belongs to the silver age.

61. **Minorem,** less than the temple of Vesta at Rome ; the fire upon the altar was supposed to have been brought by Aeneas from Troy.

63. **Valvae,** (*folding*) *doors.*

65. Atriden, *Agamemnon*, used, of course, in contempt.

Picens. The fisherman came from Picenum.

66. Focis, ablative. Cf. III, 203; *lectus Procula minor.*

Genialis, *sacred to your genius.* Every Roman was supposed to have a special guardian divinity called his *genius.*

67. Saginae; the meaning is, *make your stomach ready for the feast.*

68. As if the Fates had saved this fish for this special time.

70. Surgebant cristae, *his crest rose* with pleasure at the flattery.

71. Potestas, abstract for concrete; cf. Ital. *podesta,* and the English use of *a power = a powerful man.*

72. Derat, often written *deerat.*

Patinae mensura—i. e., *a dish large enough.*

76. Abolla. Cf. III, 115; *facinus maioris abollae.*

77. Pegasus was a celebrated lawyer of the time; he was a man of good intentions, but weak.

Vilicus, *steward*—i. e., the *praefectus* was only the emperor's *vilicus* or head slave.

78. Aliud—i. e., anything more than mere stewards, head slaves.

79. Quamquam modifies *diris.*

81. Crispi iucunda senectus. Cf. line 39. Vibius Crispus was an orator, often mentioned by Quintilian.

82. Mite ingenium, *a gentle nature.*

84. Clade et peste refer to Domitian; abstract for concrete.

86. Violentius, *more capricious.*

88. Vere, ablative of *ver.*

89. I. e., never swam against the stream, always floated with the current.

90. Civis refers to *Crispus.*

91. Vitam inpendere vero, *to risk his life for the truth.*

93. His armis—i. e., complaisance and obsequiousness.

94. Acilius. M'. Acilius Glabrio, father of the man of the same name who was consul 91 A. D. The latter was murdered by Domitian, 95 A. D., after fighting with a lion in the Alban amphitheatre. The Acilii claimed descent from Aeneas.

95. Indigno quem, *who did not deserve that . . . him.*

96. Olim = *iam dudum.* Cf. III, 163.

97. *Old age is like a miracle among the high born*—i. e., one whose birth brought him into contact with the emperor, found it difficult to live in such times.

98. Fraterculus Gigantis—i. e., one of no ancestry, sprung from the earth.

101. Artes patricias, *the tricks of the patricians.*

103. Brute. Brutus was said to have feigned stupidity to escape Tarquin's suspicion. Cf. Livy I, 56.

Barbato regi. Barbers are said to have first come to Rome about 300 B. C. *Barbatus* is used like *intonsus* (Hor. Od. II, 15, 11) for *ancient, simple.*

104. Melior vultu, *more cheerful* (Mayor).

105. Rubrius. Probably Rubrius Gallus, sent against the Sarmatians by Vespasian. *Reus = defendant.*

107. Montani venter, cf. lines 39, 81.

108. Crispinus, cf. I, 27 ; *verna Canopi Crispinus.*

109. Saevior illo, etc. Pompeius is unknown. The combination of severity and delicacy in this description has made it famous.

112. Fuscus perished in an expedition against the Dacians.

113. Veiento, cf. III, 185 ; *ut te respiciat Veiento.*

Catullo, one of Domitian's informers.

116. Dirus, *wretched.*

A ponte. The bridges were favorite places for beggars. It is hardly probable that Veiento had ever actually been a bridge-beggar.

117. Dignus qui, for the construction cf. line 95.

Aricinos. The steep hill at Aricia forced the carriages to move slowly, and thus furnished the beggars an excellent opportunity.

118. Devexae, *descending*—i. e., going down the hill.

120. Illi, ethical dative.

121. Sic pugnas, etc. The Cilician gladiators were famous ; *ictus* means the thrusts of the gladiator ; *pegma* was a part of the stage-machinery ; the *velaria* were awnings stretched over the top of the theatre.

123. Oestro, *gadfly,* so *frenzy.*

127. Arviragus, unknown.

128. Sudes, *stakes*—i. e., *fins.*

129. Fabricio—i. e., Fabricius Veiento. Cf. line 113.

130. Censes ? conciditur ? (*is it to be cut up ?*). For the tense, cf. III, 296 ; *in qua te quaero prosencha ?* "*Quidnam igitur censes*" was the usual form of a question put to the Senate.

132. Orbem, *circle, circumference.*

133. Debetur, *we need.* **Subitus,** *speedy.*

Prometheus—i. e., a potter, so *Vulcanus* is used for a smith.

134. The *rota,* as used in Egypt, is seen in Fig. 22.

135. Castra seems to have here the sense of *court.*

136. Vicit, the usual word ; his proposition was approved.

138. Pulmo may be translated *blood.*

FIG. 22.—Rota.

139. Usus, *experience.*

140. Tempestate, *tempestas* often means simply *time.*

Circeis ; the best oysters were said to come from Circeii, in Campania, from the Lucrine Lake near Baiae, and from Rutupiae (Richborough, in Kent).

142. Deprendere, translate, *in discovering.*

144. Surgitur; so we say, *the House rises.*

147. Domitian attempted to conquer these German tribes, in 84 A. D., but was defeated; in spite of this, he celebrated a triumph. Cf. Tac. Agric. 39.

149. Praecipiti pinna, probably simply = *in great haste.*

151. Quibus, its antecedent is *tempora.*

153. Cerdonibus is put for the lower classes in general. The Lamiae were a distinguished family of the Aelian gens, one of whom, Aelius Lamia, Domitian had caused to be put to death. The meaning is that, although he murdered noblemen with impunity, he perished when he began to attack the lower classes.

SATIRE V.

INTRODUCTION.—This is a description of the indignities to which a man that courts the dinner-tables of the rich is subjected.

The state of the meanest beggar is preferable to that of a parasite. In spite of your obsequious devotion, your patron seldom invites you to dinner; when he does, your dinner and his are two quite different things: he has rich old wine in gemmed goblets, you have sour grape-juice in cracked earthenware; he is waited on by a graceful slave-boy, you by a coarse, rough negro; he has fine white bread, that given you is hard and black with age. This is your reward for braving the inclement weather to attend his morning receptions. So it is with the rest of the feast: the best of everything for him, the commonest food for you. If you were to come into a fortune, what a change there would be! This is not economy, but a studied purpose to enjoy the cruel pleasure of your mortification. And, after all, you deserve no better, for you have sold your self-respect for a dinner, and will probably come to be a stage-buffoon, taking kicks and cuffs for the amusement of the audience.

2. Ut—putes. Subjunctive clause of result.

Quadra = *mensa.*

3. Sarmentus, a freedman, favorite of Augustus.

4. Caesaris—i. e., Augustus.

Gabba, probably the Aulus Gabba mentioned by Quintilian.

5. Quamvis modifies *iurato.* Cf. III, 1.

6. Novi. Notice the tense.

Frugalius, *less exacting.*

7. Puta, *suppose.*

Quod, its antecedent is *hoc ipsum.*

8. Crepido, probably = *foot-path.*

Pons—i. e., beggar's stand. Cf. IV, 116; *a ponte satelles.*

Tegetis pars dimidia brevior—i. e., *half of a beggar's mat.*

9. Tantine, etc. Is the insult of the dinner worth so much? *Iniuria cenae* is about the same as *cena iniuriosa.*

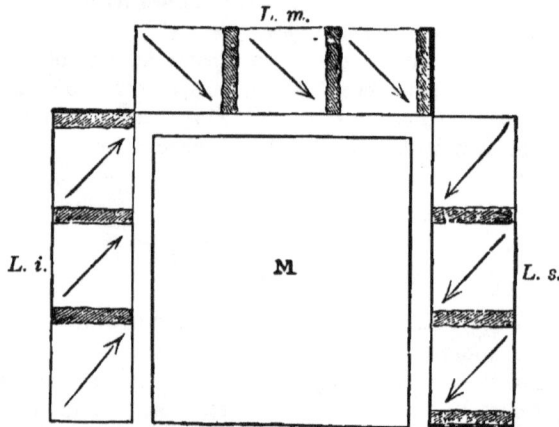

FIG. 23.—Triclinium. *M.,* Mensa ; *L. i.,* Lectus imus ; *L. m.,* Lectus medius ;
L. s., Lectus summus.

10. I. e. *Is your hunger so starving that it can endure such insults, when it might shiver and eat beggar's food?*

12. Fige, *consider.*

Discumbere iussus, *invited to din-ner.*

13. Mercedem solidam, *payment in full.*

14. Inputat, *adds to the account, credits himself with.*

Rex, *the great man, your patron.* Cf. I, 136 ; *rex ipse iacebit.*

17. Fig. 23 shows the arrangement of the *triclinium* or dining-table. The *culcitae* were the cushions, as shown in Fig. 24.

FIG 24.—Dinner-scene, showing the . culcitae.

18. Una simus. Cf. the form of invitation in Terence Haut. I, 1, 110 ; *apud me sis volo.*

19. Habet Trebius, etc.—i. e., such an invitation is reason enough for him to rouse himself early and hurry off without waiting to lace his shoes, in order that he may show the greatest respect by being early at the *salutatio.*

21. Orbem, the round of visits.

22. Sideribus dubiis. *Dubius* has the same root as *duo*. Cf. *twi-light*.

23. Serraca, *the Wain.*

24. Quod sucida nolit lana pati; the wine is so bad that even wool will not absorb it. Wool soaked in wine was used for fomentations.

25. De conviva Corybanta; the bad wine goes to his head, and *from a guest he becomes a priest of Cybele.*

28. Que connects *vos* and *cohortem.*

30. Ipse, *the master.* Cf. line 14, note.

Capillato diffusum consule—i. e., *of great age.* Cf. IV, 103 ; *barbato regi. Vinum* is, of course, understood.

32. Cardiaco, *dyspeptic.*

34. Titulum, *label.*

35. Fuligine; smoke passing through the storeroom was supposed to mellow the wine.

36. Thrasea Helvidiusque. Paetus Thrasea and his son-in-law, Helvidius Priscus, were Stoics and Independents, and as such would naturally keep the birthdays of Marcus and Decimus Brutus as festivals. Thrasea was put to death by Nero, Helvidius by Vespasian.

38. Heliadum crustas. The daughters of the Sun weeping for the death of their brother Phaethon were changed into poplars, and their tears became amber. *Crustas* is best considered = *pocula crustata.*

39. Virro, the patron.

41. Ungues observet acutos, *to watch your sharp finger-nails,* lest you pry out some of the gems.

42. Da veniam (*excuse me*), etc Probably the words of the slave to the guest. *Praeclara* is in the predicate.

45. Zelotypo, *jealous.*

Iuvenis—i. e., Aeneas, whom Dido preferred to Iarbas. It is the subject of *solebat.*

46. Vatinius, a cobbler of Beneventum, had a very long nose, whence a kind of cup with four long spouts was named for him.

48. Sulpura; old glass was exchanged for sulphur matches (cf. Martial I, 42, 4); another explanation is that the cup *called for* sulphur cement *with its broken glass.*

50. Decocta (*aqua*), water boiled and then cooled with snow.

52. Cursor Gaetulus, *an African stable-boy.*

55. Clivosae Latinae (*viae*). Cf. I, 171.

56. Flos Asiae—i. e., a beautiful slave-boy.

57. Tulli, Servius Tullius.

Census; *censeo = value, rate,* so *census = rating,* then *fortune.*

Anci, Ancus Marcius.

59. Frivola. Cf. III, 198.

61. Pauperibus miscere, to mix wine for poor men such as you.

62. Ille, the *cursor*, the black Ganymede that waits on you.

67. Cf. Fig. 25.

68. Vix fractum—i. e., made from grain so coarse that it seems hardly "cracked."

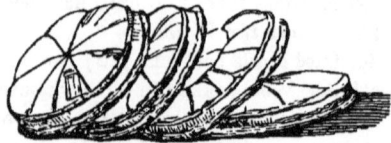

Fig. 25.—Loaves of bread found at Pompeii.

71. Dextram cohibere, etc. — i. e., don't dare to touch the fine white bread, the *artopta;* so called from the form or mold in which it was baked. Cf. Fig. 26.

73. Inprobulum, *a little forward.*

74. Vis tu, almost = an imperative like " will you?" in such expressions as " Will you let that alone ?"

77. Cucurri—i. e., to make my early morning calls.

78. Cum, conjunction.

81. Squilla, *lobster.* Cf. Fig. 27.

83. Excelsi, *tall.*

Fig. 26.—Bread-molds (artoptae).

84 f. *A crab hedged in with half an egg is placed before you. A funereal dinner in a very small dish.*

87. Olebit lanternam, etc. The patron has the best oil, that of Venafrum ; yours will have an odor of the lamp, since it is the poorer sort that comes from Africa ; such oil as makes men decline to bathe with Boccar when he has rubbed himself with it, such oil as frightens off the very reptiles.

Fig. 27.—Table delicacies, from Pompeiian frescoes.

93. Tauromenitanae rupes, on the eastern coast of Sicily.

Peractum est, *has been ransacked.*

95. Macello, the general market, on the north side of the Via Sacra.

96. Proxima, *the nearest seas.*

97. So the provinces furnish our kitchens.

98. Laenas sends dainties to Aurelia, and she sells them.

101. In carcere. Cf. Vergil's account of the winds imprisoned by Aeolus. Aen. I, 51 ff.

102. Mediam Charybdim—i. e., the most dangerous places.

104. Glacie aspersus maculis, *frost-bitten.*

Tiberinus (*lupus*), *a pike from the Tiber.*

105. Vernula. Cf. I, 26; X, 117; XIV, 169.

106. Cryptam Suburae, a branch of the *cloaca maxima*, the opening of which is seen in Fig. 28. Cf. III, 5, note.

107. Ipsi, the master, as in line 30.

Velim (*dicere*).

Fig. 28.—Mouth of the cloaca maxima.

109. Seneca, the philosopher, was very rich and very liberal; he was put to death by Nero on a charge of conspiracy, really for the sake of his property.

Piso. Calpurnius Piso was at the head of the conspiracy for alleged complicity in which Seneca was killed.

Bonus here = *generous.* Cotta is not certainly identified.

114. Anseris iecur, "*foie gras.*"

115. Altilis, from *alo*, used for anything fattened, here probably a capon.

Meleagri, for Meleager and the Calydonian boar-hunt, cf. Ovid., Meta. VIII, 270.

117. Tonitrua. Truffles were supposed to grow best in the season of thunder-storms.

118. *Keep your grain, unyoke your oxen, but send us truffles*—i. e., we will do without the necessities of life if we may have the luxuries.

120. Structorem (same root as *struo*). Properly the person that arranged the table, here the carver.

121. Chironomunta is the Greek participle χειρονομοῦντα = *gesticulating.*

122. Dictata magistri; there were schools where the art of carving was taught.

123. *Of course, it makes a great difference with what motions hares and chickens are carved.*

125. Duceris planta, *dragged out by the heels.*

Cacus. Cf. Verg. Aen. VIII, 264 ff; Livy I, 7.

126. Ponere, not infinitive, notice the quantity.

Quid—hiscere = *to open your mouth.*

127. **Tamquam habeas tria nomina.** Free Roman citizens had *praenomen, nomen, cognomen.*

Propinat, *drink to you.*

130. **Regi.** Cf. line 14, note.

131. **Pertusa laena,** ablative of characteristic.

132. **Quadringenta** (*sestertia*), cf. III, 155, note.

133. **Homuncio,** nominative.

136. **Ilibus,** *the loin.*

Praestat, *he* (the master) *offers.*

139. A parody on Verg. Aen. IV, 328, 329, "*Si quis mihi parvolus aula luderet Aeneas.*"

141. The meaning of this passage is doubtful. The best sense seems to be made by taking *Mycale* to mean the man's wife. "If you come into a fortune you will be treated with great respect, but you must take care that there be no children to inherit it, else you will lose the great man's favor; *now* your wife may have as many children as may be, and he will be amused by them." The attention supposed to be paid to the children seems out of keeping with the previous description of a poor man's treatment, but I see no better explanation. Weidner reads *sua* in line 141, and explains *parasitus* as *coaxing*.

146. **Vilibus amicis,** *poor friends.*

Ancipites fungi, *dubious mushrooms.*

147. **Boletus,** a choice sort of edible fungus.

Quales—i. e., *boletos.*

Claudius was poisoned by means of a *boletus medicatus* (illum uxoris) by his wife Agrippina, with the aid of Lucusta. Cf. I, 71, note.

150. **Poma,** the regular last course at the *cena*. Cf. Hor. Sat. I, 3, 6, *ab ovo usque ad mala.*

151. **Phaeacum.** The Phaeacians. The garden of their king Alcinous is described, Hom. Od. VII.

152. **Sororibus Afris.** The Hesperides, who cared for the golden apples.

153. Another difficult passage. The meaning seems to be, "You will have a wretched specimen of an apple, such as the monkey is fed with, when the soldiers amuse themselves by teaching him to ride a goat and throw a spear."

FIG. 29.—Culina.

Aggere seems to refer to the wall of Servius Tullius, just within which was the Praetorian camp.

157. He does this, not from parsimony, but because he enjoys your embarrassing position.

162. **Culinae.** Fig. 29 represents the kitchen in the house of *Pansa* at Pompeii.

163. Illum. *Virro.*

164. Etruscum aurum—i. e., the *bulla*, the sign of free birth: with the rich, it was a circular plate of gold worn about the neck; with the poor, it seems to have been of leather. Cf. Fig. 30, which shows a Roman school-boy wearing the *bulla*.

Puero, *as a boy.*

168. Inde, *and therefore.*

169. Omnes, *all of you.*

Stricto pane ; a play on the phrase *stricto gladio, with drawn sword.* Cf. *ense stricto*, I, 165.

170. After all, it is your own fault, and doubtless some day we shall see you taking the part of the simpleton on the stage.

FIG. 30.—Boy wearing the bulla.

SATIRE VII.

INTRODUCTION.—The Emperor is the poet's only friend. If you look elsewhere for patronage, you may as well burn your poems; the rich will praise you, but let you reach old age in poverty. The rich man is a poet himself, and thinks he does enough for you if he lends you a room for your recitations, letting you pay for hiring the chairs. And yet it is hard to break one's self of the habit of writing. The true poet should, like Horace and Vergil, be free from petty anxieties. The comic actor is the best patron in these days, and if you want to succeed you must write down to his taste. The writing of history is hardly more profitable, and the lawyers are not in much better case. Great pleaders, to be sure, receive large fees, but the majority bankrupt themselves in trying to keep up the dignity of their position. The rhetorician works hard for his money, and then very likely has to sue for it; while such triflers as music-masters reap large fortunes. Quintilian is an exception, to be sure, but his was a case of rare good luck. Schoolmasters are quite as badly off. They are expected to know everything, and to make all their pupils both wise and good; then for a year's work they receive the fee of a single victory in the circus.

1. Caesare, the Emperor, probably Hadrian, possibly Trajan.

2. Camenas. Cf. III, 16, note.

3. Respexit ; *respicio* often has the idea of *looking on with favor ;* cf. *regard.*

4. Gabiis. Cf. III, 192, note.

7. Atria (*auctionaria*), *auction-rooms.*

Clio, properly the Muse of History, here used for any of the Muses, and so for the poet.

11

8. Pieria umbra. The grove of the Muses lay on Mount Helicon, in Boeotia, between the fountains Aganippe and Hippocrene.

9. Machaerae, unknown; some auctioneer of the day.

10. Commissa auctio. The simplest explanation seems to be that *commissa auctio = auctio bonorum commissorum*—i. e., goods intrusted to the auctioneer.

12. Nothing is known of these works. The names may stand for any poor productions.

15. Quamquam (*hoc*) **faciant.** Many editors consider this line spurious, because Asiani would include Cappadoces and Bithyni, and because the first syllable of Bithyni is elsewhere long. Proper names, however, are not always used with exactness.

16. Altera Gallia—i. e., *Galatia.* These "knights" are slaves who have made fortunes in Rome.

Nudo talo. Cf. note I, 111.

Traducit; most editors take this to mean *exposes* (*for sale*). I think it means *sends over* (*to us*).

19. Eloquium vocale, *melodious words.*

Laurumque momordit, *has tasted.* Probably with reference to the chewing of laurel-leaves by the priestess of Apollo, at Delphi.

20. Circumspicit, etc. ; the subject of the verbs is *ducis indulgentia.*

22. Qua aliunde, *anywhere else.*

23. Croceae tabellae. *The yellow-stained cover.* The sheets (*membrana*) were sometimes inclosed in boards, much after the style of modern binding.

Membrana, nom. pl. neut. instead of the usual fem. form *membranae.*

24. Lignorum, partitive genitive.

25. Veneris marito—i. e., Vulcan, the god of fire.

Telesine stands for any author. The name occurs in inscriptions, and is used by Martial.

26. Clude. Juvenal uses both forms of this word, *cludo* and *claudo*— e. g., *clausam*, I, 124; *cluderet*, III, 19.

Tinea pertunde, *bore through with the book-worm*—i. e., let the book-worm destroy.

27. Calamum. Cf. Fig. 31.

Vigilata proelia—i. e., descriptions of battles, which you have sat up late to write.

28. Cella, "*den.*"

29. Venias = *prodeas.*

Imagine macra, the bust would be lean as representing a poorly fed poet.

32. Ut pueri Iunonis avem (*laudant*).

Sed defluit aetas, etc. Meanwhile your time of active life is passing away, and your eloquent but empty-handed old age is disgusted with itself and its art.

36 ff. The patron, for whose sake you desert the temple of fame, makes verses himself and yields the palm to Homer only because of his antiquity. If you want a chance to recite your poems, he offers you a long-unused apartment, and sends his freedmen as an audience; but for pay!—he will not spend enough to hire the benches.

Artes, schemes.

Ne quid—*conferat* depends on *facit* and the following verbs.

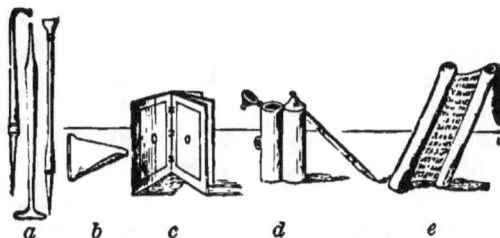

FIG. 31.—Writing materials. *a.* Various forms of the stylus; *b.* Instrument for smoothing the wax of the tablet; *c.* Tablets; *d.* Ink-stand and calamus; *e.* Papyrus-roll.

40. Maculosas, *dirty. Maculosas* is the reading of Heinrich, adopted by Macleane and Mayor. The MSS. have *Maculonus* or *Maculonis*, which must be explained as the name of the patron.

41. Longe = *diu.*

Ferrata, locked—i. e., *unused.*

Domus (as *aedes* above) = *room.*

42. Sollicitas portas, *the anxious gates (of a city in time of siege).*

45. Quanti, so-called genitive of price, probably locative.

46. *Raised seats resting on hired beams.*

47. *And the orchestra set out with hired chairs.* The room is arrayed like a theatre; the orchestra space in front, then the common benches (*subsellia*), then the raised seats. All this furnishing must be provided by the poor poet himself.

48 f. But we keep at it, plowing the sand, wasting our labor.

Sterili may be used with *aratro* by hypallage, or it may mean *unprofitable.*

52. Scribendi cacoethes. The expression has become proverbial.

53-59. The principal idea is contained in the words **animus anxietate carens vatem egregium facit.**

53. Publica vena, cf. Eng., *the popular vein.*

54. Expositum, *well known, commonplace.*

55. Communi moneta, *with the common stamp.* Cf. Hor. A. P. 59, *signatum praesente nota producere nomen.*

56. Qualem nequeo, etc. ; I can point you to no example ; I only feel what such a poet is.

58. Inpatiens, *not suffering,* so *free from.*

59. Aonidum. The Muses were called Aonides from Aonia, the ancient name of Boeotia.

60. Thyrsum. The staff of Bacchus, the symbol of poetic inspiration. Cf. Fig. 32.

61. Quo. Its antecedent is *aeris,* and it is in the ablative with *eget.*

62. The allusion seems to be to Horace's lyric poems (*"Euhoe"* may imply this), for when he wrote satires he was poor enough.

64. Dominis Cirrhae Nysaeque—i. e., Apollo and Bacchus. Cirrha was on the Corinthian Gulf. The location of Nysa is uncertain ; it was connected with the early worship of Bacchus. Note the absence of the preposition.

65. Pectora is the subject of *vexant* and *feruntur.*

66. Lodice, *a blanket.*

FIG. 32.—Figure bearing the thyrsus.

67. Attonitae, *perplexed, worried,* agrees with *mentis.*

68. Alecto, urged on by Juno, roused Turnus, the Rutulian king, to jealousy when Latinus gave his daughter Lavinia to Aeneas. Cf. Verg. Aen. VII, 420 ff; Livy I, 2.

69. Puer, *a slave ;* so παῖς, *garçon,* and *boy.*

Desset = *deesset.* Cf. *derit,* III, 303 ; *derat,* IV, 72.

70. Caderent. Not "imperfect for pluperfect," but imperfect, because Juvenal thinks of the poem, and so of Vergil himself, as existing at his own time.

71 f. We expect a poet, whose *Atreus* has driven him to the pawn-broker, to vie with the ancients. Our rich men have no money for literature, but plenty for other things.

72. Rubrenus Lappa, unknown.

Cothurno ; the *cothurnus* was a boot worn by tragic actors, as shown in Fig. 33.

79. Lucanus. *M. Annaeus Lucanus* (born 39 A. D.), author of the historical poem *Pharsalia.* He was very rich, and could therefore afford to be *" contentus fama."*

FIG. 33.—Actors wearing the cothurnus

80. Serrano, Atilius Serranus, whose debts Martial speaks of, IV, 37, 2.

Tenui here seems to mean *poor ;* cf. *et in tenui re,* Hor. Epist. I, 20, 20.

Saleio, *Saleius Bassus.* Cf. Quint. X, 1, 90. Little is known of him.

81. *What will fame, however great, be if it is only fame?*

82. Amicae, *welcome.*

83. Statins. P. Papinius Statius was the court poet of Domitian. His *Thebais* was evidently popular.

86. Fregit subsellia, *brought down the house;* for equally strong expressions, cf. *convulsa marmora* and *ruptae columnae*, I. 12, 13.

87. Intactam Agaven. *Agave* was the name of a play; *intactam* probably means before it was acted by any one else. *Paris* was a favorite actor in the time of Domitian.

88. Ille, *Paris.* Et seems to mean *even.*

89. Semestri auro, the gold (ring) which was the badge of a six-months' office, and the sign of equestrian rank.

90 f. Actors, imperial favorites, are the generous givers of our time: what is the use of courting men of rank?

92. Pelopea, Philomela, names of plays.

94. Maecenas, friend of Augustus, patron of Horace.

Proculeius, proverbial for generosity. Hor. Od. II, 2, 5.

95. Fabius and Cotta were patrons of Ovid.

Lentulus was instrumental in Cicero's recall from exile.

97. Pallere, etc.—i. e., to be pale and abstemious was profitable then.

Toto Decembri. December was the "season" in Rome.

100. Modo, *limit.*

101. Multa agrees with **papyro.**

Damnosa, *costly.*

104. Acta legenti. The *acta* were daily records of matters of interest, like our newspapers.

105. Genus ignavum—i. e., historians are lazy fellows.

106. The lawyers fare no better.

107. Fasce, *bundle.*

Libelli, *documents.*

108 ff. The lawyer makes a great noise (about his income) if one of his own creditors is listening to him, or if a client comes to consult him about a bad debt. This seems to me the simplest explanation. Others think *magna sonant* refers to his efforts in the court-room.

109. Tetigit latus, *nudges him.*

Illo—i. e., *creditore.*

110. Nomen, *debt.*

111. Cavi folles—i. e., his cheeks.

112. Conspuitur sinus. There are two explanations given. He talks so energetically that he foams at the mouth, and the folds of his toga suffer for it; or he lies so abominably that he spits (three times), to avert the wrath of the gods. I think the former is preferable.

Veram deprendere messem, etc. If you want to know what the real harvest of their labors is, put the income of a hundred lawyers on one side and the pay of a single charioteer on the other. So in our times the income of a favorite base-ball player might be compared with that of several literary men, without exciting the envy of the former.

114. Russati. The charioteers were divided into four guilds, *alba, russata, veneta, prasina* (or *viridis*), white, red, blue, green. Cf. note XI, 198, and see the excellent description of a chariot-race in Wallace's " *Ben Hur.*" For the costume of the *auriga*, cf. page 54.

Lacernae, Proper name.

115. Ovid, Meta. XIII, 1, describes the contest between Ajax and Ulysses for the arms of Achilles.

116. Bubulco iudice, *with some stupid countryman for judge.*

118. Scalarum gloria. The poor lawyer, living in an attic, adorned the staircase.

120. Pelamydum (genitive plural), a kind of cheap fish.

Epimenia, *rations.*

121. Tiberi de vectum. The better wines, on the contrary, would be brought *up* the Tiber.

122. Egisti, *pleaded.*

123. Pragmaticorum. The *pragmatici* were consulting attorneys, as distinguished from the *causidici* or pleaders.

124. Real merit has little to do with a lawyer's fees; the one that makes the greatest show gains the most.

Et, *and yet.*

127. Bellatoro, *war-horse.*

Minatur, *threatens the spear*—i. e., threatens with the spear. Cf. " he threatens fight " or " threatens a blow."

128. Lusca, *with one eye shut.* Not a dignified position; but Juvenal is not concerned with the man's dignity, but with his absurd vanity and ostentation.

129. Pedo, Matho, and **Tongilius,** imitate this extravagance and become bankrupt.

Conturbat (*rationes*), *becomes bankrupt.*

130. Rhinocerote, a rhinoceros-horn for an oil-flask.

132. Iuvenes Maedos—i. e., his litter-bearers.

133. Murrina (*vasa*).

134. Spondet—i. e., gives him credit.

Tyrio filo, ablative of characteristic.

Stlataria. *Stlata* is said to be an early form of *lata* (as *stlocus* of *locus*), and to mean a broad ship, hence *stlataria* is supposed to mean *imported;* others translate *deceptive*, taking *stlata* as a pirate-ship.

135. Vendit, *makes a market for.*

136. Amethystina (*vestimenta*).

137. Strepitu and **facie** are ablatives of manner; the preposition *cum* is not used, because the genitive *maioris census* takes the place of an adjective.

138. The extravagance of Rome makes it impossible to call a halt.

139. Eloquio. Notice that *fidere* and *confidere* are used both with the dative and with the ablative, which is explained as either ablative of source (real ablative) or locative ablative.

143. Conducta Sardonyche = *with a hired seal-ring.*

Paulus, Gallus, and **Basilus,** all poor lawyers.

144. Pluris—i. e., for a larger fee.

148. Gaul and Africa, where eloquence is well paid, are the places for you if you want to earn wealth with your tongue.

160. Vetti. Vettius was a well-known teacher of rhetoric.

151. Classis, *class.*

154. Crambe, *cabbage.* It is the same warmed-over cabbage that wears out the teacher's nerves. Cf. the Greek proverb, δὶς κράμβη θάνατος.

155. Quis color, etc. They want to know all about rhetoric, but not to pay for it.

158. Appellas, *call for, demand.*

Culpa docentis, etc. This is the ironical answer of the teacher.

159. Laevae parte mamillae (*parte = a parte*). The heart was often considered as the seat of intelligence.

161. Hannibal was a favorite subject for school declamations. Cf. X, 166: "*I demens, et saevas curre per Alpes, ut pueris placeas et declamatio fias.*"

165. Ask what you choose and take it, that his father (you) may have to listen to his declamations as often as I have.

Quod do, *for I (will) give it (gladly).*

167. Sophistae, another name for teachers of rhetoric. They throw up their teaching in disgust and go to practicing law; but it is only a jump from the frying-pan into the fire.

168. Raptore relicto—i. e., they leave the subjects of fictitious declamations.

171. Rudem. Gladiators on retiring from the arena after long service received the *rudis* as a token of honorable dismissal. Cf. Hor. Epist. I, 1, 2, *donatum iam rude.*

174. Summula, etc. The *tesserae frumenti* were about equivalent to the soup-tickets which are sometimes distributed gratuitously in modern times. Juvenal means that the teacher might as well go to the poor-house at once.

Venit, from *veneo.*

175. Tempta, *examine, consider.*

176. Chrysogonus and **Polio** were music teachers.

177. Artem, *text-book.*

Scindes, *you will tear up.* The MSS. have *scindens.* Macleane, who retains it, says it means " cutting up," and so " deriding."

Theodori, a rhetorician.

178. The rich man (*dominus*) is niggardly in his son's education, that he may furnish himself with all luxuries.

183. Algentem—i. e., the *winter sun*.

184. Quanticumque domus, *however costly the house*.

185. Condit; the change to the indicative (if the reading be correct) is rather unusual.

188. "How does Quintilian come to be rich if, as you say, rhetoricians are so ill paid?" "Quintilian," Juvenal answers, "is a favorite of fortune; when a man is born under a lucky star, all rules yield."

189. Novorum, *strange, unusual*.

192. One of the badges of senatorial rank is referred to.

194. Si = etsi. Weidner has *ni*.

199. Ventidius. P. Ventidius Bassus, consul 43 B. C., had been carried as captive in a triumph by the father of Pompey the Great.

Tullius. Servius Tullius, one of the legendary kings of Rome, was said to have been born of a slave mother.

200. Sidus, *the stars*.

203. Cathedrae—i. e., the professor's chair. Cf. the phrase *ex cathedra*.

204. Thrasymachi. The Scholiast says he hanged himself.

Secundi Carrinatis. Secundus Carrinas was banished by Caligula. He is said to have poisoned himself at Athens.

205. Hunc. Socrates.

207 f. Terram, crocos, and ver are the objects of some verb, such as *date* understood. The letters S. T. T. L., sometimes found on tombs, are for *sit tibi terra levis*.

210 ff. Metuens virgae, etc. (For the genitive, cf. *metuensque flagelli*, V, 154.) Achilles was submissive to his tutor Chiron, the centaur, and did not even make fun of the horse's tail.

214. Dixit. Subject is *iuventus*. His pupils beat him, even though they recognized his ability by calling him the "*Allobrogian Cicero*." This seems better than reading *qui* for *quem*.

215. Celadi, Palaemonis; grammarians.

218. Discipuli custos—i. e., the *paedagogus*, the slave that was put in charge of the boy.

Acoenonoetus = ἀκοινονόητος = *unfeeling, selfish*.

219. Qui dispensat. The *dispensator* was the agent or steward. Cf. I, 91.

221. Like a petty tradesman, who must pay a commission to the agent in order to secure the master's custom.

222 f. Mediae—sedisti. This clause is the subject of *pereat*.

224. Deducere, *to card*.

225-227. Provided you gain something for having endured the smoky lamps that blacken the pages of the text-books in the school-room.

227. Flaccus—i. e., Horace.

Maroni—i. e., Vergil.

228. Small as the fee is, one usually has to sue for it.

229. Vos—i. e., the parents.

230. I. e., that he make no mistakes in syntax.

233. Phoebi balnea; the scholiast says these were private baths.

235. Anchemoli. Mentioned by Vergil, Aen. X, 389.

Acestes. Vergil, Aen. I, 195.

Annis; the ablative is very often used by writers of this period to express duration—i. e., time within which.

237. Ducat, *model.*

239. Coetus, *the company*—i. e., *the scholars.*

242. "When pay-day comes, I will give you as much as a successful gladiator or charioteer gains." Cf. Note XI, 198.

SATIRE VIII.

INTRODUCTION.—The general subject is false pride of ancestry. What is the advantage of a noble name if you disgrace it by your vices? The only real nobility is that of virtue. Rubellius Blandus will find that, while he is boasting of his rank, the plebeians are becoming the orators and generals of the State. The pedigree of a horse will not save the animal from the treadmill. Do you, Ponticus, depend upon yourself, perform your own duty. If you are the governor of a province, spare your subjects. Men of noble names have been condemned for extortion, and yet what does the province gain if the next governor takes what his predecessor leaves? Consider what the provinces were and what they are.

It is not even safe to plunder warlike Spain and Africa as effeminate Greece has been plundered.

If, then, you rule your province righteously, you will be an honor to your noble ancestors, as, on the other hand, cruelty and dishonesty are less excusable in one nobly born.

The degenerate Lateranus has become a frequenter of cook-shops, and the companion of men of the lowest sort; Damasippus has gone on the comic stage, and Gracchus has disgraced himself by appearing as a gladiator.

If the people could speak, would they not prefer a Seneca to a Nero? Catiline and Cethegus, nobles by birth, were traitors to Rome; Cicero, a *novus homo*, was its preserver. So, too, Marius and the Decii deserved well of the State; and the treachery of Brutus was defeated by a slave. Go back to the earliest days, and you will find that we are all descended from shepherds or less creditable ancestors.

1. Stemmata. The *stemma* was the collection of ancestor - portraits (*imagines*) with the accompanying inscriptions (*tituli*), connected by lines showing the relationship.

6. Generis tabula, *family roll.*

Iactare, *to boast of,* followed by the accusative (*Corvinum*). Cf. Hor. Odes, I, 14, 13, *Iactes et genus et nomen.*

7. Multa contingere virga may mean *to trace through many a branch.* Others take *virga* to mean *broom;* others *wand,* used in pointing out the famous names on the stemma; others make it = *fasces.* The genuineness of the line is very doubtful.

8. Fumosos. The *imagines* were in the *atrium,* where the *focus* stood. Cf. Fig. 36.

9. Coram Lepidis—i. e., under the very eyes of one's great ancestors.

Quo = *quam ad rem.*

11. Ante Numantinos. The idea is the same as in *coram Lepidis* above. The name *Numantinus* was given to Scipio Africanus the younger after the capture of Numantia. The plural is used to make the reference general.

FIG. 34.
Cera.

13. Allobrogicis. Q. Fabius Maximus Aemilianus defeated the Allobroges 121 B. C. The *ara magna* (*maxima*) in the Forum Boarium was said to have been dedicated to Hercules by Evander. Cf. Livy, I, 7.

14. Herculeo lare. The Fabii traced descent from Hercules.

15. Euganea. The wool of Venetia, in which district the Euganei lived, was famous. Cf. Livy, I, 1.

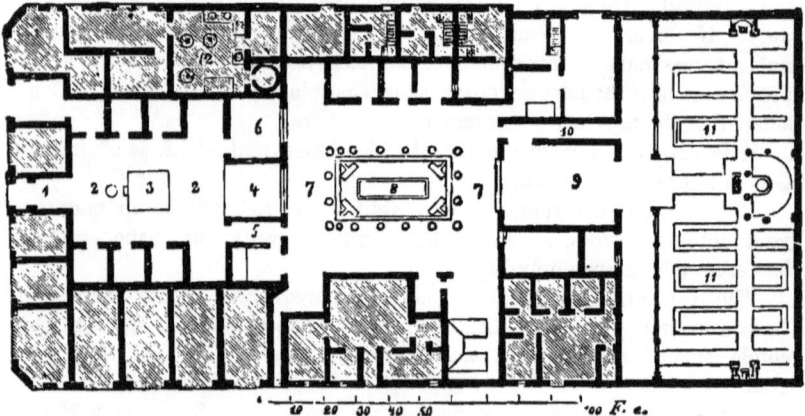

FIG. 35.—Ground-plan of the so-called "House of Pansa," at Pompeii. 1. Entrance-hall; 2. Atrium; 3. Impluvium; 4. Tablinum; 5. Passage; 6. Bibliotheca; 7. Peristylium; 8. Piscina; 9. Oecus; 10. Passage; 11. Hortus.

16. **Catinensi.** Catina was at the foot of Mount Aetna. The Romans used pumice-stone in their elaborate toilets.

17. **Traducit,** *disgraces.* For the change of meaning, cf. Eng. *traduce.*

18. **Frangenda imagine.** The statues of great criminals were publicly destroyed. Cf. X, 58, *Descendunt statuae restemque sequuntur.*

19. **Cerae;** the wax masks of ancestors. Cf. Fig. 34.

20. **Atria;** the *atrium* was the principal room in the Roman house. Cf. Figs. 35 and 36.

Sola atque unica, cf. Hor. Epist. I, 6, 1, *una solaque.*

22. **Hos** (as *illi* in the next line) refers to *mores.*

FIG. 36.—Atrium.

23. **Te consule**—i. e., when your time of power comes.

Virgas = *fasces.*

24. **Mihi debes**—i. e., *I have a right to demand from you.*

Haberi, *to be considered, held.*

26. **Agnosco procerem,** (*then*) *I recognize the nobleman*—i. e., *I acknowledge your nobility.*

27 ff. **Quocumque,** etc.—i. e., *wherever you come from, you are a fortunate acquisition, and your rejoicing country may well cry out, "Eureka!"* as do the Egyptians when they discover Osiris.

To the Romans *Osiris* was the same as *Apis.* When the bull *Apis,* whose body the god was supposed to inhabit, died, the Egyptians made great efforts to find the new creature to which the divinity had fled, and when their search was rewarded great rejoicings took place.

31. Et connects *indignus* and *insignis.*

32. Nanum, *dwarf.* As men give names in mockery, be careful lest your conduct be so inconsistent with your great name that men will call you Creticus or Camerinus only in derision.

38. Sic. Macleane has *sis,* and says, "It does not require much taste to see that Juvenal did not write *sic.*" *Sic* is the suggestion of Junius, and is adopted by Jahn, Ribbeck, Weidner, and Mayor.

39. Rubelli Blande. C. Rubellius Blandus was descended from the imperial family, through Julia, a granddaughter of Tiberius. Tiberius's brother, as well as his son, was named Drusus.

42. Ut—conciperet. Subjunctive in a clause of result. The subject of the verb is *ea,* understood as the antecedent of *quae.*

43. Conducta, *hired.* Cf. III, 225, *tenebras—conducis.*

Aggere, the wall of Servius Tullius. Cf. Livy I, 44; Sat. V, 153.

46. Cecropides—i. e., a descendent of Cecrops, the (mythical) founder of Athens.

47. Quiritem, the distinctive name of a Roman citizen. Probably used here to emphasize the contrast with *Cecropides.*

53. Truncoque Hermae. The *Hermae* were statues in which only the head, and sometimes the bust, was modeled, all the rest being left as a plain block. Cf. Fig. 37.

55. Imago—i. e., your only advantage is that you are a *living* blockhead.

58. Facili—i. e., *an easy winner.*

Palma, *hand.*

FIG. 37. Hermes.

59. Fervet, *grows warm*—i. e., by the exertion of applauding.

61. In aequore, *on the plain.*

62. Venale pecus, *(mere) market cattle.*

Coryphaei et Hirpini, famous race-horses. The genitives depend on *posteritas.*

Posteritas is in apposition with *pecus.*

66. Epiraedia. Probably heavy carts are meant.

67. Cf. Fig. 38.

68. Primum is the reading of the MSS. *Privum,* a conjecture adopted by several editors = *proprium, your own.*

69. Titulis. Cf. note, line 1.

71. Iuvenem. Cf. line 39.

72. Plenumque Nerone propinquo, *full of his relative, Nero*—i. e., puffed up by his relationship to Nero.

73. Sensus communis, not *common sense,* but *savoir faire,* a sense of the fitness of things. Cf. Hor. Sat. I, 3, 66, *Communi sensu plane caret.* Possibly, as Weidner suggests, *the sense of equality in the State.*

74. Censeri laude, for the construction, cf. line 2.

75. Pontice. Cf. line 1.

Noluerim; on this use of the perfect subjunctive to express a thing modestly and cautiously, cf. Madvig 350 b; A. and G. 311 b; H. 486, I.

Futurae laudis. The use of the "genitive of quality" was gradually more and more extended.

78. Palmes, etc. Vines were trained on elm-trees.

FIG. 38.—Roman mill.

Viduas. Cf. Horace's use of *caelebs* with *platanus.* Odes II, 15, 4.

79. Tutor, *guardian.*

81. Phalaris. The tyrant of Agrigentum and his brazen bull had become proverbial. Cf. Grote, History of Greece, V, 274.

Licet, *although.*

82. Falsus has two meanings : active, *deceitful*, and passive, *deceived ;* cf. *caecus = blind* and *dark.* *Blind* itself has also a passive sense, as in the phrase *a blind alley ;* cf. Milton, *In the blind mazes of this tangled wood.*

83. Pudori, *honor.*

85. Dignus morte perit—i. e., the man that deserves to die is, to all intents and purposes, dead. *Perit* is the perfect tense.

86. Gaurana. Mount Gaurus was near the Lucrine Lake. Cf. IV, 141.

Cosmi. Cosmus was a famous perfumer at Rome. **Aheno** is the copper (kettle) in which he prepared his perfumes.

88. Irae, dative.

90. Vacuis medullis, ablative of quality.

91. Respice, *consider.* Cf. III, 268, *Respice . . . pericula.*

Curia, the Roman Senate.

92. Maneant, *await.*

93. Et Capito et Numitor. Capito was governor of Cilicia in 56 A. D. Numitor is unknown.

94. Piratae, in apposition with *Capito* and *Numitor.*

Sed quid damnatio confert?—i. e., what good does it do the plundered provincials? Cf. I, 47 ff.

95. "*Look up an auctioneer for your rags, Chaerippus.*" Chaerippus represents the inhabitants of the province.

96. Pansa—Natta. Fictitious (?) names for provincial governors.

97. Keep quiet and make the best of it; don't spend what little you have left in paying your passage-money (*naulon*) to Rome, to bring suit against your despoiler.

99. Damnorum, *losses.*

101. Chlamys, a loose garment, shown in Fig. 39.

Conchylia Coa. The purple stuffs of Cos were especially fine.

FIG. 39.—Statue of Phokion wearing the chlamys.

102. Parrhasii. A famous Greek painter, who lived about 400 B. C.

Myronis. The celebrated sculptor, born about 500 B. C.

103. Phidiacum. Phidias (about 490–430 B. C.), the greatest sculptor of Greece. Among his works were the sculptures of the Parthenon (cf. Fig. 40), the ivory and gold statue of Jupiter, at Olympia, and that of Athena in the Parthenon.

Polycliti. Cf. III, 217.

104. Labor. Cf. Eng. *work.*

Rarae, etc. Mentor was the most famous silversmith of antiquity. For the use of the artist's name instead of his work, cf. "*a Raphael.*"

105. Dolabella. Province-plundering seems to have been the business of the family. Three of them were accused of such extortions.

Antonius. Two members of this family had unenviable reputations; C. Antonius, who plundered Macedonia 59 B. C., and his brother, who did the same for Sicily.

106. Verres. The infamous governor of Sicily (73-70 B. C.), whom Cicero prosecuted.

107. Plures, etc.—i. e., they gained more by stealing in time of peace than by capture in time of war.

FIG. 40.—View of the Parthenon.

112. Nam sunt haec maxima. In olden times the provinces were rich, and the Romans stole from them valuable works of art, etc.; now they take whatever they can find.

Despicias tu, etc. You may well despise the effeminate Greeks, but look out for Spain and Gaul.

114. Resinata. Resin was used for smoothing the skin.

116. Axis, *sky, region, land.*

117. Latus, *coast.*

118. Saturant, *furnish corn to, "provision."* He means the Africans. Cf. V, 118, note.

Circo scaenaeque, dative with *vacantem. Vacans* means *having leisure for,* then *given up to, devoted to.* For the thought, cf. III, 223, *si potes avelli circensibus.*

120. Discinxerit, *stripped, stole their very girdles.*

123. The *scutum* was a large oblong shield, while the *clipeus* (buckler) was round. The former is seen in Fig. 41.

125. Sententia, *opinion.*

128. Acersecomes, *a long-haired, young favorite.*

129. Conventus. Each province was divided into judicial districts, in each of which some town-was selected where the governor held court. Both the districts and the meetings were called *conventus.*

130. **Raptura**—i. e., *coniunx.*

Celaeno, *another Celaeno.* Celaeno was one of the harpies.

131. **Tu licet,** *you may.*

Pico. Picus, a son of Saturnus, was one of the early mythical kings of Italy.

132. **Omnem Titanida pugnam,** *the whole battle array of the Titans.* The Titans were sons of Earth; ancestry could hardly be traced further back. Prometheus was one of the Titans, and sometimes represented as the creator of man.

135. **Quod si,** *but if.*

Praecipitem—i. e., *te.*

137. **Hebetes,** *blunted, by use.*

139. **Claramque facem praeferre,** *to shed a bright light upon.*

141. **Habetur,** *is held, considered.*

142. **Quo mihi te**—i. e., *iactas.*

143. **Quae fecit avus,** *which your ancestor built.*

145. **Santonico.** The Santones were a Gallic tribe noted for their woolen manufactures.

146. **Praeter,** etc.—i. e., on the roads lined with tombs leading out of Rome. Cf. I, 171.

147. **Lateranus.** A Lateranus was consul 94 A. D.

148. **Sufflamine,** *drag-chain.*

149. **Testes,** nominative.

151. **Clara luce,** *in broad daylight.*

152. **Trepidabit,** *shun.*

Fig. 41.—Figure bearing the scutum.

153. He shows no respect for age, but salutes his aged friend with the professional coachman's turn of the whip.

154. This whole passage refers to the vulgarity of men of birth and position becoming mere horse-jockeys and grooms.

155. **Lanatas**—i. e., *oves.*

Robum = *robustum.*

156. **Iurat,** *swears by.*

157. **Eponam.** Epona was the goddess of horses.

Facies, etc.—i. e., pictures of Epona and kindred subjects.

Olida, *rank.*

Praesepia. Cf. I, 59, *cui bona donavit praesepibus.*

158. **Pervigiles.** Cf. III, 275, *vigiles fenestrae.*

Instaurare, *to frequent.*

159. **Syrophoenix,** the host.

160. This line is rejected by many editors. *Idumaeae portae* has received no satisfactory explanation. It may refer to a gate in that quarter of Rome where such taverns were plentiful.

162. Cyanis is the hostess.

Succincta. Cf. Hor. Sat. II, 6, 107, *succinctus cursitat hospes.*

168. Thermarum calices, hot drinks of wine and water are probably meant.

Inscriptaque lintea seems to refer to the curtains hanging in front of the taverns, with signs upon them.

170 f. Praestare Neronem securum, to protect the Emperor — i. e., his country.

171. Ostia, accusative plural. Ostia was the point of embarkation for foreign service.

Caesar refers to the Emperor.

173. Percussore, *cut-throat.*

175. Fabros sandapilarum, *makers of cheap coffins.*

176. Cessantia, *silent, no longer in use.*

Galli. The Galli or priests of Cybele were not noted for temperance.

180. A slave that did such things would be sent to work in the Lucanian fields (*agros* is to be supplied), or put into the Etruscan chain-gang.

181. Troiugenae. Cf. I, 100, *ipsos Troiugenas.*

182. Cerdoni. Cf. IV, 153, *postquam cerdonibus ess⁰ timendus coeperat.*

Volesos. The reference is probably to Volesus Valerius, founder of the Valerian *gens.*

186. Sipario, the curtain before the stage in the theatre.

Phasma Catulli refers to "*The Ghost,*" a *mimus* (farce), of Catullus (who should not be confused with the famous lyric poet of that name).

187. Laureolum, the name of one of the *mimi,* in which the hero, also called *Laureolus,* was crucified.

189. Frons, *shamelessness.*

Durior, translate *greater.*

190. Triscurria, *tri-* intensifies the meaning.

191. Planipedes; the actors in the *mimi* usually appeared without either the *cothurnus* of tragedy or the *soccus* of comedy.

192. Mamercorum alapas, mimic blows received by the Mamerci.

Funera, probably refers to "moral death." Ribbeck reads *munera =* *services.*

194. This verse is probably spurious. **Celsi** must refer to the exalted seat of the praetor at the games.

195. Gladios, *death.* *Gladios* and *pulpita* are the subjects of *poni.* Others read *pone,* making *pulpita* its object.

196. Quid = *utrum.*

Ut sit, a clause of result. Juvenal is almost as severe on the amateur actor as on the amateur horse-jockey.

197. Zelotypus, *the jealous husband ;* **stupidi,** *the clown.*

12

198. Citharoedo principe, as Nero was. If the prince plays the lute, the noble will play the clown. For the *cithara*, cf. Fig. 42.

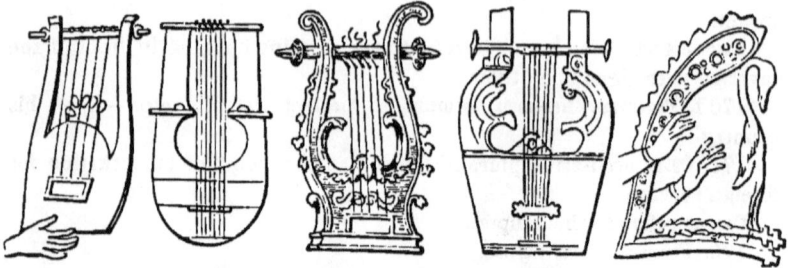

FIG. 42.—Various forms of the cithara.

Mimus, an actor of this sort is represented in Fig. 43.

199. Ludus—i. e., the gladiatorial games. Even here the degenerate noble (*Gracchus*) chooses the most disgraceful form of gladiatorial equipment, for he fights not with the arms of the *murmillo*, nor with the shield, nor with the scimiter, but as a *retiarius*, armed with a trident and a net, lightly clothed, without a helmet, and thus easily recognized. The murmillo is probably represented upon the sepulchral monument in Fig. 41; for the *retiarius* and *secutor*, cf. Fig. 17.

202. This line is rejected by several editors.

203. Galea. The form of helmet used by the gladiators is seen in Fig. 44.

205. Effudit. *cast.* The *retiarius* gathered the net in his hand and attempted to throw it so as to entangle his opponent.

207 f. Credamus tunicae, etc., *we must believe his tunic when, gold-embroidered, it stretches out from his neck and the gold cord flutters from his tall cap.* This was the costume of the Salii, priests of Mars. For the *galerus*, cf. Fig. 45.

FIG. 43.—Mimus.

212. Seneca, the philosopher, was Nero's tutor, and was murdered by the order of his former pupil.

213. Supplicio, dative with *parari*.

214. Simia—serpens—culleus. A parricide was punished by being put into a sack with a dog, a snake, a cock, and an ape, and then cast into the sea.

218. Aut. The negative idea is carried over from *nec*.

Spartani coniugii. Orestes married Hermione, daughter of Menelaus and Helen.

220. Nero's worst crimes were his artistic ones.   For the intentional anti-climax, cf. III, 7–9.

221. Troica. Nero wrote verses on the Trojan war.

Quid enim, etc.   For what that Nero did was more deserving of punishment at the hands of his enemies?

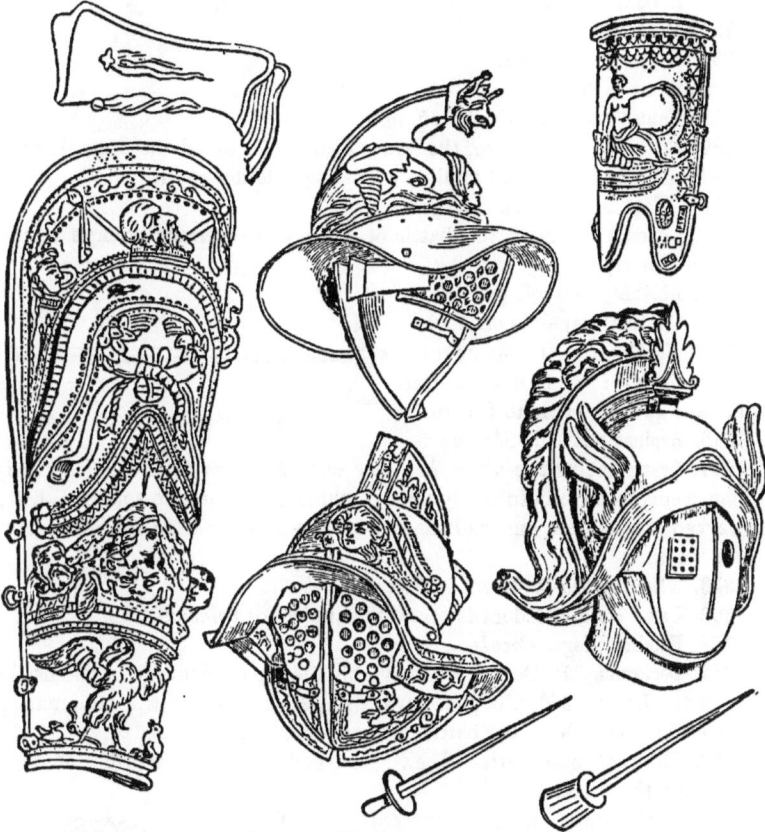

FIG. 44.—Gladiators' armor.

Verginius (*Rufus*) took up arms against Nero in Germany, (*Julius*) **Vindex** in Gaul, and (*Servius*) **Galba** in Spain.

223. Cruda, *brutal.*

224. Generosi, *nobly-born.*

225. Peregrina ad pulpita. Suetonius says that Nero appeared as a contestant in the games in Greece.

226. Prostitui. The Latin passive sometimes has the force of the Greek middle.

FIG. 45.—Galerus.

Apium, *parsley.*

227. Let him lay all these trophies of his disgraceful victories at the feet of the statues of his ancestors.

228 f. Domiti. Nero was the son of Cn. Domitius Ahenobarbus.

Thyestes, Antigone, and Melanippa were tragic parts played by Nero.

229. Syrma, the trailing robe worn by actors in tragedy.

231. Cf. line 237, note.

234. Ut, *as if you were.*

Bracatorum = *Gallorum.*

235. Tunica molesta. Cf. I, 155, note.

237. Novus Arpinas, Cicero, the *novus homo*, who saved the State, is contrasted with the men of old family, who sought to destroy it.

240 f. Tantum—nominis, *such glory.*

241. Leucade refers to the battle of *Actium* as Thessaliae campis to the battle of *Philippi.*

242. Abstulit, *bore off, gained.*

243. Caedibus depends on *udo.*

Gladio is ablative of instrument.

Sed—libera—i. e., Rome was free when she gave the title to Cicero.

Fig. 46.—Dolabra.

245. Arpinas alius, *C. Marius.*

247. Frangebat vertice vitem, *he broke with his head the centurion's rod*, which seems to have been freely used to punish the common soldiers—i. e., he served as a soldier, and had the rod broken over his head if he was slow at his work.

248. The *dolabra* is shown in Fig. 46.

252. Qui. Its antecedent is *corvi*, the subject of *volabant.*

253. Nobilis collega, *Catulus.*

254. Deciorum. P. Decius Mus gave his life for his country in the battle against the Latins, 340 B. C.; cf. Livy VIII, 9; his son, of the same name, followed his example in the battle of Sentinum. Cf. Livy X, 28.

258. Pluris, *of more value*—i. e., to the gods; so their sacrifice of their lives saved the State.

259. Ancilla natus—i. e., *Servius Tullius.* Cf. VII, 199, note.

Trabeam, the royal robe, a toga ornamented with horizontal purple stripes.

Diadema. Fig. 47 shows the form of the *diadema.*

261. Prodita claustra—i. e., the bolts that they had betrayed.

Laxabant, imperfect of "attempted action."

262. Iuvenes—i. e., the sons of Brutus, who aided in the recall of the Tarquins.

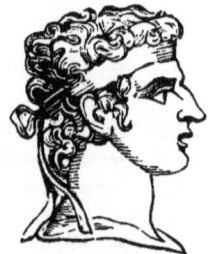

Fig. 47.—Diadema.

264. Quod. Its antecedent is *aliquid*.

Cum Coclite Mucius. *Horatius Cocles* defended the bridge against Porsenna, cf. Livy II, 10. *Mucius Scaevola* burned off his hand when arrested for an attempt to kill the same king.

Quae—natavit. *Cloelia* escaped from Porsenna and swam the Tiber to Rome.

265. Fines, in apposition with *Tiberinum* (*flumen*).

266 ff. I. e., Vindicius, the slave that discovered the plot of the sons of Brutus to the senators, deserved to be mourned as Brutus was, while these degenerate sons of Brutus deserved the punishment that they received.

268. Adficiunt. Its subjects are *verbera* and *securis*.

Legum prima securis. Their execution was the first after the establishment of laws—i. e., of the republic.

269. Thersites was a cowardly boaster in the Greek army before Troy. Cf. Il. II, 212 ff. He was killed by Achilles.

270. Aeacidae, *Achilles*, grandson of Aeacus.

272. Ut, *although*.

273. Asylo. Romulus was said to have obtained his citizens by opening an asylum for criminals. Cf. Livy I, 8.

SATIRE X.

ON THE VANITY OF HUMAN WISHES.

INTRODUCTION.—How few know what real good is; how many strive for that which serves only to injure them! Eloquence, strength, wealth, all have their victims. What wonder that Democritus laughed and Heraclitus wept at the folly of men? But the folly of those times is far exceeded in our own.

Power brings envy and ill-will; Sejanus was second to the Emperor alone; in his fall he was hated and despised. Would you not rather be a humble magistrate in some country town than have Sejanus's power and fate? Crassus, Pompey, Caesar, all illustrate the same thing.

Eloquence is fatal too. Cicero's Philippics brought upon him Antony's vengeance. Demosthenes at the forge was safe; danger and death came when he had learned to sway the people at his will.

Military glory is both delusive and destructive. Hannibal died in poverty and exile; Alexander found room for all his greatness in a coffin; Xerxes suffered ignominious defeat.

Men pray for length of days, forgetful of the infirmities and sorrows that attend it. Nestor's long life brought grief, and Peleus lived to mourn Achilles. Had Priam died before old age, he might have been spared humiliation and disgrace. Hecuba lived longer still, and met a still worse fate. Look, too, at Mithridates, Croesus, Marius, Pompey.

Since, then, human wishes are vain, leave your happiness in the hands of the gods, whose care it is. If you must offer prayers, pray for a sound mind in a sound body ; for the spirit of peace that only virtue can give.

1. Gadibus. Cadiz was the western boundary of the world to the ancients.

2. Auroram et Gangen. *Usque* without *ad* is not usual except with names of towns.

3. Illis, dative.

Remota erroris nebula—i. e., *to remove the mist of error and—*

4. Ratione, ablative of manner.

7. Domos, *families.*

8. Toga—militia, *in peace and war.*

10. Ille. I think Macleane is right in referring this to the soldier, and not, as most commentators do, to Milo of Croton, who tried to rend a tree-trunk, but was held fast and devoured by wolves.

11. Periit. The *i* in the final syllable is long.

13. Cuncta patrimonia, object of *exuperans.*

14. Quanto—i. e., *tanto—quanto.*

16. Longinum. Gaius Cassius Longinus was a famous jurist, consul, and praetor, who was banished by Nero. **Longinum** = *domum Longini,* so *Cererem* for *aedem Cereris.*

Praedivitis Senecae. Cf. V, 109, note ; VIII, 212.

17. Lateranorum ; Plautius Lateranus was accused of participation in the conspiracy of Piso.

18. Cenacula, *garrets.*

19. Licet, *although.*

Puri, *simple.*

21. Ad lunam, *in the moonlight.*

22. Vacuus, *empty-handed.*

24. Maxima, etc. The bankers (*argentarii*) had their offices in the Forum. The positions of the most important buildings are shown in Fig. 48. The heavy black lines mark existing ruins.

26. Fictilibus. Cf. III, 168, *fictilibus cenare pudet.*

Pocula gemmata. Cf. V, 43, *gemmas ad pocula transfert.*

28. Iamne igitur laudas = *quod cum ita sit, certe iam laudabis.*

Alter, *Democritus.*

30. Auctor ; *Heraclitus,* of Ephesus, about 500 B. C., who was called both the weeping and the obscure philosopher.

34. Democritus, of Abdera, 460–367 B. C.

Quamquam with the subjunctive is usual in the silver age.

Urbibus illis, etc.—i. e., in the cities of his time and country there was

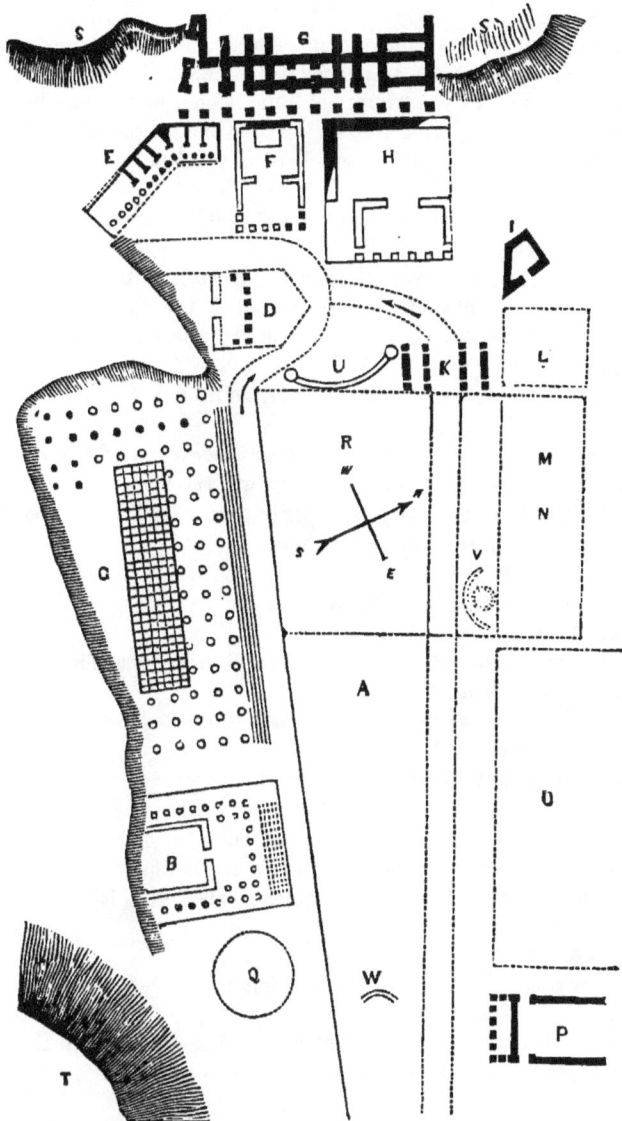

FIG. 48.—Roman Forum. (The plan is intended to give an idea of the Forum during the early empire.) A. Forum proper; B, Temple of Castor and Pollux; C, Basilica Iulia; D. Temple of Saturn; E, Porticus of the Dei Consentes; F. Temple of Vespasian; G, Tabularium; H, Temple of Concord; I, Mamertine rison; K, Arch of Septimius Severus (203 A. D.); L, Basilica Porcia; M, Curia Hostilia (burned 55 B. C.); N, Curia Iulia; O. Basilica Aemilia; P, Temple of Antoninus and Faustina; Q, Temple of Vesta; R, Comitium of the Republic; S. Capitoline Hill; T, Palatine Hill; U, Terrace (Rostra ?); V, Rostra vetera (?); W, Rostra Iulia.

no such ridiculous "pomp and circumstance"; suppose Democritus had seen the praetor at the games or a consular triumph!

38. Tunica Iovis—i. e., the triumphal tunic, which was embroidered with gold and bordered with purple. It was kept in the temple of Jupiter.

39. Aulaea, properly *curtains*, used here of the heavy folds of the triumphal toga.

Magnae coronae tantum orbem, *such a great encircling crown.*

40. Quanto, dative.

41. The crown was so heavy that it was not worn, but carried by a public slave, who took his place beside the official in the chariot, and, according to the common tradition, reminded the *triumphator* that he was but mortal, after all.

43. Da, *picture to yourself.* Cf. III, 137, *da testem.*

Volucrem—i. e., the eagle.

44. Praecedentia, etc., = *longum agmen praecedentium officiosorum.*

45. Niveos, *white-robed.* The white toga was the festal garb.

46. In loculos—i. e., he has gained their friendship by the "pensions" that they have stowed away in their coffers.

Sportula. Cf. I, 95.

47. Tum quoque, *even in those times.*

49. Exempla, object of *daturos.*

50. Vervecum, *blockheads.* Abdera, like Boeotia, was famous for the alleged stupidity of its inhabitants.

53. Mandaret laqueum, *to commend the gallows to fortune,* means, of course, to express scorn of her.

Mediumque ostenderet unguem. The middle finger was used in gestures of contempt.

54. Vel, if the reading be right, must mean *even.* The MSS. omit *vel,* which has been conjectured in order to avoid the hiatus.

55. Incerare. Petitions written on waxen tablets were laid on the knees of the statues of the gods.

57. Invidiae, dative.

Honorum pagina. The Scholiast says that this refers to a bronze tablet containing a list of titles.

58 ff. Their statues are pulled down and dragged through the streets, and even the marble representations of their horses and chariots are broken in pieces.

59. Inpacta securis, nom. sing.

61. Here follows a picture of the fate of the bronze statue of Sejanus, the ambitious favorite of Tiberius, who is selected as a striking example of the disasters incident to "*potentia.*" He is the subject of a tragedy by Ben Jonson, entitled "*Sejanus.*"

Strident, so *stridēre,* V, 160.

64. Sartago, *pan.*

65. It is an occasion of general rejoicing.

66. Cretatum = *candidum*, or refers to a custom of rubbing *creta*, white clay, on those portions of the sacrificial victim that were other than pure white.

67. What do the people, who made an idol of Sejanus, do when he falls? Listen.

69. Crimine, *accusation.*

70. Delator, *accuser.*

Teste, *witness.*

72. Capreis, the modern Capri, where Tiberius retired from Rome 26 A. D., leaving the active conduct of the State to Sejanus.

Bene habet = " *all right.*" Cf. *bene est ; bene agitur.*

73. Turba Remi. *Remus* is often used by poets for *Romulus* for the sake of the metre.

74. Nortia. An Etruscan goddess, worshiped especially at Vulsinii, the birthplace of Sejanus.

Tusco—i. e., Sejanus; dative.

75. Secura, from meaning *safe from anxiety*, comes to mean *careless.* The whole means, *if the old emperor had been caught napping.*

76. Diceret, *would be calling.* The subject is *turba Remi.*

77 f. Long ago, as soon as we lost the sale of our votes, we (i. e., *turba Remi*) threw off the cares of state. The irony in " *ex quo suffragia nulli vendimus,*" for *since the elections were transferred from the people to the senate,* is bitter indeed.

81. Panem et circenses. Cf. III, 223, *si potes avelli circensibus ;* VIII, 118. This phrase has become proverbial.

83. Bruttidius meus, *my friend Bruttidius.* Bruttidius Niger was a famous orator of the time ; perhaps he is meant.

84. Aiax—i. e., *Tiberius,* who, like Ajax conquered in his struggle with Ulysses. may rage against the supposed friends who seem to have deserted him.

87. A side blow at the power possessed by slaves, and the ease with which their testimony might ruin their masters.

90. Salutari refers to the morning reception.

91 f. Illi—**illum,** *one*—*another.*

Curules—i. e., curule offices, consulships, praetorships. Sejanus practically controlled such offices after Tiberius's retirement to Capri.

94. Grege Chaldaeo. The Chaldaeans were famous astrologers, and Tiberius was much given to that sort of superstition.

Certe, *at least.*

95. Castra domestica—i. e., the Praetorian cohorts.

96. Et qui, *even those who.*

97. Tanti. Cf. III, 54; *tanti non sit omnis harena.*

98. Ut, on condition that.

99. Qui trahitur. Cf. line 66, *ducitur unco.*

100. Fidenarum Gabiorumque. These were small towns in Latium.

101. Weights and measures were under the control of the aediles.

102. Ulubris. Another small town in Latium.

103. Quid optandum foret. Indirect question, object of *ignorasse.*

105. I. e., he was piling story on story, only that his fall might be the greater.

106. Unde = *ut inde.*

107. Praeceps is used as a noun. Cf. I, 149; *in praecipiti.* Immane is the predicate.

108. Crassos, Pompeios—i. e., such men as Crassus and Pompey. Crassus was a member of the so-called first triumvirate, and was killed in an expedition against the Parthians 53 B. C. Pompey was defeated at Pharsalos 48 B. C.

Illum. Julius Caesar.

109. Flagra. Cf. Eng., brought them under his lash.

110. Nulla non, every. *Non nulla* would mean *some.*

111. Malignis, because granting wishes that were really harmful.

112. Generum Cereris—i. e , Pluto.

114 ff. Look at another form of ambition. See the rewards of great eloquence.

115. Totis quinquatribus. The festival of Minerva (March 19-23) was a school holiday.

116 f. I. e., every little boy that goes to school.

117. Vernula. Cf. I, 26; *verna Canopi Crispinus.*

120. Ingenio, etc. *Genius lost head and hands.* After Cicero's murder, his head and hands were cut off by the order of Antony and fixed upon the rostra.

121. Causidici, *pettifoggers.* Cf. I, 32; *causidici Mathonis.*

Rostra. Cf. Fig. 49.

122. A line written by Cicero. Dryden imitates it in—

FIG. 49.—Rostra.

"Fortune foretuned the dying notes of Rome
      Till I thy consul sole consoled thy doom."

123. Juvenal says that if Cicero had never been more eloquent than in the line quoted, he might have been quite safe from Antony. Cf. Cicero's words in the second Philippic, "*Contempsi Catilinae gladios, non pertimescam tuos.*"

124. Ridenda, etc.—i. e., I would rather write such poor poetry and save my life, than write the famous second Philippic at the expense of my head. Cicero's attacks on Antony in the Philippic orations were the immediate cause of his murder.

126. Volveris a prima quae proxima, *unrolled next to the first.*

Illum, Demosthenes.

128. Torrentem, so we speak of a torrent of eloquence.

Moderantem frena—i. e., curbing, guiding, the passions of the people.

FIG. 50.—Tropaeum.

FIG. 51.—Currus, showing the temo.

130. This description of the father of Demosthenes as a blacksmith is a rhetorical exaggeration. He was the proprietor of a sword factory.

131. Gladios, object of *parante.*

133. Truncis tropaeis. A *tropaeum* in early times consisted of the armor

FIG. 52.—Trireme, showing the three banks of oars.

FIG. 53. — Position of rowers in a trireme.

of the conquered warrior arranged on a block of wood, or part of a tree-trunk. Cf. Fig. 50.

135. Curtum temone iugum. *Curtum* is about = *carens*, hence the use of the ablative. The *currus*, with the *temo* (pole) and the bolt, which kept the *iugum* (yoke) in place, is seen in Fig. 51.

Triremis. Cf. Figs. 52 and 53.

136. Aplustre = ἄφλαστον, the fan-shaped ornament on the stern of a ship. Cf. Fig. 54.

Arcu, *triumphal arch*, cf. cut, page 23.

137. Maiora—i. e., *bona maiora.*

138. Graius = *Graecus.*

Induperator, an older form of *imperator.*

143 f. Laudis titulique depend on *cupido ;* **haesuri** agrees with *tituli ;* **saxis** is the dative with *haesuri ;* **custodibus** is in apposition with *saxis.*

147. Expende Hannibalem, *weigh Hannibal.* Cf. Hamlet, Act V, Scene I.

148. Africa, etc.—i. e., Africa, which stretches from the Moorish sea to the Nile, and back to the land of the Ethiopians.

Mauro Oceano refers to that part of the Atlantic that washes the west coast of Africa.

FIG. 54.—Ship, showing the aplustre.

151. Hispania. The Carthaginians had many colonies in Spain, and their power there was strengthened by Hannibal. The following lines refer to his campaign in Italy after the fall of Saguntum in 219 B. C.

153. Montem rumpit aceto. Cf. Livy XXI, 37 ; *ardentia saxa infuso aceto putrefaciunt.*

155. Poeno milite. Note the absence of a preposition, and cf. the usage in I, 54 ; *mare percussum puero.*

Portas—i. e., the gates of Rome.

156. Subura. Cf. III, 5 ; note.

158. Gaetula belua, *elephant.*

Luscum : Hannibal lost one of his eyes through disease contracted in the marshes south of the river Po. Cf. Livy XXII, 2.

159. Ergo, *then.* Cf. I, 3.

Vincitur, by Scipio at Zama, 202 B. C.

161. Mirandus, *to be stared at.*

Cliens, *suppliant.*

162. Bithyno tyranno—i. e., Prusias, to whose court Hannibal fled.

Libeat, the subjunctive, because there is an idea of purpose in *donec = until.*

163. Animae, dative.

Quae res humanas miscuit olim, *which once threw the world into confusion.*

164-166. Ille—anulus. Hannibal is said to have taken poison from a ring, which is here called the *avenger of Cannae*. There is probably an allusion to the story that after the battle of Cannae (216 B. c.) a peck of rings was taken from the slain Roman equites.

168. Pellaeo iuveni. Alexander the Great, who "sighed for more worlds to conquer." He was born at Pella, 356 B. c., and died at Babylon, 323 B. c.

170. Gyari, Seripho. For the former, cf. I, 73; *aude aliquid Gyaris dignum. Seriphus* was another of the Cyclades.

171. A figulis munitam urbem—i. e., Babylon, built by the brick-makers.

172. Fatetur, *discloses, betrays.*

174. Velificatus Athos. Xerxes cut a canal between Mount Athos and the mainland, the remains of which have been discovered in modern times.

Fig. 55.—Bridge of boats.

175. Constratum (*esse*) **suppositumque** mare is the subject of *creditur*.

176. Rotis, dative with *suppositum*. The reference is to the bridge of boats by which the army of Xerxes crossed the Hellespont. Fig. 55 represents the passage of Trajan's army over the Danube by such a bridge.

177. The rivers that the Medes drank dry were probably rivers by courtesy.

178. Madidis alis. There are two explanations: one, that he struggled so hard that the wings of his fancy were wet with sweat; another, that they were made damp and heavy by wine. The latter is preferable. Cf. Ovid Meta. I, 264; *Madidis Notus evolat alis.*

Sostratus, unknown.

179. Ille—i. e., Xerxes, the man that accomplished all this.

180 f. Xerxes assumed *more* power over the winds than even their master Aeolus.

181. Hoc, accusative.

182. Ennosigaeum, Homer's name for Poseidon. To punish him for destroying his bridge of boats, Xerxes caused fetters to be thrown into the sea.

183. With all his assumed control, it is a wonder that he did not punish him even more severely.

184. No wonder the gods rebelled !

188. Another common desire is length of days.

189. Recto vultu—i. e., *in health*, opposed to *pallidus*.

192. Dissimilem sui. " After *similis* Cicero uses the genitive of living objects, and either the genitive or dative of things " (A. and G. 234, d. 2).

Cutis is a man's skin, pellis is a beast's hide.

194. Thabraca, a town in Numidia; the surrounding forests were full of monkeys.

199. Lēve, *bald*.

200. Misero, dative of apparent agent.

Gingiva inermi, *toothless gums*.

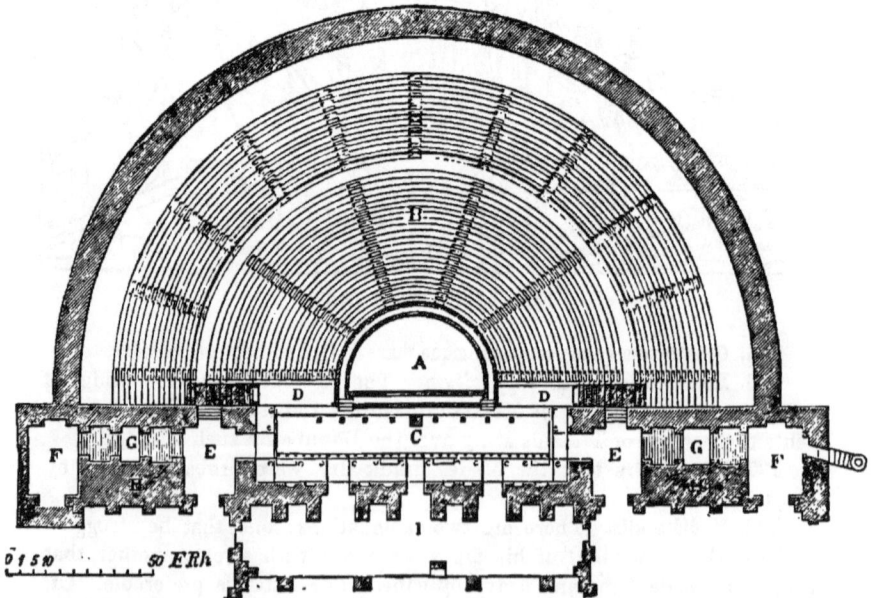

Fig. 56.—Ground-plan of the theatre of Herod at Athens. A, Orchestra ; B, Cavea ; C, Pulpitum (stage) ; D, D, Parodoi ; I, One of the three entrances through the stage-wall (scaena). The exact use of the various rooms adjoining the stage is not known.

202. Such a disgusting object that even Cossus, who would be likely to stand a great deal for the sake of an expected legacy, is driven from the field. This may be the Cossus mentioned in III, 184.

209 f. Partis alterius, *the other sense*—i. e., hearing.

210 f. Cantante citharoedo, ablative absolute. *Cantare* is used of both vocal and instrumental music.

211. Seleuco. Seleucus is unknown.

212. Aurata lacerna, for the elegance of theatrical dress, cf. Hor. A. P. 215.

213. Theatri. Cf. Fig. 56.

214. The *cornu* (a large curved horn) is seen in Fig. 55; the *tuba* or straight horn, in the representation of a sacrifice, in Fig. 57.

216. Dicat, subjunctive in an indirect question.

Quot horas, *what time.* Cf. *Quota hora est = what time is it?* Time-pieces were not in common use, and it was the duty of a slave to announce the hour from a public sundial or water-clock.

FIG. 57.—A sacrificial scene, showing the tuba.

218. Agmine facto. The same phrase III, 162, also in Vergil.

226. This line occurs also I, 25.

233. Damno, ablative of separation with the comparative.

FIG. 58.—Rogus.

FIG. 59.—Funeral-urn.

237. Suos—i. e., his natural heirs. **Suos** is the subject of **esse, heredes** the predicate.

240. Ut, *although.*

Ducenda. Cf. I. 146; *ducitur funus.*

241. Rogus. Cf. Fig. 58, which represents the funeral pyre of Patroclus.

242. Urnae—i. e., *aspiciendae sunt.* For the form of the urn, cf. Fig. 59.

243. Haec data poena; here *data* has its usual force; *this penalty is as-signed.* For the technical use of *poenas dare*, cf. III, 279.

244. Domus, genitive.

246. Rex Pylius—i. e., Nestor, who was said to have lived to see three generations of men.

247. A cornice secundae, *next to the crow.*

248. Qui, *in that he.*

249. Dextra. Units and tens were counted on the left hand, hundreds on the right.

253. Antilochi barbam ardentem—i. e., the funeral pyre of Antilochus. The cut on page 61 represents the friends of Antilochus lifting his body into a chariot.

257. Alius, Laertes, the father of Ulysses, of Ithaca.

Cui fas, *whose fate it was.*

258. Incolumi Troia, ablative absolute.

Venisset is the conclusion of the condition expressed in *si foret exstinctus,* line 263.

259. Assaraci, the great-uncle of Priam.

260. Cervicibus, ablative absolute with *portantibus* implied.

261 f. Ut—inciperet, result clause, imperfect for vividness.

264. Aedificare carinas; notice the loss of original meaning in *aedi-fico.*

265. Dies meaning *time* is usually feminine.

267. Miles tremulus—i. e., Priam.

270. Ab ingrato aratro. The plow is personified, hence the use of the preposition.

271. Yet Priam's death was that of a human being, while Hecuba, who outlived him, was changed into a cur, and died a beast's death.

273. Regem Ponti, Mithridates, King of Pontus, 130–63 B. C.

274 f. Croesum. The story of Croesus, King of Lydia, 560–548 B. C., and Solon is told by Herodotus I, 29 ff.

276–282. Marius is referred to.

278. Illo cive, ablative with *beatius.*

282. De Teutonico curru. Marius defeated the Teutons 102 B. C., and the Cimbri in the following year. Cf. VIII, 249.

Vellet. Cf. ἔμελλεν, *was about to.*

283. Provida, *foreseeing, wise.* Pompey was ill of a fever at Naples, 50 B. C. Public prayers were offered for his safety.

286. Victo—i. e., after his defeat by Caesar. Dative with *abstulit.*

287. Lentulus, Cethegus, and **Catilina,** who died in comparative youth, escaped this ignominy.

347. Permittes, the future has the same force as in *optabunt* above.

Expendere, *to weigh out,* so *to decide.*

353. Notum (*est*).

354. Et and **que** are correlative.

Sacellis, *shrines.*

355. Et connects *exta* and *tomacula.*

Tomacula, mince-meat, made of sacrificial pork.

356. This line has become proverbial.

358. Spatium extremum. Cf. lines 188, 275.

Munera, *burdens.*

362. Et—et—et serve to co-ordinate the ideas.

Venere—cenis—pluma. Ablatives with the comparative *potiores.*

Sardanapalli, the last king of Assyria. He furnished a typical instance of luxurious living.

365 f. These lines occur also XIV, 315, 316.

SATIRE XI.

INTRODUCTION.—In this satire, which is written in the form of an invitation to dinner, sent to his friend Persicus, Juvenal shows the folly of those who, with small means, attempt to imitate the luxury of the rich.

People are all talking of Rutilus, who has ruined himself by his extravagant luxury. He is one of many. Such a man cheats his creditors and pawns his silver or his mother's portrait to purchase table delicacies. This conduct arises from ignorance of self, and of individual limitations. The bankrupt's only regret is that his enforced exile deprives him of the pleasures of the circus. Come and dine with me, and I will show you that I practice what I preach. You shall have a simple meal, such a one as in former times would have contented a senator, although in our day it would be despised by a slave. In the early times there was no search for treasures of art; men used silver in their armor, earthenware on their tables. Then, when Jupiter's statue was of clay, the gods were nearer men. Now the most luxurious furniture is thought necessary, but at my table you will find simplicity in everything. Lay aside the anxieties that belong to modern city life, and seek rest and refreshment with me.

1. Atticus, may refer to Ti. Claudius Atticus, who was a rich man of the time of Nerva, or to T. Pomponius Atticus, the friend of Cicero.

Lautus, *fine, elegant.*

2. Rutilus, unknown. Some spendthrift noble.

3. Apicius. M. Fabius Apicius lived in the time of Tiberius. He was famous for his luxurious table.

4. Convictus = *convivia.*

13

Stationes, *clubs, lounging places.*

6. Galeae—i. e., *for military service.*

7. I. e., the tribune had not put him into bankruptcy, and so driven him to this, but he had not interposed to save him.

8. Scripturus (*esse*), etc.—i. e., to sign the conditions and agree to the "royal" commands of the trainer—i. e., to become a hired gladiator. Cf. III, 158.

10. Macelli, *the market.* The creditor was sure to find them looking after table delicacies.

12. Egregius, a comparative form, as if from *egrex.*

13. Et connects *miserrimus* and *casurus.*

Perlucente ruina; the metaphor is taken from a building so shattered that the light shines through the cracks.

14. Gustus, abstract for concrete = *relishes.*

15. Animo, *fancy.*

Interius si attendas, *if you look more closely.*

17. Perituram, *to be squandered.*

Arcessere, *to raise.*

18. Oppositis (*pignori*), *pawned.*

19. Condire gulosum fictile, *to season a dainty-filled dish*—i. e., *to load a dish with dainties.* The adjective is proleptic.

20. Miscillanea ludi, *the messes of the gladiator's school.*

21. Paret, subjunctive, indirect question.

22. Est; the subject of est, sumit, and trahit (line 23), is implied in *haec eadem paret.*

Ventidio, some well-known rich man, perhaps Ventidius Bassus.

23 ff. He is properly an object of contempt, who does not see that a safe differs from a purse as much as Atlas from all the mountains of Libya.

25. Hic, strict grammar would require *qui.*

26. Arca. Cf. I, 90 ; *posita luditur arca.*

27. Γνῶθι σεαυτόν, "*know thyself*" ; a famous saying used by Socrates. Cf. Xen. Mem. IV, 2, 24.

29. In parte, *in the ranks.*

30. Thersites knew himself too well to ask for the armor of Achilles.

31. Se traducebat may mean *made himself ridiculous,* or simply *showed himself.* The latter seems preferable. The story of the contest between Ajax and Ulysses for the armor of Achilles is told by Homer, Iliad II.

32. Magno discrimine, *of great importance.* Ablative of characteristic.

33. Adfectas, *undertake.* The indicative is used because, owing to the parenthesis, *neque—Ulixes,* the sentence becomes independent.

Consule, imperative.

34. Curtius et Matho. The former is unknown, the latter is mentioned I, 32.

Buccae, *puffed-out cheeks*, so *wind-bags*, *blowers.*

37. Gobio, a small, cheap fish.

38. Deficiente crumina—i. e., your purse growing smaller as your appetite grows larger.

43. Anulus, the badge of the knight or senator.

Pollio, unknown.

45. Luxuriae is the dative of apparent agent, with *metuenda* supplied from the following clause.

46. Conducta pecunia, *conducere* = *to borrow, to hire.* Cf. III, 225.

47 f. Paulum nescio quid, *a little something.*

48. Faenoris auctor—i. e., the lender.

49. Qui vertere solum. Literally, *those who have changed their soil.* The meaning is, they run away from Rome.

50. Cedere foro, *to become bankrupt*, cf. *to go out of the street*—i. e., Wall Street.

51. To move from one part of the city to another.

53. Anno uno. For the ablative, cf. VII, 235; *quot vixerit annis.*

Circensibus. Cf. III, 223, *avelli circensibus;* VIII, 118; X, 81.

54. Morantur, transitive, *seek to detain.*

56. What precedes is an introduction to the following invitation.

Pulcherrima dictu, *fine to talk about;* so Livy says *speciosa dictu.* What case is *dictu?*

58. Occultus ganeo, *a glutton in secret.*

59. Dictem. *Dictare* for the classical *imperare.*

60 f. Habebis Evandrum, etc.—i. e., I shall be as simple a host to you as Evander was to Hercules (*Tirynthius*) or to Aeneas, who, though inferior to Hercules, was also of divine descent.

69. Posito fuso, *laying aside her spindle.*

70. Tortoque calentia faeno, *warm (fresh) from the nest.*

72. Parte anni, *through half the year.* For the ablative, cf. VII, 235; XI, 53.

73. Signinum Syriumque pirum. Signium was a town in Latium. Syrian pears grew at Tarentum.

74. Aemula Picenis mala. The apples of Picenum are mentioned by Horace, Sat. II, 3, 272, and 4, 70; *Picenis cedunt pomis Tiburtia.*

76. Autumnum—i. e., the crudeness that they had in autumn.

77. Iam luxuriosa—i. e., after it had gone beyond the still simpler fare of Curius.

78. Curius (*Dentatus*) conquered the Samnites.

79 ff. Quae nunc, etc. In these days even the slave in chains despises such fare, remembering the delicacies of the cookshop.

82. Suis, genitive singular of *sus.*

Rara crate, *wide-barred rack.* Horace uses *rarus* of a net (Epodes II, 33).

84. **Natalicium,** translate *on birthdays.*

85. **Si quam dabat hostia**—i. e., if there had been a recent sacrifice.

88. **Solito maturius,** *earlier than usual,* because it was a festal day.

89. **Erectum**—i. e., on his shoulder.

90. **Tremerent,** the subject is general, *they.* The verb has transitive force.

Fabios, etc. The names here used belong to representatives of the severe simplicity of early Rome.

93. **Habendam** (*testudinem*).

94. **Qualis—nataret,** indirect question.

95. **Troiugenis.** Cf. I, 100; note.

Fulcrum is probably the head-piece of a couch; here it may be used for the couch itself. Cf. Fig. 60.

96. *Nudo latere* and *parvis lectis* may be taken as ablatives of characteristic modifying *frons aerea,* which, as the important idea, is made the subject; or *lectis* modified by *parvis* and by *nudo latere* may be considered as the ablative of place without the preposition.

97. **Vile,** *cheap, common, roughly fashioned.*

Coronati. The head of an ass, an animal sacred to Bacchus, was often crowned with vine leaves, when used as an ornament.

98. *Which the rude country boys laughed at.*

103 ff. **Ut cassis**—ostenderet is a clause of purpose depending on *frangebat. Simulacra, Quirinos,* and *effigiem* are the objects of *ostenderet* (line 107).

FIG. 60.
Fulcrum.

Phaleris. Cf. Fig. 61.

104. **Mansuescere,** intransitive.

105. **Imperii fato**—i. e., by the fate that watched over the future of the Roman Empire.

Quirinos. Romulus and Remus are called Quirini, as Castor and Pollux are called Castores.

106. Clipeo et hasta, ablatives of accompaniment. The *clipeus* was a round shield, as seen in Fig. 62.

107. Pendentis, *hanging, hovering* in the air between heaven and earth.

108. Tusco catino, much of the earthen table ware used at Rome came from Etruria.

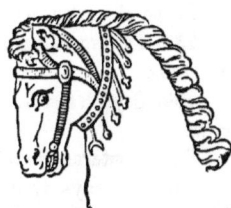
Fig. 61.—Horse adorned with phalerae.

Farrata—i. e., food made from meal.

111. Praesentior. Cf. III, 18; *quanto praesentius esset numen.*

112. Cf. Livy V, 32: *Eodem anno M. Caedicius de plebe nuntiavit tribunis, se in nova via, ubi nunc sacellum est supra aedem Vestae, vocem noctis silentio audisse clariorem humana, quae magistratibus dici iuberet, Gallos adventare.*

114. His—i. e., by such means.

116. Violatus. Cf. III, 20.

118. Hos agrees with *usus.* Others read *hoc.*

120 ff. It became the fashion in Rome to collect rare and costly tables. Two specimens are shown in Figs. 63 and 64. Juvenal here has in mind one of the *orbes* (round tables, the tops of which were of a single section of expensive foreign wood or marble), supported on a single shaft (hence called *monopodia*), consisting of an ivory leopard, rampant. Cf. I, 137; *de tot pulchris et latis orbibus.*

Fig. 62.—Figure bearing the clipeus.

124. Porta Syenes. Syene was a town on the Nile, on the border between Egypt and Ethiopia.

125. Mauro obscurior Indus, *the Indian duskier than the Moor.*

126. Deposuit, *shed.* Juvenal's natural history is at fault.

Nabataeo saltu. Probably Napata, the capital of Ethiopia, is meant.

127. Orexis, *appetite.*

128 f. I. e., a silver table-leg is to them no more than an iron finger-ring, such as were worn by the common people.

131. Adeo nulla, *so far am I from having.* Cf. III, 84.

133. Quin, *nay even.*

136. Structor. Cf. V, 120.

137. Pergula, *(carving) school.* Cf. V, 122.

Fig. 63.—Orbis.

Trypheri, unknown.

138. Pygargus, *a white-backed antelope.*

139. Scythicae volucres, *pheasants.*

Phoenicopterus, *flamingo.*

140. He says that this very fine supper made of elm is cut up with a dull knife, and the clatter is heard all over the Subura. The carving - teachers seem to have used wooden models.

Oryx, *gazelle.*

142. Subducere, *to steal.*

Afrae avis; so Hor., Epod. 2, 53. Probably a Guinea-hen.

143. Noster, *my servant.*

144. Inbutus, *tainted with—* i. e., *accustomed to.*

Ofellae, diminutive of *offa = a scrap.*

146. A frigore tutus, warmly clad, not dressed in the Eastern fashion.

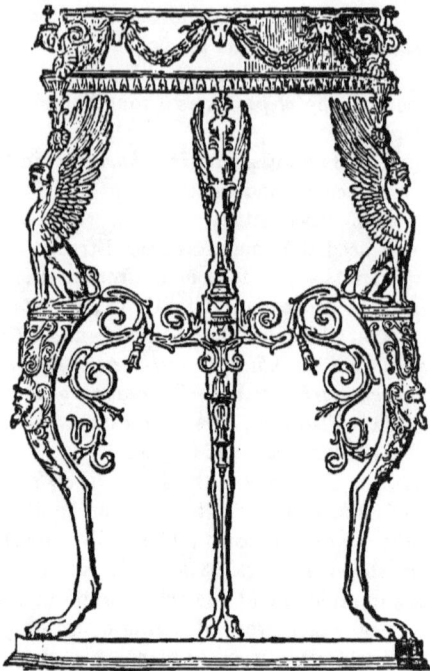

FIG. 64.—Orbis.

147. Mangone, *slave-dealer.*

148. Magno—i. e., *magno poculo,* but the whole passage *non—magno* is rejected by several editors. *Weidner's* conjecture *mangone . . . Armenio* suits the context very well.

155. Ardens purpura, the dress of the sons of free citizens.

159. Diffusa, *drawn off,* bottled.

179. In the omitted passage Juvenal has described some of the less reputable forms of amusement.

181. Dubiam palmam—i. e., Vergil's poetry vies with that of Homer.

190. I. e., leave all your cares outside the door.

191. Domum, *household.*

Illis, for the omission of *ab,* cf. I, 54, *mare percussum puero.*

193. Mappae. A napkin or scarf was dropped by the praetor as a signal for the games to begin.

194. Idaeum sollemne. The *Megalesia* were in honor of Cybele, the Idaean mother. Cf. III, 137, note.

Colunt—i. e., the people at Rome.

Similisque triumpho—i. e., *similis triumphanti.*

195. Praeda, *a victim,* because the horses cost him so much.

Pace, *by the leave of.* It is a bold statement, but under Vespasian the Circus is said to have had seats for 250,000 persons.

198. Eventum, *success.*

Viridis panni. Cf. note, VII, 114. In republican times there were two parties among the charioteers, the red and the white; later two others came into existence, the blue and the green; Domitian added the gold and the purple. These colors appeared in the tunics of the drivers, and the whole city seems to have divided itself into partisans of the various colors. The drivers consisted for the most part of slaves or freedmen, who were trained in regular schools. The chariots were drawn by two or by four horses, rarely by three. The charioteers frequently became very rich, their profits coming from prizes and from their share of the money wagered in the race. The greatest of Roman jockeys, Diocles, left his son a fortune of about a million and a half. For the charioteer's costume, cf. page 54. The green seems to have been the favorite color at this time.

Quo colligo, *whence I gather.*

201. Consulibus, L. Aemilius Paulus and C. Terentius Varro, 216 B. C.

Audax sponsio, *bold betting.*

203. I. e., it is better for old people like us to take sun-baths and give up evening dress.

204. Salva fronte, *without shame, without violating the proprieties.*

Quamquam—sextam, *although it be only eleven o'clock.* The usual hour was 2 P. M.

208. Commendat, *enhances, gives zest to.*

SATIRE XII.

INTRODUCTION.—A letter to Corvinus, describing the safe arrival of Juvenal's friend Catullus, with some intentional exaggeration of his dangers and fears. The Satire closes with a statement of the disinterested character of Juvenal's enthusiasm, which leads to a description of the arts of the professional legacy-hunter.

I have made ready a sacrifice to celebrate my friend's safe return. If I were richer, the offering should be costlier. He has passed through great dangers, and was in great terror, so great that he was willing to throw all his possessions overboard; fancy, in these days, a man who will give up his wealth to save his life! Finally, the mast must be cut away. At last they have arrived at the harbor of Ostia. Make ready, then, for the sacrifice. Does all this joy seem suspicious? No, it is not mercenary, for Catullus has three children, and is, therefore, not a good subject for legacy-hunters. Let a childless rich person have the slightest illness, and men will go to the most extravagant lengths to show their grief and fear; will offer a hundred oxen, would offer an elephant if one were to be found—nay, even a slave or a child! May such men enjoy the reward they deserve, wealth and lack of love!

1. Natali die, (*my*) *birthday.* Ablative with the comparative. Birthdays are mentioned as festivals, V, 37; XI, 84.

Lux for *dies* is common.

2. Caespes, *turf* (*altar*).

3. Reginae, *Juno ;* dative.

4. Vellus, *fleece.*

Pugnanti Gorgone Maura. Minerva, who put the head of the Gorgon, killed by Perseus, on her shield. Some traditions placed the Gorgon Medusa in Africa, hence *Maura.* *Pugnanti Gorgone* does not mean *fighting against the Gorgon*, but *fighting with the Gorgon-shield.*

6. Coruscat, about the same as *vibrat.*

10. Affectibus = *amori ;* post-classical. *Adf-* is more common in Juvenal.

11. Hispulla, noted for size and weight.

13. Clitumni, in Umbria.

Sanguis—i. e., *a blooded beast.*

14. A grandi ferienda ministro. This is quoted as one of the rare instances of *a* and the ablative to express the agent with the gerundive. I am inclined to think that wherever *real* agent, without any notion of "person interested" is expressed, the ablative with the preposition is used, otherwise the dative.

16. I. e., surprised to find himself still alive.

17. Et = *etiam.*

19. Nube una—i. e., there were no breaks; the whole sky was dark.

Antemnas, *the yard-arms.* Probably "St. Elmo's fire" is referred to.

21. Conferri, *to be compared to.*

22. Omnia fiunt, etc. It was a real poet's shipwreck, with no harrowing detail omitted.

24. Discriminis, *danger.*

25. Cetera—i. e., what follows.

27. Quam, its antecedent is *pars.*

28. Ab Iside. The Egyptian goddess Isis was, in imperial times, the favorite divinity of traders; votive tablets to her were a source of income to the painters. Cf. Hor. Odes I, 5, 13 ; A. P. 20. She is represented in Fig. 72.

30. Medius alveus, *the middle of the hold.*

31. Alternum latus, *first one side and then the other.*

32. Arbori incertae, the reading is doubtful. The MSS. have *arboris ;* *arbori* is Lachmann's conjecture.

33. Decidere is a law-term meaning *to compound, to compromise.*

Iactu, *by throwing overboard.* Cf. III, 125.

34. Coepit, its subject is implied in *rectoris*.

39. Teneris—Maecenatibus, *an effeminate Maecenas.* Cf. I, 66, note.

40. Quarum depends on *pecus* (= *wool*), which is the object of *infecit* (= *tinged*).

41. Sed et, *but also*.

42. Baeticus. The *Baetis* was the modern Guadalquiver.

43. Lances, *dishes, plate*.

44. Parthenio, unknown.

Urnae, used here of a measure.

45. Pholo. Pholus was one of the centaurs.

Coniuge Fusci, unknown.

46. Bascaudas, a Keltic word, from which Eng. *basket* is derived; probably vessels covered with wicker-work are meant.

Escaria, from *esca*, so dishes of some sort.

Multum caelati, *much chased ware.* *Caelati* is partitive genitive.

47. Emptor Olynthi, Philip of Macedon, who gained possession of Olynthus by bribing two of its citizens.

48 f. *What other man* (than Catullus), *what man in what part of the world, would dare to prefer his safety to his silver, his weal to his wealth ?*

50 f. These verses are often considered as an interpolation, apparently on the principle that whatever in Juvenal savors of the commonplace is spurious. I see no reason for rejecting them.

51. Vitio, avarice.

53. Damna, *sacrifices*.

Illuc reccidit, *he was reduced to this*.

55. Angustum; cf. " *in a strait.*"

Quando, etc.—i. e., when we throw away part of the ship to save the rest.

57. Dolato, *rough-hewn*.

59. Taeda, *plank*.

60. Ventre lagonae ; cf. *Montani venter*, IV, 107.

61. Sumendas, *to be used*.

63. Vectoris, *the traveler*.

64. Meliora—pensa, *kindlier threads, a happier lot*.

65. Staminis albi, white threads were favorable.

67. Miserabilis modifies *prora* (line 69).

69. Velo suo—i. e., the sail that belonged to the prow, the *dolon*, or foresail.

71. Atque connects *gratus* and *sublimis*.

Novercali—praelata Lavino, *preferred* (by him) *to his step-mother's Lavinium.* Iulus leaving Lavinium was guided to the site of Alba Longa by a white sow with thirty pigs. Cf. Verg., Aen. III, 390.

Lavino, the usual form is *Lavinio*.

73. **Phrygibus**—i. e., the Trojans with Iulus.

74. **Clara,** refers to *scrofa.*

75. The artificial harbor formed at Ostia by Claudius, 42 A. D.   Cf. Fig. 65, a restoration by Canina.

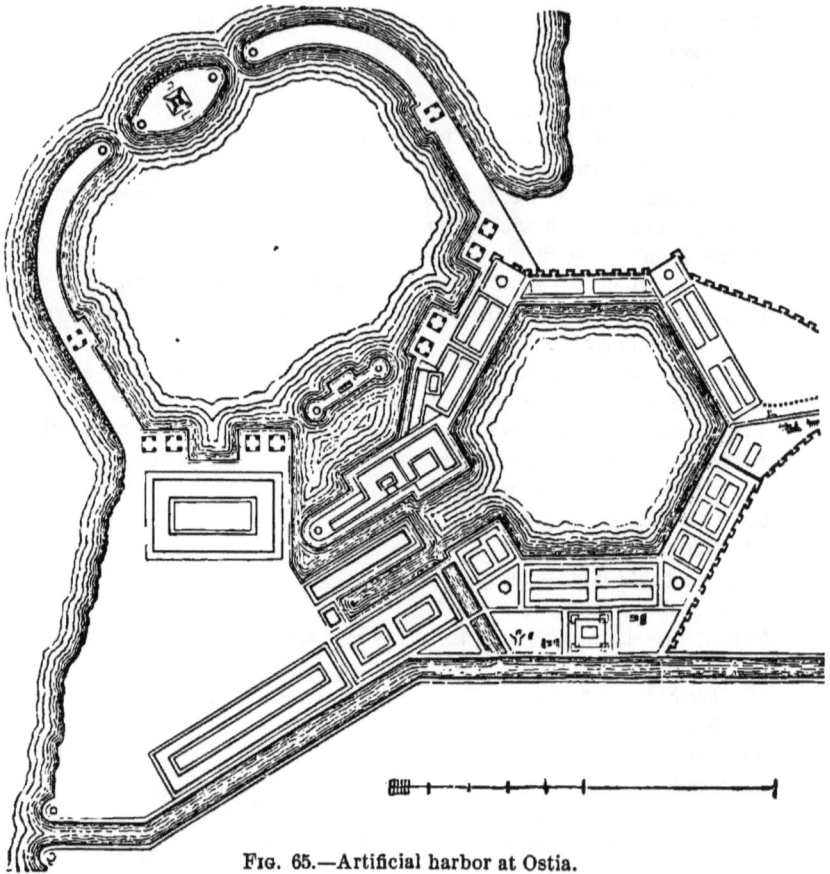

FIG. 65.—Artificial harbor at Ostia.

76. **Tyrrhenamque pharon**—i. e., a lighthouse like that on the island of Pharos, near Alexandria.   Cf. Fig. 66, which is from a medal of the Emperor Commodus.

Porrectaque bracchia rursum, the breakwaters ran out into the sea and then curved inward, as seen in Fig. 65, upper left-hand corner.

78. **Italiam**—i. e., the shore.

79. I. e., more wonderful than any natural harbor.

80. Interiora, the inner harbor built by Trajan. Fig. 67, from a coin struck in 103 A. D., shows the warehouses surrounding this inner harbor.

Pervia, *navigable.*

Cumbae, dative with *pervia.*

81. Tuti stagna sinus, *the quiet waters of a safe bay.*

Vertice raso. Men cut off their hair as a votive offering. Cf. III, 186.

83. Linguis animisque faventes—i. e., with a strict religious silence. Cf. Hor., Odes III, 1, 2.

84. Serta, *garlands.*

Farra—i. e., the sacrificial meal with which the knives were sprinkled.

85. Mollis focos, the turf altars.

90. I. e., *violets of every color.*

91. Longos, etc ; cf. *pone domi laurus,* X, 65.

92. Matutinis—i. e., lighted before daybreak.

Operatur = *operam dat, celebrates.*

Festa (*ianua*).

FIG. 66.—Pharos.

93 ff. This sounds like legacy-hunting, but Catullus has three children, so you see my devotion is disinterested.

95. Libet expectare, *I should like to see.*

96. Claudentem oculos, *blind.*

98. Pro patre—i. e., for a man that is a father.

Sentire calorem—i. e., *to feel the approach of fever.* We might say *to have a chill.*

99. Coepit, singular because each subject is thought of separately.

100. Legitime, *in due form.*

Libellis = *votorum tabulis.*

101. Porticus, either of the house or of some temple.

Hecatomben—i. e., a hundred oxen; he goes on to say that they would make it elephants if they could.

102. Quatenus, *since.*

103. Sidere, *sky.*

104. Furva gente—i. e., from India.

Petita agrees with *belua.*

105. *In the Rutulian forests and the land where Turnus reigned.*

FIG. 67.—Inner harbor at Ostia.

106. Caesaris armentum. Herds of elephants were kept by the emperors for use in the public shows.

107. Siquidem almost = *for.*

Tyrio Hannibali. Carthage was a colony from Tyre.

108. Nostris ducibus—e. g., Scipio.

Regique Molosso, Pyrrhus, King of Epirus.

110. Partem aliquam belli, *an important part of the war.*

111. *Novius and Hister Pacuvius* (legacy-hunters) *would not hesitate to offer up elephants at the shrines of their patrons.*

115. Alter, *the latter*, as shown by the use of his name again in line 125.

119. Iphigenia, etc.—i. e., he would be as ready to sacrifice his own daughter as was Agamemnon, even without the hope that a deer would be furnished at the last moment to take the maiden's place, as the tragedians represented in the case of Iphigenia. Cf. Fig. 68.

121. Civem, *fellow-citizen.*

Nec comparo, etc.—i. e., how much better to sacrifice one's daughter for

FIG. 68.—Sacrifice of Iphigenia.

a legacy than for a thousand ships; referring, of course, to the Greek fleet in the story of Iphigenia.

122. Libitinam, the goddess of funerals, so death; cf. Hor., Odes III, 30, 6, *multa pars mei vitabit Libitinam.*

123. Inclusus carcere nassae, *imprisoned in the net.* The *nassa* was a sort of lobster-pot, as seen in Fig. 69.

127. Ingulata Mycenis—i. e., the sacrifice of his "Iphigenia."

128. Nestora totum, a sort of cognate accusative; for the sense, cf. X, 246.

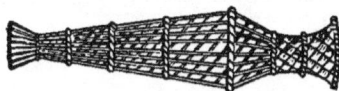

FIG. 69.—Nassa.

SATIRE XIII.

INTRODUCTION.—Juvenal writes to his friend Calvinus, who is much distressed by the loss of a small sum of money through breach of trust. The strength of the Satire lies in its ethical teaching, and its vigorous description of the terrors of a guilty conscience.

Crime is its own punishment; then, too, you are rich enough to bear this loss with equanimity. Why are you so overwhelmed by a misfortune which in these evil days is so common? In the golden age, when there were fewer gods, there was more virtue; now an honest man is a rarity. Men break their oaths without hesitation, some believe in no gods, others hope to escape divine vengeance. Consider how many suffer more serious losses than yours; look at the criminal courts. No one wonders at that which is common, why wonder at dishonesty in Rome? Do you seek revenge? That is unphilosophical, the mark of a petty mind. Leave your enemy to the punishment of his own conscience; it will give him no peace, will torture him under all circumstances, but it will not deter him from further crimes, and you will some day have the satisfaction of seeing him the victim of his own ill-doing.

1. Exemplo—malo, ablative of characteristic.

2. Se iudice, etc. Each *iudex* (juryman) was furnished with three tablets marked respectively A. (*absolvo*), C. (*condemno*), and N. L. (*non liquet = not proven*), one of which he cast into the urn, whence they were taken and counted by the praetor.

3. Inproba gratia, *corrupt influence.*

5 ff. You have the sympathy of your friends, your wealth is still great, and you have plenty of company in your misfortunes.

6. Crimine, *charge.*

8. Iacturas. The paradox, "*burden of a loss*," is probably intentional.

10. Et e medio, etc., *taken from the middle of Fortune's heap*—i. e., taken at random.

13. Quamvis levium, *however slight.*

16. There is some doubt as to the subject of *stupet.* I think it is not Juvenal, but Calvinus.   •

17. Fonteio. One Fonteius was consul 59 A. D., another 67 A. D.; the latter is probably meant.

20. Sapientia means philosophy as contrasted with experience (*vita*).

23. Cesset, *fail.*

25. Pyxide, *box,* here a box containing poison. The peculiar lid of the *pyxis* is seen in Fig. 70.

27. Thebarum portae, Boeotian Thebes had seven gates, and the Nile had seven mouths.

28. Nunc aetas. Ovid calls the iron age the fourth; no wonder, then, that no metal could be found base enough to designate the present.

Agitur, *is passing.* **Saecula,** the subject of an implied *aguntur,* is the antecedent of **quorum.**

31. Fidem ; *fides* means that which may be trusted; *we make as much noise about honor and religion—*

32. Faesidium. Faesidius was a rich lawyer; hence *agentem, pleading.*

Vocalis sportula—i. e., those persons whose applauding voices had been bought by the *sportula.*

33. Bulla, worn by children. Cf. V, 164, note (Fig. 30).

FIG. 70.—Pyxis.

37. Rubenti—i. e., with the blood of victims.

39 f. Saturn fleeing from Jupiter, who had deprived him of his crown, came to Latium and taught the people agriculture.

41. Privatus, *a simple citizen, one without office.*

Idaeis antris ; Jupiter's early boyhood was passed on Mount Ida, in Crete.

42 ff. The simplicity of those early times was found in heaven as well as on earth.

43. Puer Iliacus, Ganymede, who came from the Troad.

Herculis uxor, Hebe.

44. Ad cyathos—i. e., as cup-bearer.

45. Liparaea ; Vulcan's forge was sometimes located in Lipara, a volcanic island north of Sicily. Cf. I, 8, note. Fig. 71, from a bas-relief, represents Vulcan in his workshop affixing the handle to a shield.

46. Nec turba deorum. The Roman pantheon became very much crowded

FIG. 71.—Vulcan's workshop.

in later times by the importation of a host of Asiatic and Egyptian divinities, and the deification of emperors, heroes, and abstract ideas.

48. Atlanta. "*Poor Atlas*" was supposed to support the heavens on his shoulders.

49. Triste profundi imperium, *the gloomy empire of the abyss.*

50. Aut, the negation continues.

Sicula—coniuge, Proserpina, whom Pluto carried off from Enna in Sicily. Cf. Ovid, Met. V, 391 ff.

51. Rota, saxum, and **vulturis atri poena** refer to Ixion, Sisyphus, and Tityus respectively.

53. Admirabilis, *a wonder.*

54. Quo (*aevo*).

57. Notice the incidental reference to the simplicity of living.

59. Lanugo, *down.*

61. Follem, *purse.*

62. Tuscis libellis. The Etruscans were famous for their skill in augury. Cf. Livy, I, 34.

64. An honest man in these days is a wonder and a prodigy.

Bimembri seems to mean *half-man, half-beast*, or it may be *two-headed.*

68. Uva is often used for a "cluster" of bees.

70. Miris seems tame, but *miniis* (Porson's conjecture, followed by Ribbeck) is improbable.

71. Decem sestertia, about $400.

73. Arcana = intrusted without witnesses or receipt.

74. Quam patulae, etc.—i. e., so large a sum that there was no room for it in his money-chest.

76. Quanta voce, *how loudly.*

78. Tarpeia fulmina, *the thunderbolts of Tarpeian* (i. e., Capitoline) *Jupiter.*

79. Frameam, the Teutonic word for lance. Cf. Tacitus, Germ. VI, and Fig. 72.

Cirrhaei vatis, Apollo. Cf. VII, 64.

80. Venatricis puellae, Diana.

82. Herculeos arcus, the bow that Hercules gave to Philoctetes.

84. Et, *too, as well.*

Flebile—i. e., *deeply as it would pain me.* *Flebile* agrees with *sinciput.*

85. Que connects *elixi* and *madentis.*

88. *For nature brings about the changes of day and night, and of the seasons.*

Fig. 72.—Figure hurling the framea.

93. Isis. The Egyptian goddess Isis was a popular divinity at Rome during the empire. Cf. XII, 28, note, and Fig. 73.

Sistro. The *sistrum* was a sort of musical instrument. Cf. Fig. 73.

94. Vel, *even.*

Abnego, *deny*—i. e., disclaim knowledge of.

96. Sunt tanti—i. e., are not too much to pay (for wealth).

97. Ladas, a famous runner at the Olympic games.

Anticyra was a town noted for hellebore, which was considered a specific for madness. Cf. Hor., A. P. 300.

98. Archigene. Archigenes was a specialist in mental disorders.

99. Esuriens, the olive branch brings fame but no food.

Pisaeae, the Olympic games were held near Pisa, in Elis.

100. Ut, *although.*

107. Ad delubra vocantem—i. e., to hear his oath. So eager is he to take the false oath, that he hurries on before you, and is even ready to insist on your going.

109. Superest, *supports.*

110. Fiducia is contrasted with *audacia.*

Mimum. *Mimus* may mean the play-writer, the play itself, or a single *rôle* in the play.

111. Catulli. Cf. VIII, 186.

112. Stentora, the Greek herald whose voice was equal to that of fifty men.

113. Gradivus Homericus | Mars, as Homer says, shouted as loudly as ten thousand men (Il. V, 859).

116. Carbone tuo—i. e., *on thy altar.*

Charta soluta refers to the paper parcel in which the incense was brought.

118. Omenta, *entrails.*

Fig 73.—Isis with the sistrum.

14

119. Vagelli, unknown.

120. Hear what a plain man, no philosopher, can say for your comfort.

121. Et qui, *even he who.*

122. Tunica. The Cynics wore a heavy cloak and no tunic.

125. Your case, however, is simple, and may be intrusted to a mere tyro. **Philippi.** Probably some physician of little reputation.

132. Vestem diducere summam, *to tear (only) the upper part of his garment.*

135. Fora, *courts.*

136. If, after their agreements have been read over and over (*deciens* seems to be used for any large number) by the other side (i. e., by their opponents).

137. They, whom their own signature (*littera*) and best sardonyx seal (*gemma*) convict, assert that the writing of the invalid (*supervacui*) tablet is not binding.

140. O delicias, *my dear fellow.*

141. Quia tu, etc. ; because you, forsooth, are of an exceptional breed !

145. Conductum, *hired.*

Sulpure atque dolo, one idea.

146. Primos cum, etc., a proof that the house was set on fire.

148. Adorandae robiginis, genitive of characteristic. *Robigo = rust,* and thus *antiquity.*

152. Bratteolam, one of the leaves or plates of gold with which the statue was overlaid.

155. Deducendum—i. e., one that ought to be thrown.

Cum quo, etc. Cf. VIII, 214, note.

157. Quota pars, *how small a part !* Cf. III, 61, *quota portio.*

Gallicus. Rutilius Gallicus was *praefectus urbi* in the time of Domitian.

162. Tumidum guttur, goitre, a common disease in the Alps.

165. *Which twists its tufts in damp curl*—i. e., the hair twisted into wet, curly tufts.

Fig. 74.—Pygmies and cranes.

167. Thracum volucres—i. e., cranes ; their contests with the pygmies are mentioned by Homer, Il. III, 3 ff. Cf. Fig. 74.

168. The tradition concerning a race of pygmies, like other popular traditions, seems to have had a certain basis in fact. Recent investigations seem to prove the existence in Africa of a race of fully developed human beings whose stature does not exceed four feet. Juvenal's disbelief in the canal at Mount Athos has been shown to have been unfounded (cf. X, 174), and it may be that the much-ridiculed story of Hannibal's use of heated vinegar to soften the rocks in his passage of the Alps (cf. X, 153 ; Livy XXI, 37) is not so absurd, after all.

176. Nostro arbitrio, *as we choose.*

179. Invidiosa, *odious.*

Minimus sanguis, *a drop of blood.*

180. Vindicta, *revenge.*

Bonum, substantive in the predicate.

181. Indocti, supply *dicunt.*

184. Chrysippus, etc. Philosophers such as these will teach you that revenge is ignoble.

185. Senex, Socrates.

187. Plurima vitia. *Vitia* are faults of nature, *errores* faults of practice.

Felix is used as a masculine substantive = *sapiens.*

Fig. 75.—Flagellum.

190. Voluptas is in the predicate.

191. Continuo, *straightway, unhesitatingly.*

194. Attonitos, *terrified.*

Surdo verbere, *the unheard blow,* so **occultum flagellum,** *the unseen lash.*

195. Tortore is in apposition with *animo,* which is in the ablative absolute with *quatiente.*

Flagellum. Cf. Fig. 75.

197. Caedicius is said to have been a cruel judge in the time of Nero.

Rhadamanthus with Minos and Aeacus gave judgment in the lower world. Cf. I, 10.

199 ff. This story of Glaucus is told by Herodotus, VI, 86. He wanted to keep from the sons money entrusted to him by their father, and consulted the oracle as to the probable effect.

204. Moribus, *principle.*

205. Adyti, *of the sanctuary.*

206. Extinctus—i. e., his destruction with that of his whole race proved, etc. *Extinctus* is the participle.

207. Quamvis longa, *however far removed.*

210. Cedo (an old imperative form), *come, tell me* (what penalties he incurs).

212. Ut morbo—i. e., as if he were ill.

213. Cibo, ablative absolute with *crescente.*

Sed, *but even.*

214. Albani senectus—i. e., old Alban wine.

215. Densissima ruga, cf. *densissima lectica.* I, 120.

216. Acri Falerno. The Falernian wine was sharp, and was usually mixed with honey.

221. **Imago,** *apparition*, called *sacra*, because connected with the idea of an avenging deity.

224. **Primo quoque,** *the very first.*

228. **Velut hoc dilata sereno,** *as if but deferred by this clear weather.*

229. **Vigili cum febre,** *with sleepless fever.*

233. **Balantem,** *bleating.*

234. **Nocentibus** = *noxiis, criminals.*

236. **Malorum,** masculine.

237. **Superest,** cf. line 109, note.

239. **Ad mores damnatos,** to the practices condemned by conscience.

242. **Attrita,** *hardened.*

244. **Dabit,** etc., *will step into the snare*—i. e., will be caught.

245. **Uncum,** cf. X, 66, *Seianus ducitur unco.*

246. **Rupem scopulosque;** cf. I, 73.

248. **Nominis** is used for the man himself.

Laetus, *with joy.*

249. **Tiresian** = *caecum*, for Tiresias was the blind prophet of Thebes.

SATIRE XIV.

THE EFFECT OF EVIL EXAMPLE.

INTRODUCTION.—Parents often unconsciously teach their children to be gamblers or gluttons. Can Rutilus, who treats his slaves with cruelty, expect his son to be humane? It is easier to teach vice than virtue. Reverence the innocence of childhood, else you will have no right to censure your son's faults when he grows up. Will you not make as great efforts to keep your home pure for the sake of your child as you make to keep it clean for the sake of your guests? Children, like birds, show their training in after-life. Cretonius is extravagant, his son is still more so. Another man is tolerant of superstitions, his son becomes a fanatic. Most faults the young are ready to learn; avarice must be forced upon them, and, alas! it is but too often taught, first by little acts of meanness, then by greater ones. What folly is such avarice! In early times a little land was enough to support a family, now we must have more than that for a pleasure-garden. Hear the advice of the simple Samnite father. Now the father urges his son on in the race for wealth. The rising generation learns its lesson well, and is apt in forgery, even in murder. "I never taught him that," you say. No, but you planted the seed that produces such a harvest. The follies of the avaricious are more amusing than any drama. There are various forms of madness, and your indifference to danger in the pursuit of wealth is one. Then, too, what hard work you have to keep what you have gained! My advice is: Be content with little; if you begin to seek much you will end by wanting more.

1. **Fuscine,** unknown.

2. **Maculam haesuram,** *a lasting stain.*

5. **Bullatus.** Cf. V, 164 (Fig. 30);
XIII, 33.

Arma, *implements ;* cf. *armiger,* I, 92.

Fritillo, *dice-box.* Cf. Fig. 76.

7. **Radere tubera terrae,** *to peel truffles.*

8. **Eodem iure,** *in the same sauce* (as the mushrooms).

FIG. 76.—Fritillus.

9. **Mergere,** *to dip.*

Ficedulas, small birds, *beccaficoes.*

10. **Gula,** as well as *parente* (line 9), is ablative absolute with *monstrante.*

13. **Lauto—paratu.** The usual word is *apparatus ;* cf. Hor., Odes I, 38, 1, *Persicos odi puer apparatus.*

15. **Aequos,** almost = *indulgent.*

16. **Atque** connects *praecipit* and *putat ; Rutilus* is the subject of both. Bücheler's conjecture of *utque* here and *putet* in line 17 seems good.

Nostra materia—i. e., of the same material as ours.

17. **Putat** seems awkward; it must have something of the idea of *praecipit.*

20. **Antiphates,** etc.—i. e., *the dreaded tyrant of his household. Antiphates* was the fierce king of the Laestrygones. Hom., Od. X, 80.

22. Thievish slaves were branded on the forehead with the letter F (*fur*).

24. **Quem,** its antecedent is the subject of *suadet,* implied in *laetus.*

Inscripti, *branded slaves.* The *ergastulum* is the slaves' prison.

35. **Meliore luto,** *finer clay.*

Titan, Prometheus, who was often considered as the creator of man. Cf. IV, 133.

37. **Trahit,** its object is *reliquos.*

Orbita means the track made by the wheel. then *path, course.*

40. **Imitandis turpibus ac pravis,** ablative of specification.

41 f. Catiline has many imitators, Brutus and Cato none.

42. **Quocumque,** *any.*

Axe, *sky.* Cf. VIII, 116 ; *Gallicus axis.*

43. **Bruti avunculus,** Cato the Younger.

51. **Se dederit,** *shall show himself.* For *filius* in the next line we might expect *filium.*

53. **Omnia** does not modify *vestigia.*

54. **Corripies,** " *catch up,*" so *blame. reprove.*

55. **Tabulas mutare,** *to alter your will.*

56. Frontem may bc the brow of authority as Mr. Lewis translates it, but I think it means *impudence*, as usually. Cf. German *Stirne.* So too *forehead*, e. g., *With what forehead do you speak this to me?* Beaumont and Fletcher, Beggars' Bush, I, 2.

57. Vacuum cerebro, *empty of brains.*

58. Cucurbita, *cupping-glass*, so called from the likeness of its shape to that of a gourd (cf. Fig. 77). It is called *ventosa*, from the movement of the air as it is drawn out to form the vacuum. It was (and is) used in diseases of the brain to relieve the pressure of blood.

Quaerat, *is looking for*—i. e., *needs ;* subject is *caput.*

59 ff. You are anxious to have your home swept and garnished when guests are expected: have you no care that it should be morally pure in the eyes of your son?

59. Tuorum (*servorum*).

61. Arida, *dry, withered.*

Cum, preposition.

Tela, *web.*

67. Scobis, *sawdust.*

71. Si facis, if you bring it about.

74. Pullos, *her young.*

76. Sumptis pinnis—i. e., as soon as they can fly.

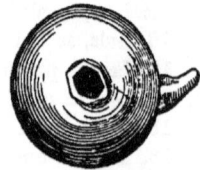

Fig. 77.—Cucurbita.

77. Relictis—i. e., having eaten such food, the vulture carries a portion of it back to her young ones. Of course, *crucibus* refers to the bodies of criminals.

79. Quoque, *also.*

81. Famulae Iovis, the eagle was the bird of Jupiter.

Generosae aves is simply another name for eagles.

82. Cubili, *the nest.*

86. Aedificator, cf. I, 94 ; *Quis totidem erexit villas?* X, 225 ; Hor. Epist. I, 1, 100.

Cretonius, the orthography of the name is doubtful. **Modo—nunc—nunc.**

87. Caietae (modern Gaeta), on the coast of southern Latium, a favorite place for villas.

Tiburis. Cf. III, 192 ; *proni Tiburis arce.*

88. Praenestinis. Cf. III, 190 ; *gelida Praeneste.*

89. Graecis marmoribus ; instrumental ablative. The principal sources of the supply of Greek marble, largely used by the Romans during the empire, were Hymettus, Pentelicus, and the island of Paros.

Longeque—i. e., from Numidia, Phrygia, and Egypt.

90. Fortunae ; there was a famous temple of Fortune at Praeneste.

Herculis. Martial mentions the temple of Hercules at Tibur.

91. Capitolia ; for the plural, cf. X, 65 ; *duc in Capitolia.*

Posides was a favorite freedman of Claudius.

95. The Roman villas were often very extensive; cf. Fig. 78.

96 ft. So, too, in religious matters; if the father has a leaning toward Jewish superstitions, the son becomes an actual convert.

97. I. e., no statues.

100. This was the chief complaint against the Jews at Rome, that they held themselves bound to obey the Jewish rather than the Roman laws. Some slight similarity may be seen in the alleged recognition by the Roman Catholics in the United States of the Church as a higher authority than the State.

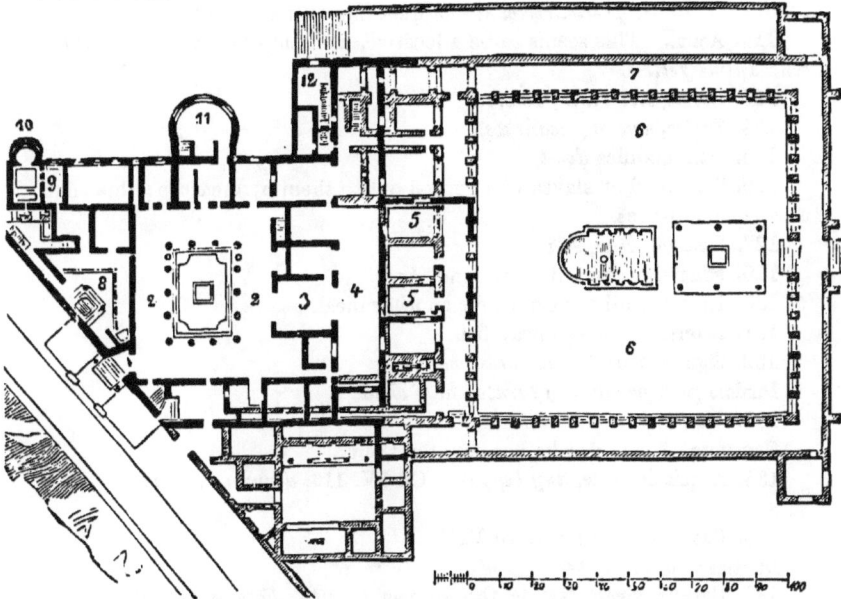

Fig 78.—Ground-plan of the so-called villa suburbana of Diomedes, at Pompeii. 1. Entrance ; 2. Peristylium ; 3. Tablinum ; 4. Gallery : 5. Occus ; 6. Court ; 7. Cryptoporticus ; 8. Court ; 9. Tepidarium ; 10. Calidarium ; 11. Sleeping-room ; 12. Staircase.

103. Monstrare and deducere (line 104) depend on some such word as *solent* implied in the preceding verbs.

Eadem sacra colenti—i. e., to one of their own sect. The reference is to the esoteric character of the Jewish teaching.

104. Quaesitum fontem—i. e., the fountain of truth.

105. In causa, a rare use, = *causa* (nominative).

Lux ignava, *a lazy day.*

106. Attigit. Most editors say that the subject is *pater ;* it seems to me that it is *septima quaeque lux.*

107. Sponte, *of their own accord.*

108. Quoque, *even*, modifies *inviti*.

109 ff. For avarice is called wise economy.

111. Nec dubie, *unhesitatingly*.

Frugi. Cf. III, 167, note.

114. Hesperidum serpens; the dragon that guarded the golden apples of the Hesperides.

Ponticus (*serpens*), the dragon that guarded the golden fleece.

117. Cf. Hor., Epist. I, 1, 65:

" *Rem facias, rem,*
Si possis, recte, si non quocumque modo rem."

119. Animi. This seems to be a locative, as in *aeger animi*, etc. Others read *animi felicis*.

122. Sectae, *sect*—i. e., *doctrine*.

124. Sordes, *acts of meanness*.

125. Mox modifies *docet*.

126. The food of slaves was served out to them by measure; this man uses false measures.

127. Sustinet, *bear, endure*.

129. Minutal, a minced compound, *hash*.

130. He saves all the scraps for another meal.

131. Lacerti, a coarse, cheap fish.

132. Signatam, *sealed up, preserved*.

Dimidio putrique siluro, *a tainted half shad*.

133. Fila, *shreds* or *slices*.

Numerata—i. e., after he has counted them.

134. Aliquis de ponte, *any beggar*. Cf. IV, 116, *dirusque a ponte satelles;* V, 8.

135. Quo = *quam ad rem*, so VIII, 9.

Divitias; supply *habes*.

137. Egentis vivere fato is the subject of *sit*. *Fato* is the ablative of manner, *egentis* supplying the place of the adjective.

142. Cf. Hor. Sat., II, 6, 8:

"*O ! si angulus ille*
Proximus accedat qui nunc denormat agellum."

144. Densa oliva, cf. *densissima lectica*, I, 120.

145. If you can not buy your neighbor's fields, you turn your cattle in among his growing corn.

146. Famelica (from *fames*), *starved*.

148. Novalia, *standing crops*. *Novale* originally means *newly-plowed*.

151. Venales fecerit, *has forced to be sold*.

152. Quam foede bucina famae, some verb, as *sonabit*, may be understood. *Fama = common report*.

153 ff. Quid nocet haec, etc. What does that harm me? I don't care a bean-shell for the applause of the whole county if I must gain it by reaping small harvests.

156. Scilicet, etc., is ironical.

160. Sub Tatio—i. e., in the times of early Rome.

161. Mox, *afterward.*

Fractis ac passis, indirect objects of *dabantur.*

162. Gladios Molossos, cf. XII, 108.

163. Tandem, *at last.*

Iugera bina, a little over an acre.

165. Meritis minor, *less than their deserts.*

Aut, etc., nor that their country had been ungrateful and broken faith with them.

167. Casae, *cottage.*

168. Unus vernula. A single slave-child, who played about the house with the master's children.

169. Fratribus dative.

170. Scrobe, *ditch.*

180. Marsus (cf. III, 169), **Hernicus, Vestinus.** These people all belonged to the Sabellian stock, famous for severity and simplicity.

182. Hoc—i. e., such a course.

183. Gratae post munus aristae, etc.—i. e., after the welcome gift of grain, men despised the acorns that had been their former food.

185. Fecisse for the tense, cf. Hor. Odes, I, 1, 4, *collegisse iuvat.*

186. Per glaciem, *through the winter.*

Perone, a rough boot.

187. Inversis—i. e., with the hair-side in.

188. Quaecumque est. *Purpura = fine clothing,* so he adds, *of any sort.*

189. Minoribus, *their children.*

191. Ceras, writing tablets, coated with wax. Cf. Fig. 4.

192. Rubras maiorum leges. The title at the head of the law was in red ink; hence the laws themselves were sometimes called *rubrica,* whence the English word *rubric.*

193. Vitem posce libello, *ask for the vine-staff (of the centurion,* cf. VIII, 247) *in a petition*—i. e., seek a centurion's commission.

194 f. But use your personal influence as well, and be sure that the officer in charge (*Laelius*) sees what a great rough fellow you are.

Buxo—i. e., the comb, made of box-wood.

195. Alas, *shoulders.*

196. Brigantum the Brigantes occupied the north of England.

197. Aquilam. The eagle was carried by the first centurion of the first cohort. Various forms of the standard are shown in Fig. 79.

199. Trepidum solvunt ventrem, seems to refer to a certain "gone" feeling sometimes produced by fear.

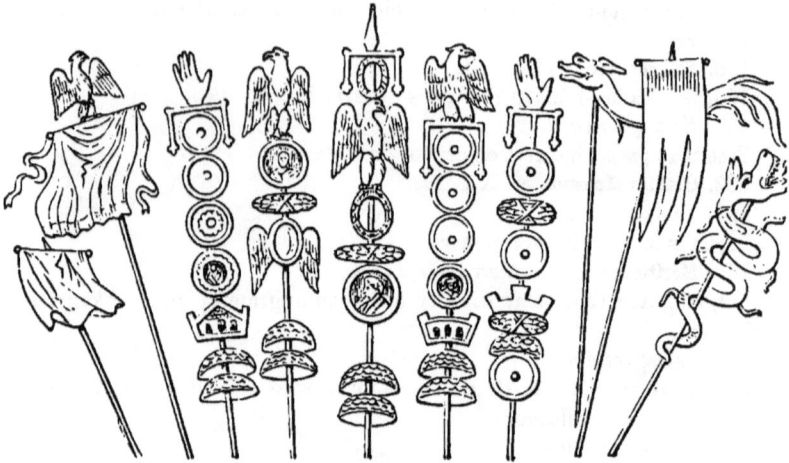

Fig. 79.—Roman standards.

201. Pluris dimidio, *at more by half.* The genitive *pluris* is probably used by analogy with such forms as *tanti, quanti,* which are really locative, but came to be considered as genitive. Cf. Roby, II, lvii ff.

202. Certain trades of a disagreeable sort (e. g., tanning) were relegated to the less thickly settled right bank of the Tiber.

206. Iove poeta. *Poeta* almost = *auctore.*

208. Assae, *nurses.* Cf. Hor., Epist. I, 4, 8.

212 ff. I. e., your son thus taught will outdo you as Ajax and Achilles surpassed their fathers.

Praesto, *I warrant.*

219. Exigua modifies *summa.*

220. Elatam, *borne out to burial.* She is sure to be murdered if her dowry makes it worth while.

223. Illi—i. e., *that son of yours.*

228. Producit, *educates.*

229. This line has no grammatical connection with the context, and is doubtless spurious. Weidner reads *conduplicandi.*

231. Quem refers directly to *curriculo,* which really represents the son—i. e., the *illi* of line 223.

232. Metis; the *metae* were the conical posts set up at each end of the *spina* or dividing wall in the circus. Cf. Fig. 80.

235. Stultum—i. e., *esse eum.*

237. Circumscribere, *to cheat.*

239. Quantus implies *tantus.*

Deciorum. Cf. VIII, 254; *plebeiae Deciorum animae.*

240. Si Graecia vera, *if Greece tells the truth.* Cf. X, 174; *Graecia mendax.*

Menoeceus is said to have given his life for Thebes.

241. Quorum—i. e., *Thebanorum.* The Thebans sprang from the dragon's teeth sown by Cadmus. Cf. Ovid, Metaph. III, 104 ff.

247. Alumnus, originally a participle from *alo.*

248. Mathematicis, dative.

249. Colus, acc. pl. fem.

251. Cervinaı the stag, like the crow, was proverbial for long life.

252. Archigenen. Cf. XIII, 97 ; *si non eget Archigene.*

Mithridates was said to have compounded a very efficacious antidote to poisons, and to have taken so much of it that when he wanted to poison himself he could not.

253. Aliam decerpere ficum—i. e., to see another autumn.

254. Medicamen—i. e., as preventive antidote.

257. Aequare, *compare.*

258. Quanto capitis discrimine, *what danger of life.*

260. Fiscus is here used in a general sense for money.

Ad vigilem Castora. The temple of Castor was used as a safe-deposit building.

261. Ex quo, *since.* The temple of Mars seems to have been either robbed or burned.

FIG. 80.—Circus Maximus at Rome.

262 f. Florae, Cereris, Cybeles. The games referred to, accompanied by dramatic representations, occurred on the following dates: The *Floralia*, April 28-May 3; the *Cerealia*, April 12-19; the *Megalesia* (cf. XI, 193), April 3-10.

265 ff. Your struggles to gain wealth are as amusing as those of a gymnast.

265. Petauro. The *petaurus* was probably some sort of a spring-board.

266. Rectum funem, *tight-rope.* Cf. Fig. 14.

267. Corycia. Corycus was a promontory in Cilicia, famous for saffron, which seems to be meant by *sacci olentis* (line 269).

268. Tollendus, *tossed about.*

269. Perditus, *desperate, reckless.*

270. Pingue passum, *rich raisin-wine.*

271. Municipes Iovis; Jupiter was said to have been born in Crete. According to another legend, he was hidden in a cave on Mount Ida in that island. Cf. XIII, 41; *Idaeis Iuppiter antris.*

272. Hic, the rope-dancer.

Ancipiti planta, *doubtful, hesitating foot.*

273. Brumamque famemque are the objects of *cavet.*

276. Plus hominum, *the greater part of mankind.*

278. Carpathium. Carpathos was an island between Crete and Rhodes.
Gaetula, used for the African coast.

279. Calpe, Gibraltar.

280. Herculeo gurgite—i. e., the Atlantic Ocean, where it was thought the sun sank beneath the waves and hissed as it sank.

281. Tenso folle, *with full purse.*

282. Aluta, *money-bag.*

283. Iuvenes marinos—i. e., the mermen.

284 ff. Madness does not always show itself in the same way: Orestes fancies he sees the Eumenides, Ajax thinks he hears Agamemnon and Ulysses; so a man may need a keeper even though he does not tear his clothes.

289. Tabula (cf. XII, 58; *dolato ligno*) is ablative of instrument; **unda** ablative of separation.

291. A contemptuous description of money.

294. Fascia nigra, *black belt* (of clouds).

295. Aestivum tonat; it is only summer thunder.

297. He swims with his right hand and holds his girdle (*zonam*), containing his money, in his left hand and his teeth.

298. Modo, *just now*—i. e., a few hours ago.

Suffecerat; notice the tense.

299. Tagus. Cf. III, 55; *omnis harena Tagi.*

Pactolus, in Lydia; like the Tagus, it was supposed to have gold in the sand of its bed.

300. Sufficient; *ei* is understood as indirect object, the subject is *panni.*

302. Picta tempestate. Cf. XII, 27, note. A rude picture of the shipwreck was carried about to excite pity.

305. Amis, *fire-buckets.*

306. Licinus. Cf. I, 109; *possideo plus Pallante et Licinis.*

Attonitus, *anxious.*

307. Electro, *amber.*

308. Testudine. Cf. XI, 94; *qualis testudo nataret.*　　　　.

Dolia, *jars* (made of clay). They were sometimes very large, having a capacity of several barrels. Fragments three inches thick have been found at Antium. Diogenes, the Cynic, is said to have used a *dolium* as a house. When Alexander the Great saw him he pitied his poverty and told him to express some wish that he might grant it. Diogenes asked only that the great ruler would stand out of his light.

Nudi; perhaps because the Cynics did not wear the tunic. Cf. XIII, 122; *a Cynicis tunica distantia.*

310. Plumbo commissa, *patched up with lead.*

311. Illa refers, as often, to something well known.

315. This line occurs X, 365.

318. In quantum; for the usual prose construction *quantum;* cf. English, *to ask a reward,* and *to ask for a reward.*

319. Epicurus is said to have gathered his scholars about him in his garden; the Epicurean school of philosophy is sometimes called "the Garden," as the Stoic is called "the Porch." Cf. XIII, 120 ff.

320. Ante, temporal adverb. Socrates died 399 B. c., Epicurus 270 B. c.

321. Nature and true philosophy always teach the same lesson.

322. Te cludere, *to hem you in.*

323. Effice, *procure.*

324. Bis septem ordinibus—i. e., for the knights, who occupied the first fourteen rows of seats in the theatre, in accordance with the law of Otho, passed 65 B. c. Cf. Hor. Epist. 1, 1, 67.

Dignatur, *thinks fitting.*

325. If you frown and pout at this.

326. Duos equites—i. e., two equestrian fortunes.

329. Narcissi. The favorite freedman of Claudius. His wealth was proverbial. He gained such control of his imperial master, that Claudius had Messalina put to death at his bidding.

SATIRE XV.

A CASE OF CANNIBALISM.

INTRODUCTION.—The superstitions of the Egyptians are well known; they revere certain animals and abstain from certain vegetables, but they eat human flesh. When Ulysses told his stories of cannibals, they were thought incredible, but I have such a tale of recent times. Ombi and Tentyra were waging a religious war. The Ombites were attacked in the midst of a festival by their enemies; first their fists were their weapons, then they hurled such stones as the weak muscles of the present race of men can lift, then swords and arrows are used. One man as he falls in flight is seized and his flesh devoured. True, the Vascones ate human flesh when a long siege had brought famine, but that was before the philosophy of Zeno had taught men that some things are worse than even death. Other peoples of whom like tales are told had excuse, but this Egyptian tribe had none. Nature teaches men mercy and pity, thus they are distinguished from the beasts. This common sympathy holds peoples together, but now it seems that men may be more cruel than the beasts themselves. What would Pythagoras have said to such a tale?

1. **Volusi,** unknown.
2. **Crocodilon.** Cicero, de Nat. Deor. I, 36, mentions the crocodile among the objects of Egyptian animal-worship; he says of the ibis, "*Ibes maximam vim serpentium conficiunt.*"
4. **Cercopitheci,** *long-tailed ape.*
5. **Dimidio Memnone.** The Greeks related that music proceeded from the colossal statue of Memnon at sunrise. For *dimidio,* cf. VIII, 4.
6. **Thebe,** nom. sing. The usual form is *Thebae.*
Centum portis; ablative of characteristic.
7. **Aeluros,** *cats.* I have not ventured to change the text, but am strongly inclined to think that the reading of the MSS. *caeruleos* (= *sea-fish*) [P. has *aeruleos*] is correct.
9. **Caepe,** *onion.*
15. **Alcinoo.** When Ulysses was telling his adventures at the court of Alcinous, king of the Phaeacians, and described the cannibal Laestrygones and Cyclopes, some of his hearers declared they were ready to believe all his other adventures more readily than these.
16. **Moverat**—i. e., *had roused,* even while he was speaking.
Aretalogus, used of a degenerate, parasitic philosopher, it came to mean *boaster, babbler.*
19. **Concurrentia,** *clashing.*

20. Cyaneis (*fluctibus*) is probably dative. The Cyaneae were islands in the Bosporus.

21. Percussum agrees with *Elpenora*.

Circes, genitive.

22. Some of Ulysses's companions were changed to swine by the wand of Circe.

24. Minimum temetum, *very little wine.*

27. Nuper consule Iunco. Iuncus was consul 127 A. D.

28. Super, *above*—i. e., higher up the river.

Copti. Coptos was near the Nile, about ten miles north of Thebes.

29. Cothurnis—i. e., than the terrible deeds of the tragic drama. Cf. Fig. 83.

30. A Pyrrha—i. e., from the time of the flood. Cf. I, 81, note.

Syrmata, *tragic robes* = tragedies.

33. Finitimos, *neighbors ;* but Ombi and Tentyra were about one hundred miles apart. Perhaps Juvenal made a mistake, and perhaps he did not intend to be exact.

Simultas, *feud.*

36. Volgo, dative.

40. Primoribus ac ducibus, dative.

42. Sentirent, subject is *their neighbors.*

43. Pervigili toro. Cf. VIII, 158, and Fig. 8.

Quem ; its antecedent is *toro.*

44. Horrida sane, etc. These lines are authority for the statement that Juvenal had visited Egypt.

46. Barbara turba, *the barbarian horde—* i. e., the Egyptians in general.

Fig. 81.—Tibicen.

Canopo, a town at the mouth of the Nile, famous for dissolute luxury.

47. Adde connects what follows with line 40.

48. Blaesis, properly used of persons that lisp, applies here to those whose utterance was thick from intoxication.

Inde, *among the one people ;* **Hinc** (line 51), *among the other.*

49. Tibicine. Cf. Fig. 81.

52. Tuba = *signal,* so *beginning.* Cf. I, 169.

54. Malae, *cheeks.*

55. Vix cuiquam aut nulli, *scarcely any one,* or (rather) *no one.*

57. Alias—i. e., *changed, unrecognizable.*

60. Calcent. Why not indicative ?

61. Quo, *to what purpose.*

63. Inclinatis lacertis—i. e., *stooping down.*

65. Turnus et Aiax ; these ancient heroes hurled mighty rocks.

66. Tydides, Diomedes.

72. A deverticulo, *after this digression.*

73. Aucti and pars altera refer to the same party—i. e., the Ombites.

75. Praestant, its subject is *ii*, to be supplied as the antecedent of *qui* in line 76.

82. Veribus, *spits.*

Usque adeo, *so very.*

84. Hic, adverb.

86. Te—i. e., Volusius; others make it refer to the fire.

88. Sustinuit. Cf. English, "I can not *bear* to do it," and XIV, 127.

90. Prima gula, *the first palate*—i. e., the first one that tasted the dreadful food.

93. Vascones, the Basques. The inhabitants of Calagurris were reduced by famine to cannibalism.

94. Produxere animas = *produxere vitam.*

95. Bellorum ultima, *the extremities of war.*

Casus extremi, *the climax of misfortune.*

97. Huius, *such.*

Quod nunc agitur—i. e., when men are driven to it by famine. The antecedent of *quod* is *exemplum ; agere* means *to treat of.*

98. Sicut, *as, for instance.*

Mihi, dative of apparent agent.

Gens, subject of *lacerabant.*

100. Hostibus—miserantibus, ablative absolute.

102. Esse, from *edo.*

104. Urbibus; this seems to be the reading of the best MS., and is certainly better than *viribus* or *ventribus.*

105. Quibus = *iis quibus.*

108. Sed Cantaber, etc.—i. e., how can we expect Zeno's stern philosophy from the Cantabrians, especially in ancient times?

109. Metelli. Q. Metellus Pius fought against Sertorius in Spain.

110 ff. In these times culture extends over the whole world.

110. Nostras Athenas = *Romam.*

112. Thyle stands for the northern limit of the world.

113. Nobilis ille populus—i. e., Calagurris.

114. Zacynthos (commonly *Saguntum*), a town in Spain, the attack upon which by Hannibal was the ostensible cause of the second Punic war.

115. Tale, *habet* must be understood; its subject as well as that of *excusat* is *populus-et-Zacynthos.*

Excusat = *allege in excuse.*

Maeotide ara. Diana had an altar in the Tauric Chersonese, on which shipwrecked strangers were sacrificed.

117. Ut iam—credas. Cf. XIV, 240; X, 174.

Carmina is nominative.

119. Modo is variously explained. I think it is temporal *=just now*.

120. Hos, the Egyptians.

122. Terra Memphitide sicca—i. e., if the land of Memphis were oppressed with drought.

123. Invidiam, *insult.* Could they offer greater insult to the Nile under the greatest provocation than to commit such a crime?

Fig. 82.—Phaselus.

124. Qua—i. e., *rabie.*

125. Sauromatae and **Agathyrsi,** Scythian tribes.

127. Fictilibus phaselis. Some of the Egyptian boats were made of a sort of clay ; were shaped like a bean (*phaselus,* cf. Figs. 82 and 83), and gaudily painted.

128. Pictae testae, used contemptuously of such a boat as those described above.

134. Causam dicentis, *pleading his case. Squalorem* refers to the custom of a defendant putting on a mourning garment. With this reading *amici* and *rei* both depend on *squalorem.* Others with less authority read *casum lugentis.*

136. Circumscriptorem, a technical term for an unfaithful guardian. Cf. XIV, 237.

Cuius, antecedent is *pupillum.*

137. Puellares capilli. Boys wore their hair long until they put on the *toga virilis.*

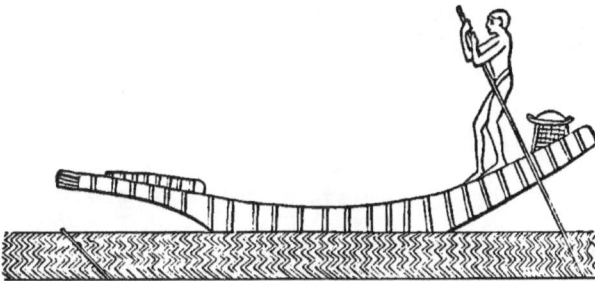

Fig. 83.—Egyptian phaselus.

Incerta ; the boy is so young that his long hair makes him look like a girl.

140. Minor igne rogi, *too small for the funeral pyre.* The bodies of very young children were buried not burned. For the construction, cf. *lectus Procula minor,* III, 203.

Face dignus arcana. In the Eleusinian mysteries there was a procession with torches.

15

141. *Such as the priest of Ceres wishes him to be*—i. e., pure and good.

142. Aliena sibi, *foreign, of no interest to him;* so *Terence Haut.* 77, *humani nil a me alienum puto.*

143. Venerabile may mean *"reverential"* (Macleane), but there seems little authority for the use.

Soli, *we* (i. e., men) *alone.*

147. Cuius, its antecedent is *sensum.*

Prona, etc.—i. e., *beasts.*

149. Animas—animum. *Anima = life; animus = intellect.*

152. Proavis, dative of apparent agent.

156. Nutantem, *staggering.*

157. Defendier, archaic form of the infinitive *defendi.*

159. But men have less kindliness toward each other than the brutes themselves.

160. Cf. Hor. Epod. VII, 11.

164. Convenit, impersonal.

Ursis, dative.

165. Ferrum letale, *death-dealing weapon.*

166. Parum est, *it is not enough.*

Cum, *although.*

167. Coquere, *to forge.*

168. Extendere, has about the force of *producere* above.

171. Crediderint. Weidner says that *sed crediderint* seems to stand for *sed qui crediderint.*

173. Pythagoras was a strict vegetarian.

174. Indulsit, *permitted.*

SATIRE XVI.

THE ADVANTAGES OF MILITARY LIFE.

INTRODUCTION.—Great are the prizes of the soldier that is born under a lucky star. He may beat his civilian enemy without fear of justice, for, though the centurion may hear the complaint, his fellow-soldiers will see to it that their comrade's accuser is made to smart for his temerity. Then, too, it is easier to find men that will give false witness in a civil court than those that will witness to the truth against a soldier. Civilians must wait the law's delay; the soldier's case is speedily tried. Another of his advantages is that he may dispose of his own property without his father's control, so that a rich soldier may have his own father for a legacy-hunter. His promotion, too, is in accordance with his deserts, for it is the general's interest that the bravest be advanced.

1. **Galli,** some unknown friend of Juvenal.
2. **Subeuntur,** *subire* = *enter.*
Castra. Cf. Figs. 84 and 85.
3. **Excipiat,** optative subjunctive.
Secundo sidere = *under favorable auspices.*
6. **Genetrix,** Juno had a temple at Samos.
8. **Ne,** *quod non* would be more usual.
Togatus, *civilian.*
10. **Excussos—dentes.** Cf. III, 301.
11. **Offam,** *a bruise.*
12. **Medico nil promittente**—i. e., the physician gives no assurance of recovery.
Relictum modifies *oculum.*
13. **Bardaicus iudex,** etc. If a civilian seeks redress against a soldier, he

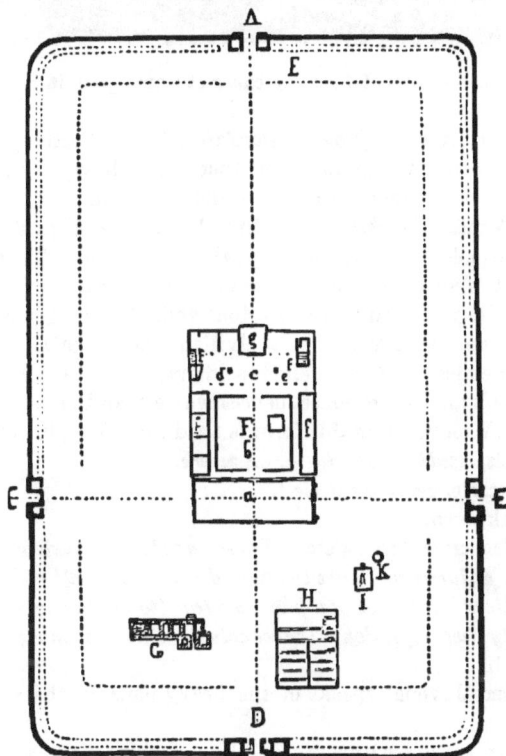

FIG. 84.—Plan of Roman fortified camp. A. Porta praetoria; D. Porta decumana;
F. Praetorium.

Fig. 85.—Ruins of a Roman camp at Gamzigrad, in Servia.

has a rough centurion for judge. *Bardaicus* is an adjective, said to be derived from *Bardaei,* an Illyrian people that used a heavy, coarse boot.

14. **Grandes,** etc., refers to the size of the centurion.

15. **More Camilli,** L. Furius Camillus during the siege of Veii (405–396 B. c.) kept the soldiers under arms all the year round. There is no historical account of such a special rule as is here referred to.

17. It is quite just then that centurions should be judges where soldiers are concerned, and doubtless I, as a civilian, shall receive redress; but I shall make enemies of all his fellow-soldiers, and they will see to it that the revenge I obtain brings consequences worse than the original harm.

20. **Chors;** Weidner says this form is used for *cohors,* in contempt.

21. **Curabilis,** *needing remedy*—i. e., *severe.*

23. **Mulino corde,** *asinine intellect.*

Vagelli, unknown.

24. **Cum duo crura habeas,** etc. These words are variously explained: *With all your injuries you have two sound legs left, don't risk them against so many soldiers' boots;* or *you have two legs* (*to run away with*); or *since you have only two legs, don't try conclusions with so many.* I think the last is preferable.

25. **Clavorum,** Juvenal speaks of the heavy nails in the soldiers' boots, III, 248.

Quis, etc.—i. e., as a witness.

Procul must be ironical, for the Praetorian camp which seems to be meant was close to the city. Cf. V, 153, note.

26. Pylades. The friendship between Pylades and Orestes was proverbial, like that between Damon and Pythias.

29. Da testem, *produce your witness;* so III, 137.

31. Dignum, etc.—i. e., phenomenally brave and loyal. The ancient Romans wore beard and hair long; cf. *capillato consule,* V, 30.

33. Paganum, *villager* and so *civilian.*

34. Pudorem, *honor, good name.*

35 ff. The soldier has another advantage in that his lawsuit is settled quickly, while that of a civilian is drawn out by tedious delays.

36. Sacramentorum almost = *militum.* The *sacramentum* was the oath of allegiance taken by the soldier.

38. Sacrum saxum, *the boundary stone.*

39. I. e., where I have sacrificed every year, at the feast of the *Terminalia,* on the 23d of February.

40. Pergit non reddere, *insists upon not returning.*

41. Cf. XIII. 137.

42. Qui lites inchoet, *which begins the lawsuits of a whole people*—i. e., a civilian's suit must wait a whole year before it is even reached on the docket.

44. Subsellia, *judicial benches,* cf. l. 14.

Tantum sternuntur, *are only spread* with coverings—i. e., not actually used.

47. Lenta fori harena, *the tedious arena of the court.*

48. Balteus, *sword-belt.* Cf. Fig. 86.

50. Sufflamine, *drag-chain.* Cf. VIII, 148, *rotam astringit sufflamine.*

FIG. 86.—Soldier wearing the balteus.

51. The soldier is also free from some forms of the *patria potestas*—e. g., he may dispose of his own property even during the lifetime of his father.

53. Placuit, *it has been decided.* **Census,** *property;* genitive.

56. Captat, *pays court to.* Cf. X, 202. **Hunc** refers to Coranus.

Favor. The MSS. all have *labor,* but it seems inexplicable. *Favor* is Ruperti's conjecture. *Favor aequus* is *the favor he has earned.*

57. Et pulchro, etc., seems to mean, *makes his toil sweet by giving it its deserved rewards.*

58. Referre (with the genitive), *to be advantageous to.*

60. Phaleris; *phalera* seems to have been used for a necklace as well as for a part of the ornamental trappings of the war-horse. Cf. Fig. 61.

Torquibus, a gold collar, or neck-chain. Cf. Fig. 41.

The fragment ends abruptly; the last sentence is incomplete.

LIST OF PASSAGES IN WHICH THE PRESENT EDITION DIFFERS FROM BÜCHELER'S TEXT.

			B.
I.	122.	praegnans	praegnas
III.	38.	et cur non omnia?	et cur non ? omnia
	218.	Phaecasiatorum	Haec Asianorum
IV.	67.	saginae	sagina
V.	38.	berullo	berullos
	39.	phialas	phiala
	42.	illic	illi
	116.	fumat	spumat
	169.	iacetis	tacetis
VII.	16.	Gallia	gallica
	40.	maculosas	Maculonis
	114.	Lacernae	Lacertae
	121.	lagonae,	lagonae.
	134.	stlataria	stlattaria
	136.	illis	illi
	159.	laevae	laeva
	165.	quod	quid
	198.	fies	fiet
VIII.	68.	primum	privum
	90.	regum	rerum
	112.	nam	iam
	162.	Cyanis	Cyane
	176.	Galli	galli
	207.	credamus tunicae	credamus, tunicae
	234.	Bracatorum	bracatorum
	239.	gente	monte
X.	54.	vel	quae
	150.	altosque	aliosque
	193.	pendentisque	pendentesque

			B.
XI.	55.	effugientem	et fugientem
	57.	vel	nec
XII.	32.	arbori	arboris
	116.	et	aut
XIII.	65.	miranti	mirandis
	224.	exanimes	exanimis
XIV.	16.	atque	utque
	17.	putat	putet
	24.	inscripti, ergastula	inscripta, ergastula
	47.	reverentia. Si quid-ne	reverentia, si quid-nec
	119.	felices	felicis
	152.	foede	foedae
	217.	longi	longae
	254.	rosas. Medicamen	rosas, medicamen
	296.	cadit	cadet
XV.	75.	praestant, instantibus Ombis	praestantibus omnibus instans

INDEX OF PROPER NAMES.

ALPHABETICAL LIST OF OBJECTS ILLUSTRATED.

16

THE END.

STANDARD LATIN SERIES.

Harkness's Standard Latin Grammar.
"The most complete, philosophical, and attractive Grammar evei written." Adapted to all grades. 12mo. Introduction price, $1.12.

Harkness's New Latin Reader.
Especially adapted for use with the "Standard Latin Grammar." 12mo. Introduction price, 87 cents.

Harkness's Complete Course in Latin for the First Year.
Comprising an Outline of Latin Grammar and Progressive Exercises in Reading and Writing Latin, with Frequent Practice in Reading at Sight. Designed to serve as a complete introductory book in Latin—no grammar being required. 12mo. Introduction price, $1.12.

Harkness's Cæsar's Commentaries.
New Pictorial Edition. With full Dictionary, Life of Cæsar, Map of Gaul, Plans of Battles, Outline of the Roman Military System, etc., and Notes to the author's Standard Latin Grammar. Containing numerous colored plates, showing the movements of armies, military uniforms, arms, standards, etc., which, in point of beauty, are superior to any edition of Cæsar yet published. 12mo. Introduction price, $1.20.

Harkness's Cicero's Orations.
With full Notes, Vocabulary, etc. 12mo. Introduction price, $1.22.

Harkness's Course of Latin Prose Authors.
New Pictorial Edition. With full Notes and Dictionary. The work contains four books of "Cæsar's Commentaries," the "Catiline" of Sallust, and eight of Cicero's Orations. 12mo. Introduction price, $1.40.

Frieze's Editions of Vergil.
THE ÆNEID, with Notes only. 12mo. $1.40.
THE ÆNEID, with Notes and Dictionary. 12mo. $1.30.
SIX BOOKS OF THE ÆNEID, GEORGICS, AND BUCOLICS, with Notes and Dictionary. 12mo. $1.30.
VERGIL COMPLETE, with Notes and Dictionary. 12mo. $1.60.

Sallust's Jugurthine War with full Explanatory Notes,
References to Harkness's Standard Latin Grammar, and a copious Latin-English Dictionary. By CHARLES GEORGE HERBERMAN. 12mo. Introduction price, $1.12.

(SEE NEXT PAGE.)

Cornelius Nepos.

Prepared expressly for the Use of Students Learning to Read at Sight. With Notes, Vocabulary, Index of Proper Names, and Exercises for Translation into Latin. Illustrated by numerous Cuts. By THOMAS B. LINDSAY, Ph. D., Professor of Latin in the Boston University. 12mo. Introduction price, $1.22.

THE SAME, for Sight-Reading in Schools and Colleges, with English-Latin Exercises and Index of Proper Names. By THOMAS B. LINDSAY. 12mo. Introduction price, $1.00.

Selections from the Poems of Ovid.

With Notes. By J. L. LINCOLN, LL. D., Professor of Latin in Brown University. The text is very carefully annotated and references made to Harkness's Standard Grammar. 12mo. Introduction price, $1.00.

THE SAME. With Notes and Vocabulary. 12mo. Introduction price, $1.22.

Livy.

Selections from the First Five Books, together with the Twenty-first and Twenty-second Books entire; with a Plan of Rome, a Map of the Passage of Hannibal, and English Notes for the Use of Schools. By J. L. LINCOLN, LL. D. 12mo. Introduction price, $1.22.

Horace.

With English Notes, for the Use of Schools and Colleges. By J. L. LINCOLN, LL. D. 12mo. Introduction price, $1.22.

Sallust's Jugurtha and Catiline.

With Notes and a Vocabulary. By NOBLE BUTLER and MINARD STURGUS. 12mo. Introduction price, $1.22.

Germania and Agricola of Tacitus.

With Notes, for Colleges. By W. S. TYLER, Professor of the Greek and Latin Languages in Amherst College. 12mo. Introduction price, 87 cents.

Mailed, post-paid, for examination, at introduction prices. Send for full descriptive circulars.

AMERICAN BOOK COMPANY, Publishers,

NEW YORK, · : · CINCINNATI, · : · CHICAGO.

STANDARD GREEK TEXTS.

Xenophon's Anabasis: with Explanatory Notes for Use of Schools and Colleges in the United States. By JAMES R. BOISE, Ph. D. (Tübingen), LL. D., Professor in the Theological Seminary at Morgan Park, Illinois. 12mo. 393 pages. Introduction price, $1.40.

The First Four Books of Xenophon's Anabasis: with Explanatory Notes with grammatical references to Hadley-Allen's, Goodwin's, and other Greek Grammars; a copious Greek-English Vocabulary; and Kiepert's Map of the Route of the Ten Thousand. By JAMES R. BOISE. 12mo. 451 pages. Introduction price, $1.32.

This work takes the place of the *Three Book* and *Five Book* editions of the Anabasis heretofore published.

THE SAME. Without Vocabulary. 12mo. 324 pages. Introduction price, $1.08.

The First Three Books of Homer's Iliad, according to the Text of Dindorf; with Revised Notes, Critical and Explanatory, and References to Hadley-Allen's, Crosby's, and Goodwin's Greek Grammars. By HENRY CLARK JOHNSON, A. M., LL. B. 12mo. 180 pages. Introduction price, $1.12.

THE SAME. With Vocabulary. 12mo. Introduction price, $1.32.

Selections from Herodotus: comprising mainly such Portions as give a Connected History of the East, to the Fall of Babylon and the Death of Cyrus the Great. By HERMAN M. JOHNSON, D. D., Professor of Philosophy and English Literature in Dickinson College. 12mo. 185 pages. Introduction price, $1.05.

The Œdipus Tyrannus of Sophocles; with English Notes. By HOWARD CROSBY, D. D., formerly Professor of Greek Language and Literature in Rutgers College, and Professor in the University of the City of New York. Revised edition, with Notes to Hadley-Allen's and Goodwin's Greek Grammars. 12mo. Introduction price, $1.05.

The Greek Prepositions, Studied from their Original Meanings as Designations of Space. By F. A. ADAMS, Ph. D. A short but comprehensive treatise on the meanings of the verbs as compounded with the prepositions. 12mo. 131 pages. Introduction price, 60 cents.

Specimen copies of the above books, for examination, will be sent, postpaid, to teachers of Greek, on receipt of introduction price.

AMERICAN BOOK COMPANY, Publishers,

NEW YORK, · : · CINCINNATI, · : · CHICAGO.

BY

ALBERT HARKNESS, Ph. D., LL. D.

A Complete Latin Course for the First Year.

Progressive Exercises in Reading and Writing Latin, with Frequent Practice in Reading at Sight.

An Introductory Latin Book. 12mo.

A Latin Grammar. Edition of 1874. 12mo.

A Latin Grammar. Standard edition of 1881. 12mo.

The Elements of Latin Grammar. 12mo.

A New Latin Reader. 12mo.

A Latin Reader. 12mo.

A Latin Reader. With Exercises in Latin Composition. 12mo.

A Practical Introduction to Latin Composition. 12mo.

Caesar's Commentaries on the Gallic War. 12mo.

Cicero's Select Orations. 12mo.

Cicero's Select Orations. With Explanatory Notes and a Special Dictionary. 12mo.

Sallust's Catiline. With Explanatory Notes and a Special Vocabulary. 12mo.

Preparatory Course of Latin Prose Authors. Large 8vo. Contains Four Books of Cæsar's Commentaries, Sallust's Catiline, and Eight of Cicero's Orations.

AMERICAN BOOK COMPANY, Publishers,

NEW YORK, · ː · CINCINNATI, · ː · CHICAGO.

BY

HENRY S. FRIEZE,

Professor of Latin in the University of Michigan.

I.

The Complete Works of Vergil. With Notes and Special Dictionary.

II.

The Aeneid of Vergil. With Notes, etc. Large type.

III.

The Aeneid of Vergil. With Notes and Dictionary.

IV.

The Bucolics and Georgics, and Six Books of the Aeneid. With Notes and Dictionary. 12mo.

V.

A Vergilian Dictionary. Embracing all the words found in the Eclogues, Georgics, and Aeneid of Vergil, with numerous references to the text verifying and illustrating the definitions.

VI.

The Tenth and Twelfth Books of Quintilian. With Notes. 12mo.

AMERICAN BOOK COMPANY, Publishers,

NEW YORK, · : · CINCINNATI, · : · CHICAGO.

GREEK LESSONS,

PREPARED TO ACCOMPANY THE GRAMMAR OF
HADLEY AND ALLEN.

By ROBERT P. KEEP, Ph. D.,
Principal of the Norwich (Connecticut) Free Academy.

The Greek Grammar of Hadley and Allen has won for itself the position of a standard Manual of the Greek language, and is widely recognized as a book which every American student of Greek should possess. The only question is whether it should be purchased at the very outset, or whether a beginning should be made with a smaller and less complete grammar, this latter to give place after a year or two to the fuller treatise. It was with the design of making the path to the acquaintance with the new Hadley clear, sure, and not unnecessarily difficult, that the preparation of these Lessons was undertaken.

A good FIRST LESSONS is really an abridged grammar, constructed upon the lines of the larger treatise and employing precisely its language. Dr. Keep has done, in these Lessons, the work of abridging the new Hadley, and he has done it with such judgment as would have been expected from his knowledge of the needs of the beginner in Greek, and from his intimate familiarity with the grammar of Professor Hadley, both in its older and its more recent form.

The publishers commend this elementary Greek book to American teachers with great confidence that it will be found to possess important advantages above other books of its class.

AMERICAN BOOK COMPANY, Publishers,

NEW YORK, · : · CINCINNATI. · : · CHICAGO.

FIRST FOUR BOOKS OF

XENOPHON'S ANABASIS.

BY

JAMES R. BOISE, Ph. D., LL. D.,

Professor in the Theological Seminary at Morgan Park, Illinois

WITH OR WITHOUT VOCABULARY.

As our colleges, with but one or two exceptions, require three or four books only of the Anabasis for admission, the majority specifying four books, we have substituted a *Four-Book* edition of "Boise's Anabasis" for the *Three-Book* and *Five-Book* editions heretofore published. This edition is thoroughly revised and up to date; has references to Hadley-Allen's, Goodwin's, and other Greek grammars; contains tables of grammatical references and exercises, Kiepert's Map of the Route of the Ten Thousand, tables of illustrations, etc. It is issued in two forms, viz., *with* and *without* vocabulary.

It is believed that this work will be found to be the most accurate, comprehensive, and attractive edition of the Anabasis heretofore published.

Introduction price, with vocabulary   - $1.32.

"   " without vocabulary - 1.08.

Specimen copies sent, post-paid, to teachers, for examination, at the introduction prices. Send for full descriptive circulars of Latin and Greek Text-books.

AMERICAN BOOK COMPANY, Publishers,

NEW YORK,   · : ·   CINCINNATI,   · : ·   CHICAGO.

THE FIRST THREE BOOKS OF HOMER'S ILIAD.

With Notes, Critical and Explanatory, and references to
Hadley-Allen's, Crosby's, and Goodwin's Greek Grammars,
and to Goodwin's Greek Moods and Tenses; together
with an Appendix, containing an Outline of the
Homeric Question, A Sketch of the Versification
and the Dialect of Homer, and a number of
Selected Passages for Sight-Reading.

By HENRY CLARK JOHNSON, LL. B.,

Principal of the Philadelphia High-School, formerly Professor of the Latin
Language and Literature in the Lehigh University.

SECOND EDITION, REVISED AND REWRITTEN.

12mo, 180 pages. Introduction price, $1.12.

THE SAME WITH LEXICON.

Being a combined edition of JOHNSON'S FIRST THREE
BOOKS OF HOMER'S ILIAD and BLAKE'S LEXICON
OF THE FIRST THREE BOOKS OF
HOMER'S ILIAD.

12mo, 509 pages. Introduction price, $1.32.

Teachers and students will find this to be one of the most
complete and valuable editions of that part of the Iliad ever pub-
lished.

*Either book will be sent to teachers of Greek, for examination, on
receipt of the introduction price.*

AMERICAN BOOK COMPANY, Publishers,
NEW YORK, · : · CINCINNATI, · : · CHICAGO.

PRACTICAL LANGUAGE-STUDY.

A Complete Graded Course in English Grammar and Composition. By BENJAMIN Y. CONKLIN, Principal of Grammar School No. 3, Brooklyn, N. Y. A practical working manual for both teacher and pupil. Prepared on the inductive method. Adapted to lowest grammar grades as well as advanced pupils. Introduction price, 65 cents.

Grammar and Composition. For Common Schools. By E. O. LYTE, A. M., Principal State Normal School, Millersville, Pa. Introduction price, 65 cents.

Quackenbos's Illustrated Lessons in our Language. Designed to teach children English Grammar without its Technicalities, in a common-sense way, chiefly by practical exercises. 16mo, 200 pages. Introduction price, 42 cents.

Quackenbos's English Grammar. 12mo, 288 pages. Introduction price, 42 cents.

It is brief and clear in definition, lucid in arrangement, happy in illustration, practical in its exercises.

Quackenbos's Advanced Course of Composition and Rhetoric. *Revised edition.* 12mo, 453 pages. Introduction price, $1.05.

Bain's English Composition and Rhetoric. *Revised and enlarged edition.* PART I. Intellectual Elements of Style. PART II. Emotional Qualities of Style. Introduction price, per part, $1.20.

The Sentence and Word Book: A Guide to Writing, Spelling, and Composition. By JAMES JOHONNOT. Introduction price, 24 cents.

Sample copies mailed, post-paid, for examination, at the introduction price. Send for full descriptive circulars of language books.

AMERICAN BOOK COMPANY, Publishers,

NEW YORK, · : · CINCINNATI, · : · CHICAGO